BABY'S IN BLACK

My thanks for their help, time and patience go to Astrid, Ulf, Micha, Sascha and Jan-Frederik – and above all to Line and Matti: you know what for.

First Second

Translated from the German by Michael Waaler

Published by First Second
First Second is an imprint of Roaring Brook Press, a division of Holtzbrinck Publishing Holdings Limited Partnership
175 Fifth Avenue, New York, New York 10010

Originally published in Germany by Reprodukt under the title *Baby's in Black: The Story of Astrid Kirchherr & Stuart Sutcliffe* (2010)

Cataloging-in-Publication Data for the hardcover edition is on file at the Library of Congress

ISBN 978-1-59643-918-4

First Second books may be purchased for business or promotional use. For information on bulk purchases please contact Macmillan Corporate and Premium Sales Department at (800) 221-7945 x5442 or by email at specialmarkets@macmillan.com.

FIRST EDITION

First American hardcover edition 2012
American paperback edition 2014
Book design by Colleen AF Venable
Printed in the United States of America

10 9 8 7 6 5 4 3 2 1

BY ART WE LIVE

Arne Bellstorf

BABY'S IN BLACK

Astrid Kirchherr, Stuart Sutcliffe, and The Beatles

:01

First Second

New York & London

»Grosse Freiheit«

October 1960

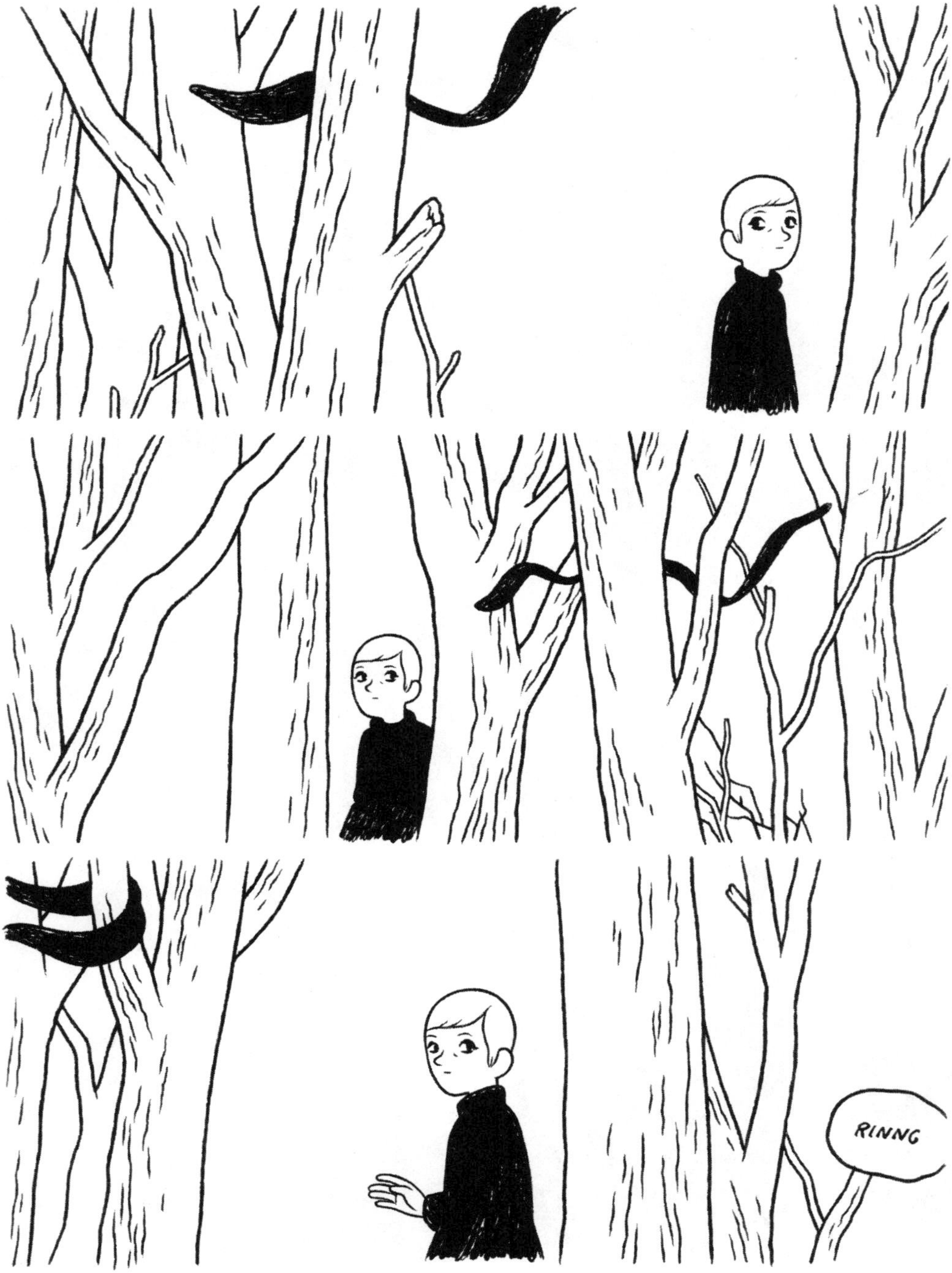
RINNG

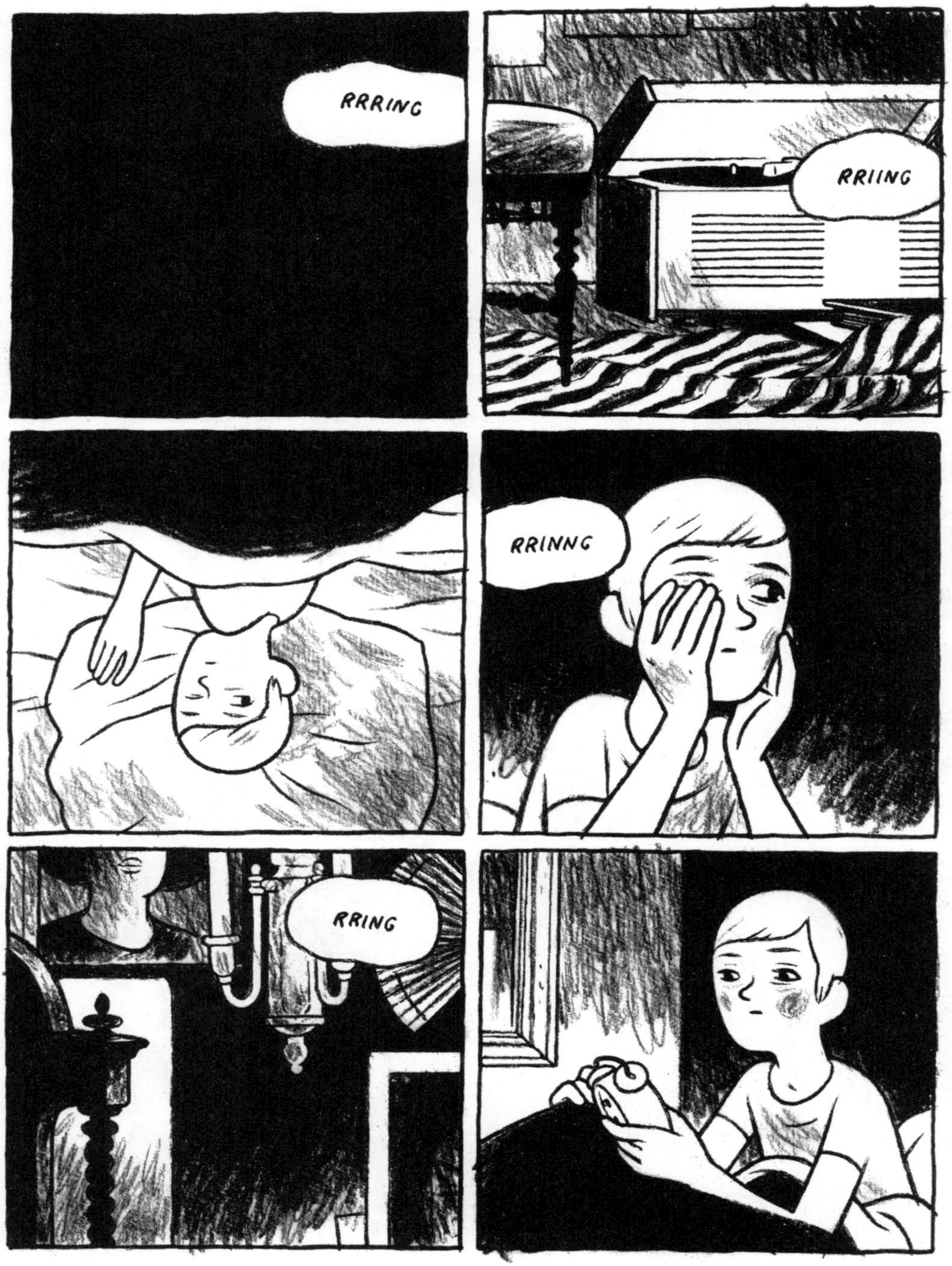
RRRING
RRIING
RRINNG
RRING

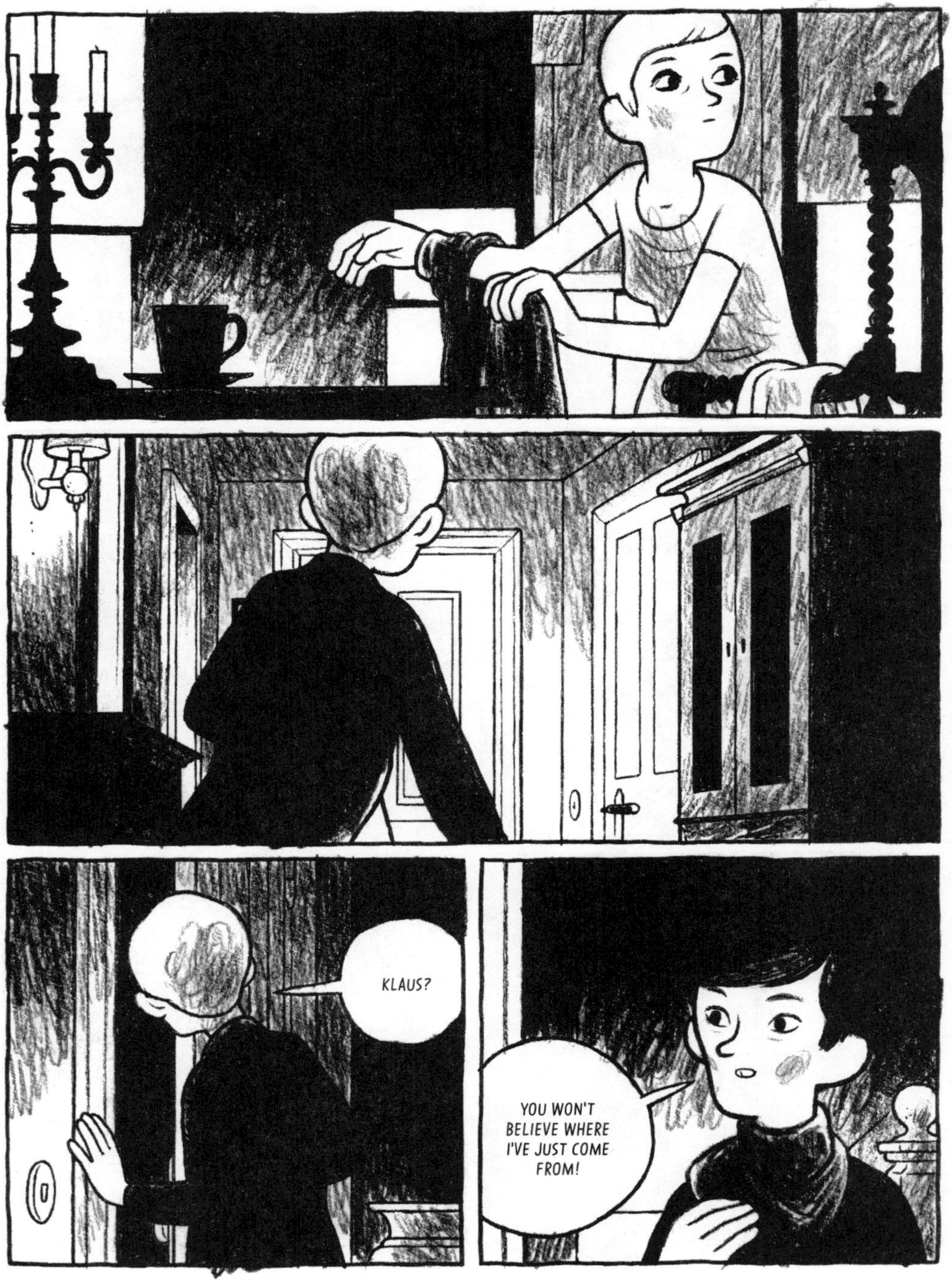
KLAUS?
YOU WON'T BELIEVE WHERE I'VE JUST COME FROM!

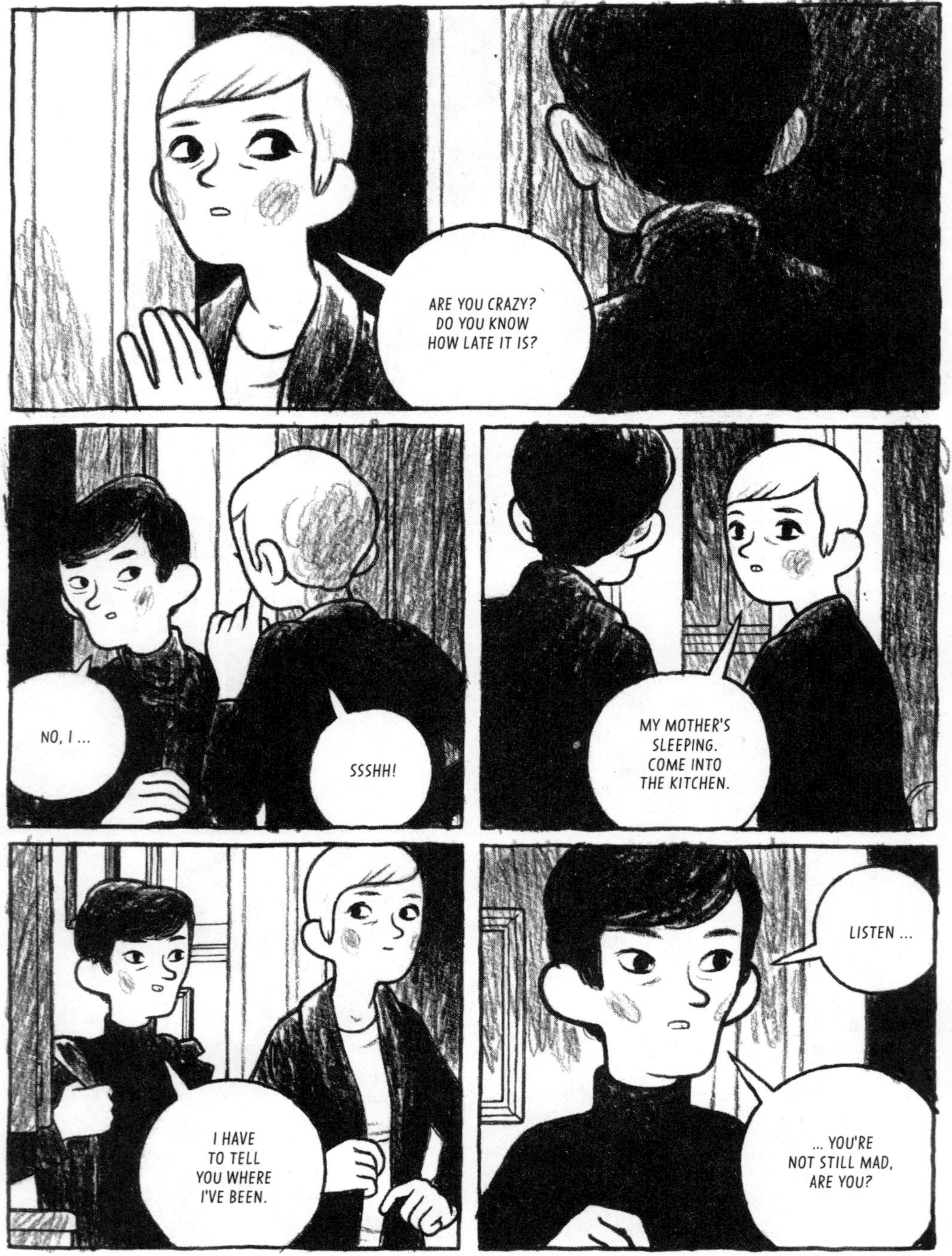
ARE YOU CRAZY? DO YOU KNOW HOW LATE IT IS?
NO, I ...
SSSHH!
MY MOTHER'S SLEEPING. COME INTO THE KITCHEN.
I HAVE TO TELL YOU WHERE I'VE BEEN.
LISTEN ...
... YOU'RE NOT STILL MAD, ARE YOU?

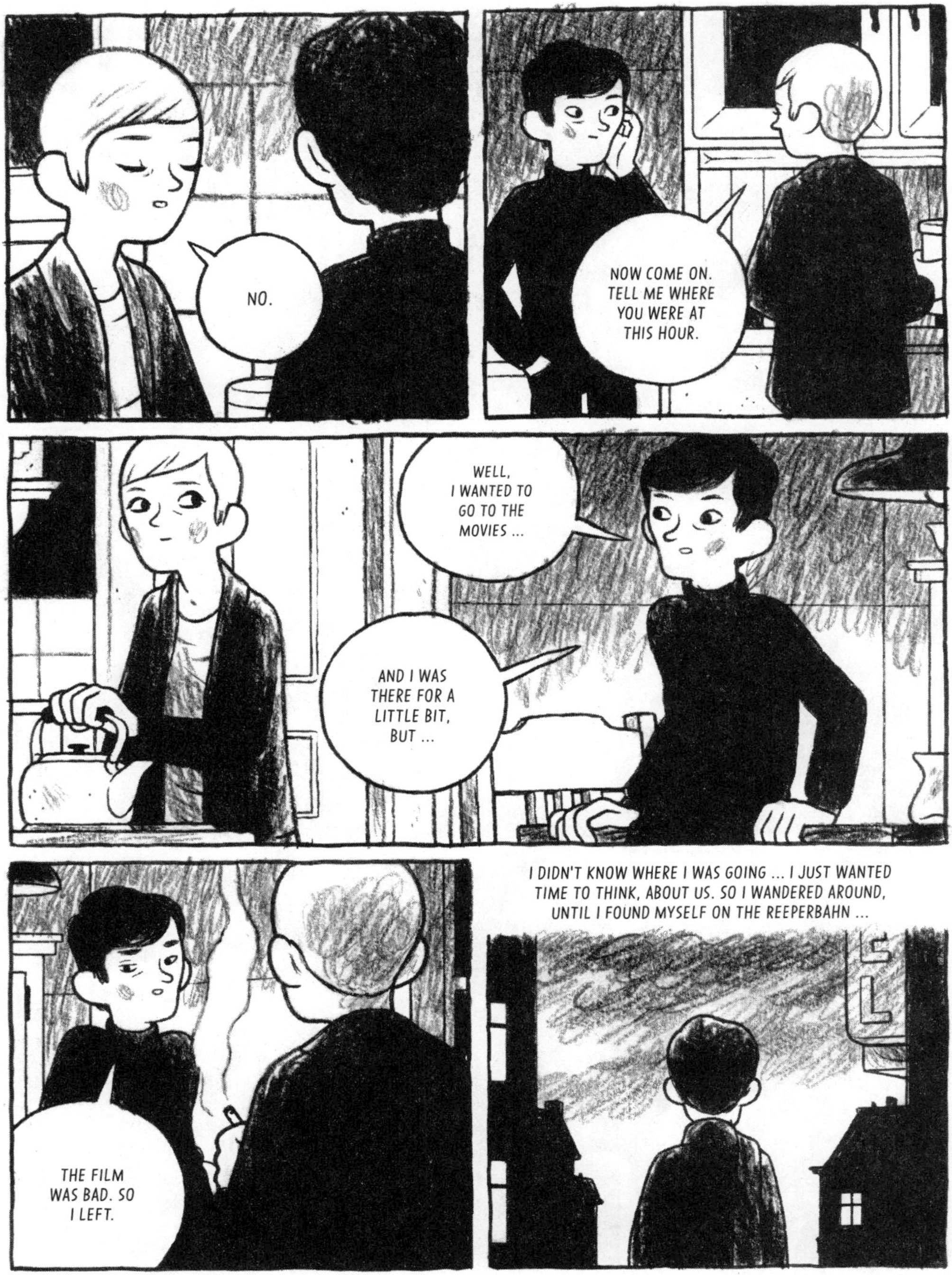
NO.
NOW COME ON. TELL ME WHERE YOU WERE AT THIS HOUR.
WELL, I WANTED TO GO TO THE MOVIES ...
AND I WAS THERE FOR A LITTLE BIT, BUT ...
THE FILM WAS BAD. SO I LEFT.
I DIDN'T KNOW WHERE I WAS GOING ... I JUST WANTED TIME TO THINK, ABOUT US. SO I WANDERED AROUND, UNTIL I FOUND MYSELF ON THE REEPERBAHN ...

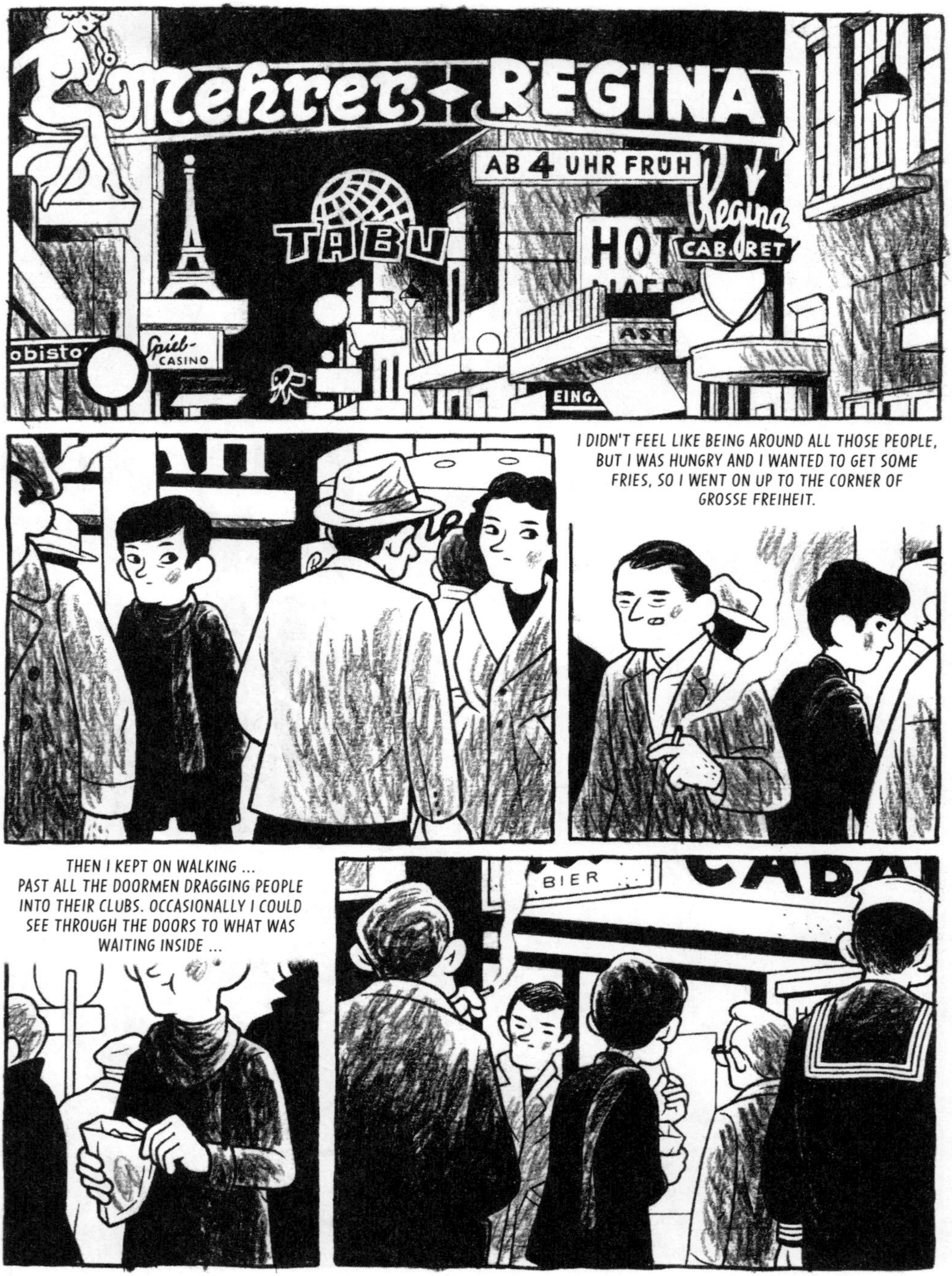

Mehrer - REGINA
AB 4 UHR FRÜH
Regina
CAB RET
HOT
TABU
Spiel-
CASINO
obisto
AST
EINGA
I DIDN'T FEEL LIKE BEING AROUND ALL THOSE PEOPLE, BUT I WAS HUNGRY AND I WANTED TO GET SOME FRIES, SO I WENT ON UP TO THE CORNER OF GROSSE FREIHEIT.
THEN I KEPT ON WALKING ... PAST ALL THE DOORMEN DRAGGING PEOPLE INTO THEIR CLUBS. OCCASIONALLY I COULD SEE THROUGH THE DOORS TO WHAT WAS WAITING INSIDE ...
BIER
CABA

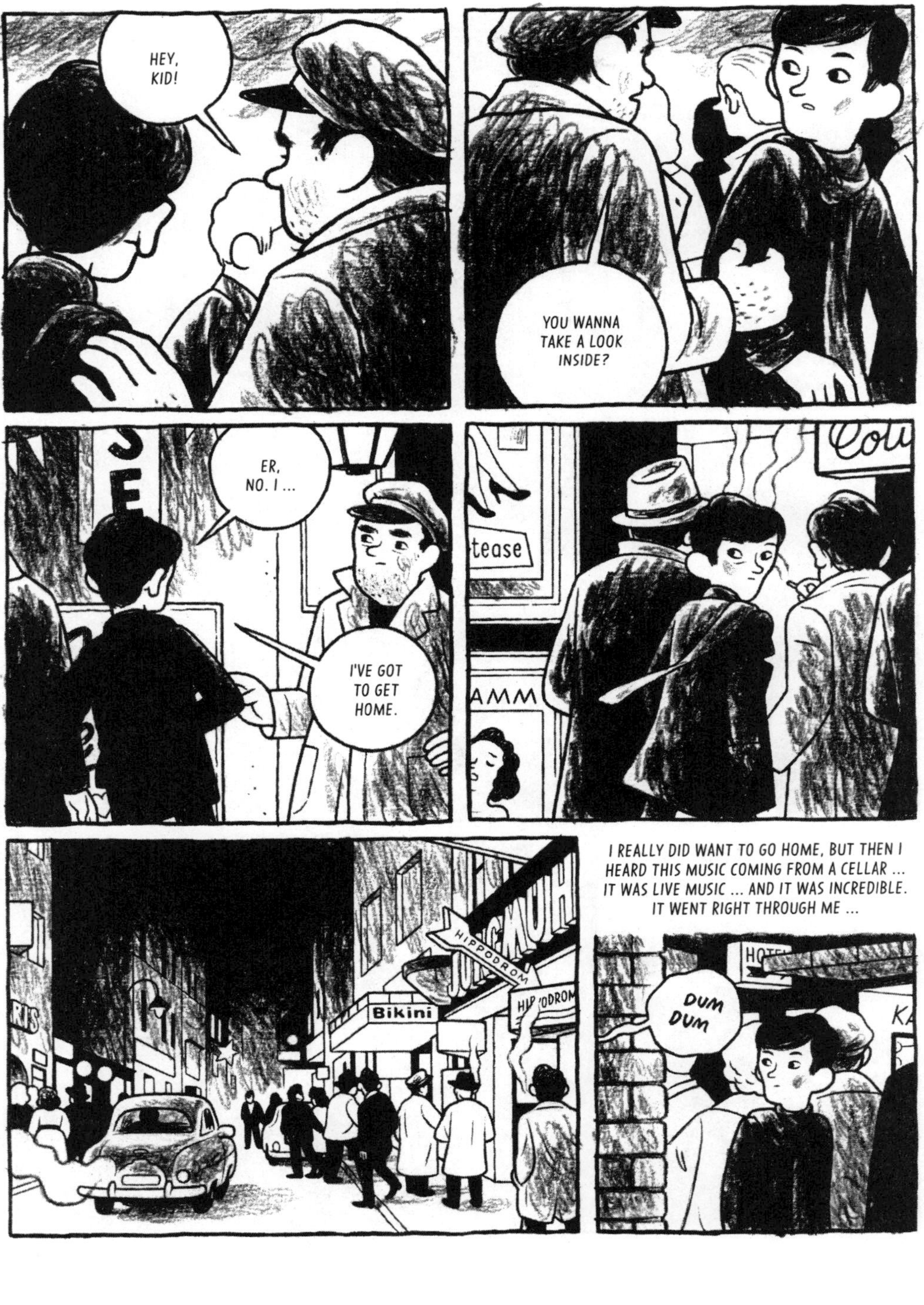
HEY, KID!
YOU WANNA TAKE A LOOK INSIDE?
ER, NO. I ...
I'VE GOT TO GET HOME.
tease
AMM
HIPPODROM
Bikini
I REALLY DID WANT TO GO HOME, BUT THEN I HEARD THIS MUSIC COMING FROM A CELLAR ... IT WAS LIVE MUSIC ... AND IT WAS INCREDIBLE. IT WENT RIGHT THROUGH ME ...
DUM DUM

I JUST HAD TO GO IN AND TAKE A LOOK ... SOMEHOW, I MANAGED TO BUILD UP THE COURAGE AND PUSHED PAST A BUNCH OF TOUGH-LOOKING GUYS, INTO THE ENTRANCE.
NOT SO FAST!
I GOTTA STAMP YOUR HAND.
OH YEAH, RIGHT.
COME ON OVER BABY ...
WHOLE LOTTA SHAKIN' GOIN' ON

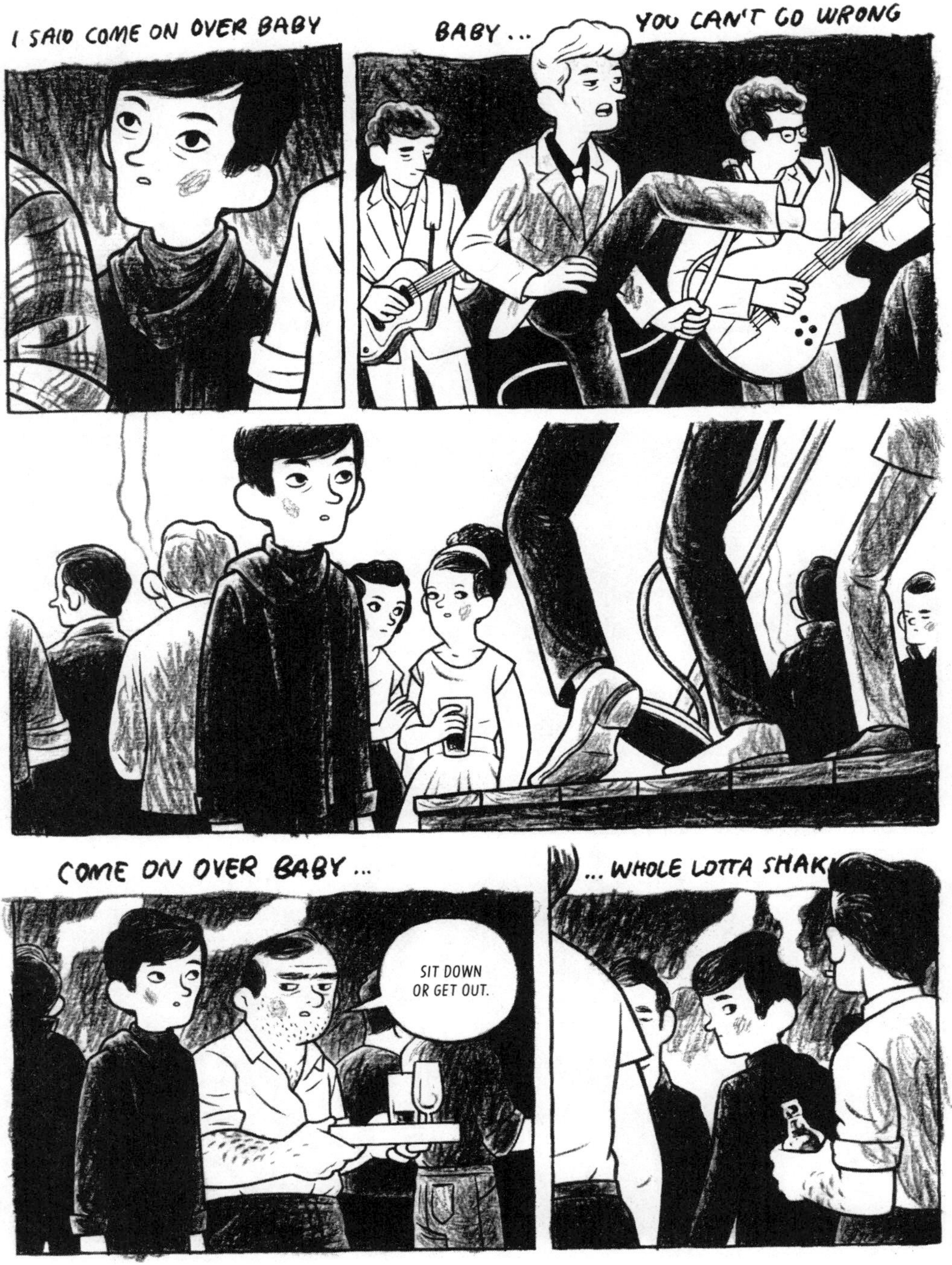
I SAID COME ON OVER BABY
BABY ...
YOU CAN'T GO WRONG
COME ON OVER BABY ...
SIT DOWN OR GET OUT.
... WHOLE LOTTA SHAK

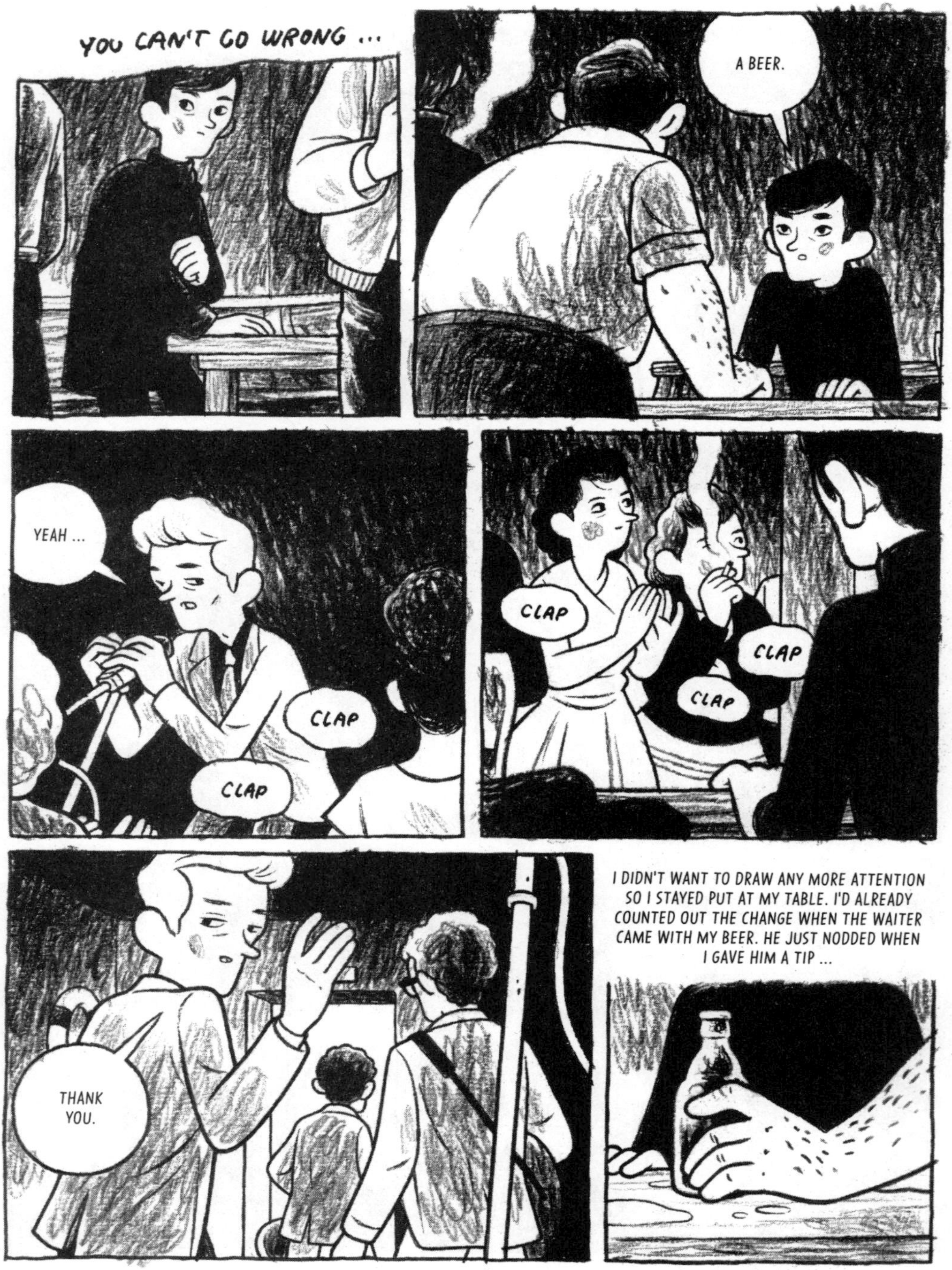
YOU CAN'T GO WRONG ...
A BEER.
YEAH ...
CLAP
CLAP
CLAP
CLAP
CLAP
THANK YOU.
I DIDN'T WANT TO DRAW ANY MORE ATTENTION SO I STAYED PUT AT MY TABLE. I'D ALREADY COUNTED OUT THE CHANGE WHEN THE WAITER CAME WITH MY BEER. HE JUST NODDED WHEN I GAVE HIM A TIP ...

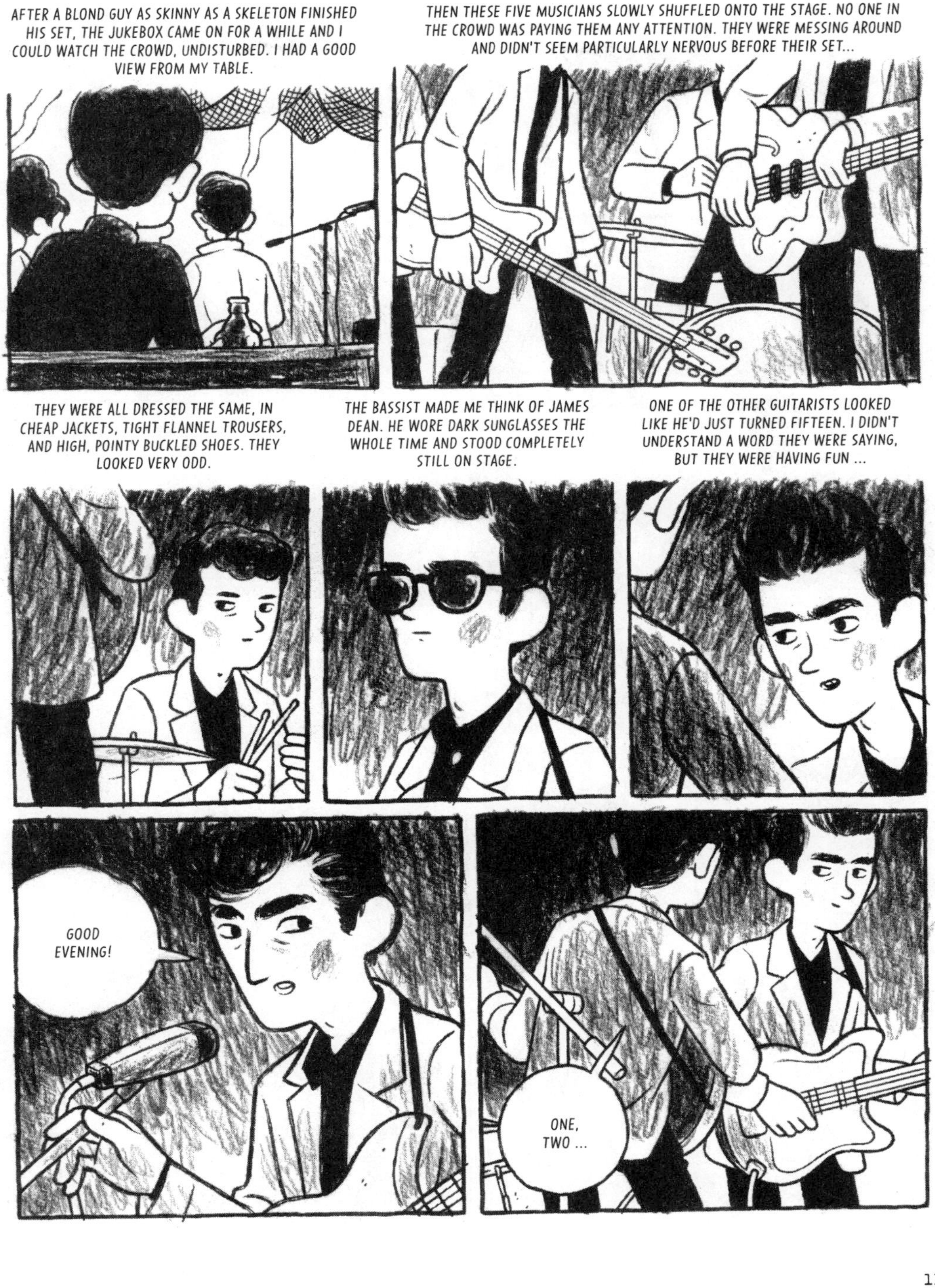
AFTER A BLOND GUY AS SKINNY AS A SKELETON FINISHED HIS SET, THE JUKEBOX CAME ON FOR A WHILE AND I COULD WATCH THE CROWD, UNDISTURBED. I HAD A GOOD VIEW FROM MY TABLE.
THEN THESE FIVE MUSICIANS SLOWLY SHUFFLED ONTO THE STAGE. NO ONE IN THE CROWD WAS PAYING THEM ANY ATTENTION. THEY WERE MESSING AROUND AND DIDN'T SEEM PARTICULARLY NERVOUS BEFORE THEIR SET...
THEY WERE ALL DRESSED THE SAME, IN CHEAP JACKETS, TIGHT FLANNEL TROUSERS, AND HIGH, POINTY BUCKLED SHOES. THEY LOOKED VERY ODD.
THE BASSIST MADE ME THINK OF JAMES DEAN. HE WORE DARK SUNGLASSES THE WHOLE TIME AND STOOD COMPLETELY STILL ON STAGE.
ONE OF THE OTHER GUITARISTS LOOKED LIKE HE'D JUST TURNED FIFTEEN. I DIDN'T UNDERSTAND A WORD THEY WERE SAYING, BUT THEY WERE HAVING FUN ...
GOOD EVENING!
ONE, TWO ...

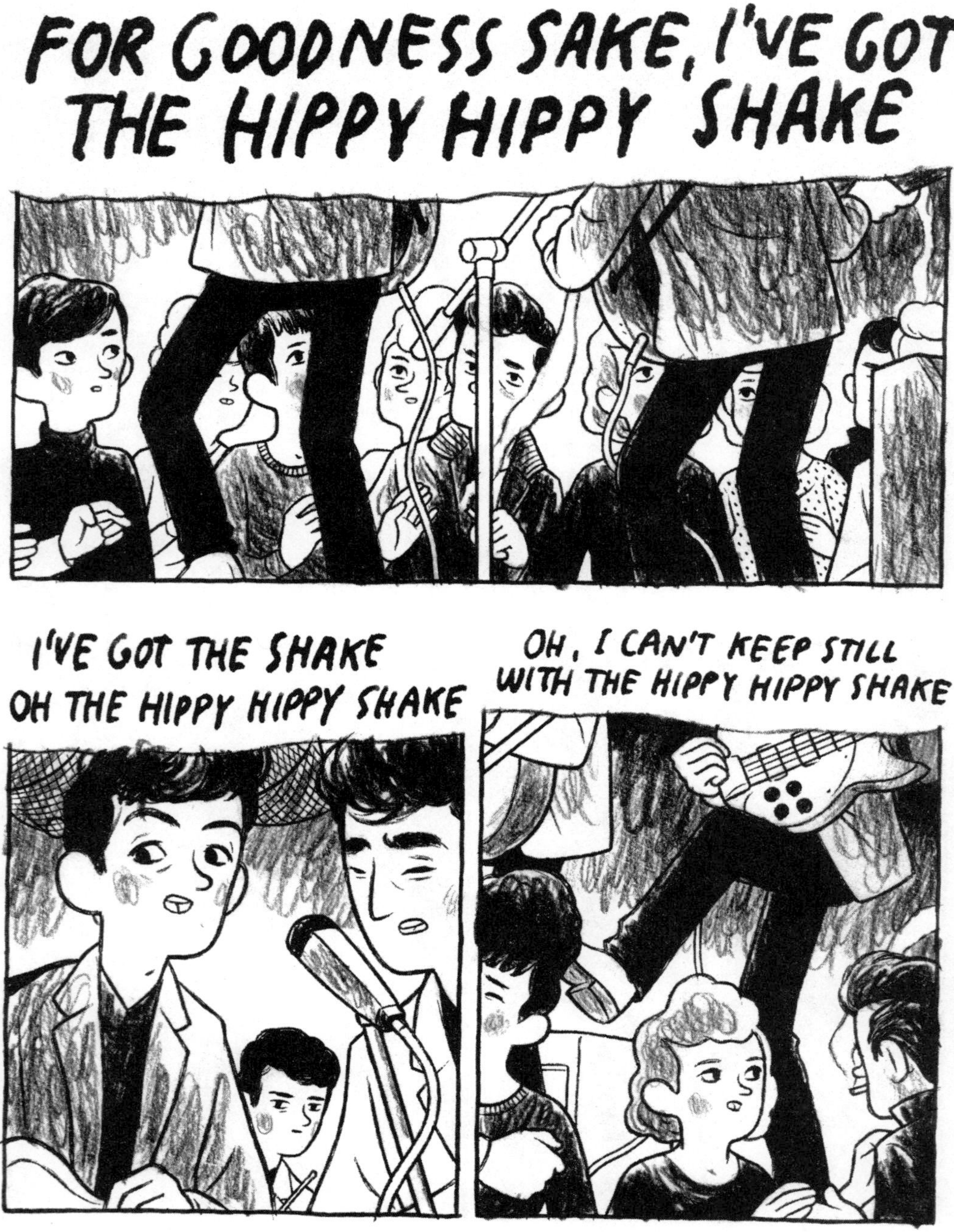
FOR GOODNESS SAKE, I'VE GOT
THE HIPPY HIPPY SHAKE
I'VE GOT THE SHAKE
OH THE HIPPY HIPPY SHAKE
OH, I CAN'T KEEP STILL
WITH THE HIPPY HIPPY SHAKE

OOH... THE HIPPY HIPPY SHAKE

EVERYONE STARTED DANCING AND I DRIFTED TOWARD THE STAGE. IT WAS INCREDIBLE ... THE ATMOSPHERE. IT FELT LIKE THE ENTIRE ROOM WAS MOVING TO THE RHYTHM OF THE MUSIC.

THEY PLAYED ONE SONG AFTER ANOTHER WITHOUT STOPPING. THE SINGER WITH QUIVERING NOSTRILS GOT LOUDER AND LOUDER AND WAS SCREAMING HIS HEART OUT ...

ONE OF THEM WAS SO HYPED UP HE WAS BOUNCING UP AND DOWN LIKE A RUBBER BALL ... BOUNCING UP TO THE CEILING, LIKE HE WAS ON A TRAMPOLINE. HE DID THE SPILTS IN THE AIR ... WHILE PLAYING HIS GUITAR!

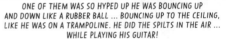

I STOOD THERE DRENCHED IN SWEAT, SPEECHLESS BUT HAPPY. I'D FORGOTTEN EVERYTHING AROUND ME ...

THANK YOU VERY MUCH!

CLAP

CLAP

CLAP

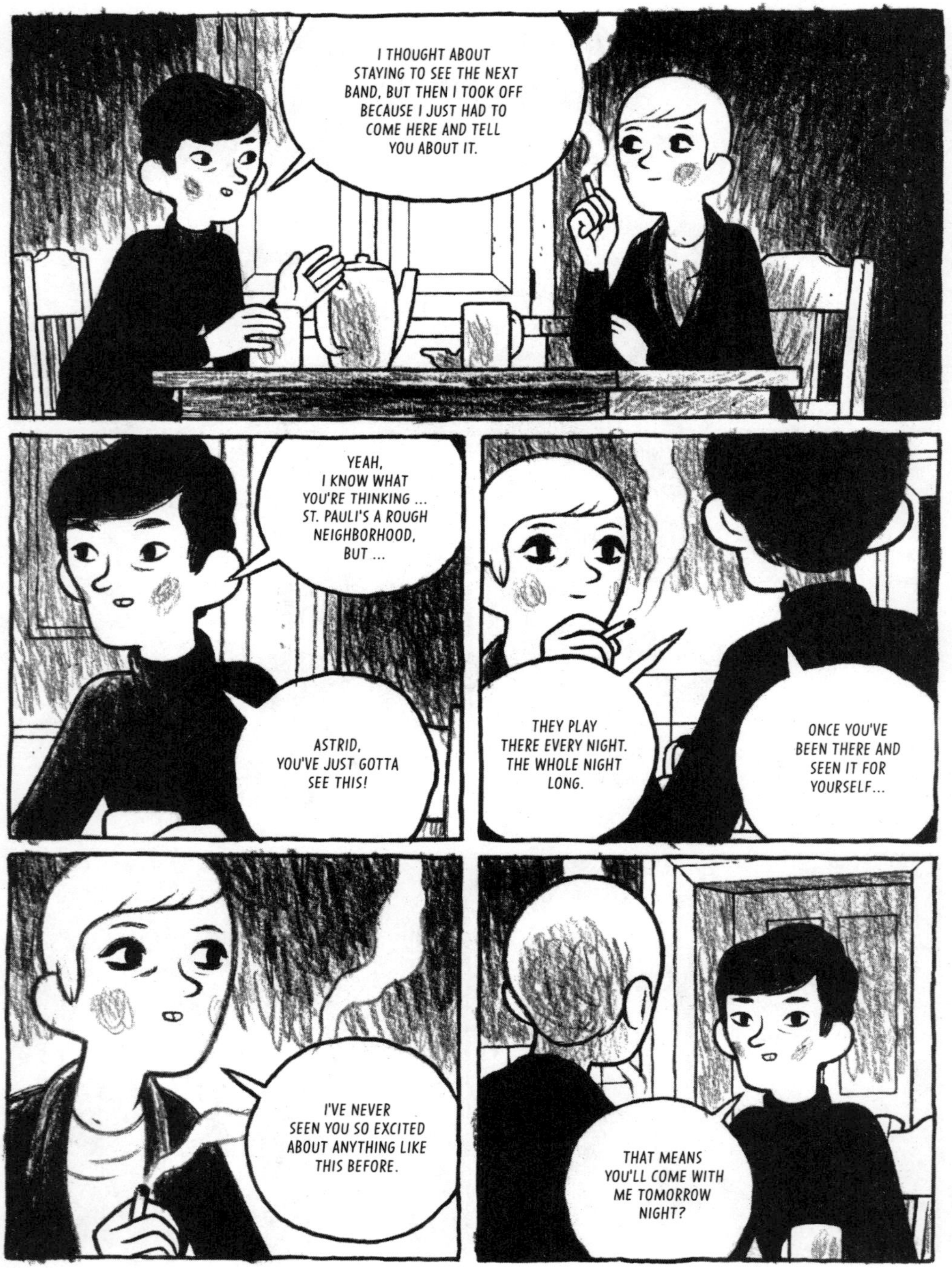
I THOUGHT ABOUT STAYING TO SEE THE NEXT BAND, BUT THEN I TOOK OFF BECAUSE I JUST HAD TO COME HERE AND TELL YOU ABOUT IT.
YEAH, I KNOW WHAT YOU'RE THINKING ... ST. PAULI'S A ROUGH NEIGHBORHOOD, BUT ...
ASTRID, YOU'VE JUST GOTTA SEE THIS!
THEY PLAY THERE EVERY NIGHT. THE WHOLE NIGHT LONG.
ONCE YOU'VE BEEN THERE AND SEEN IT FOR YOURSELF...
I'VE NEVER SEEN YOU SO EXCITED ABOUT ANYTHING LIKE THIS BEFORE.
THAT MEANS YOU'LL COME WITH ME TOMORROW NIGHT?

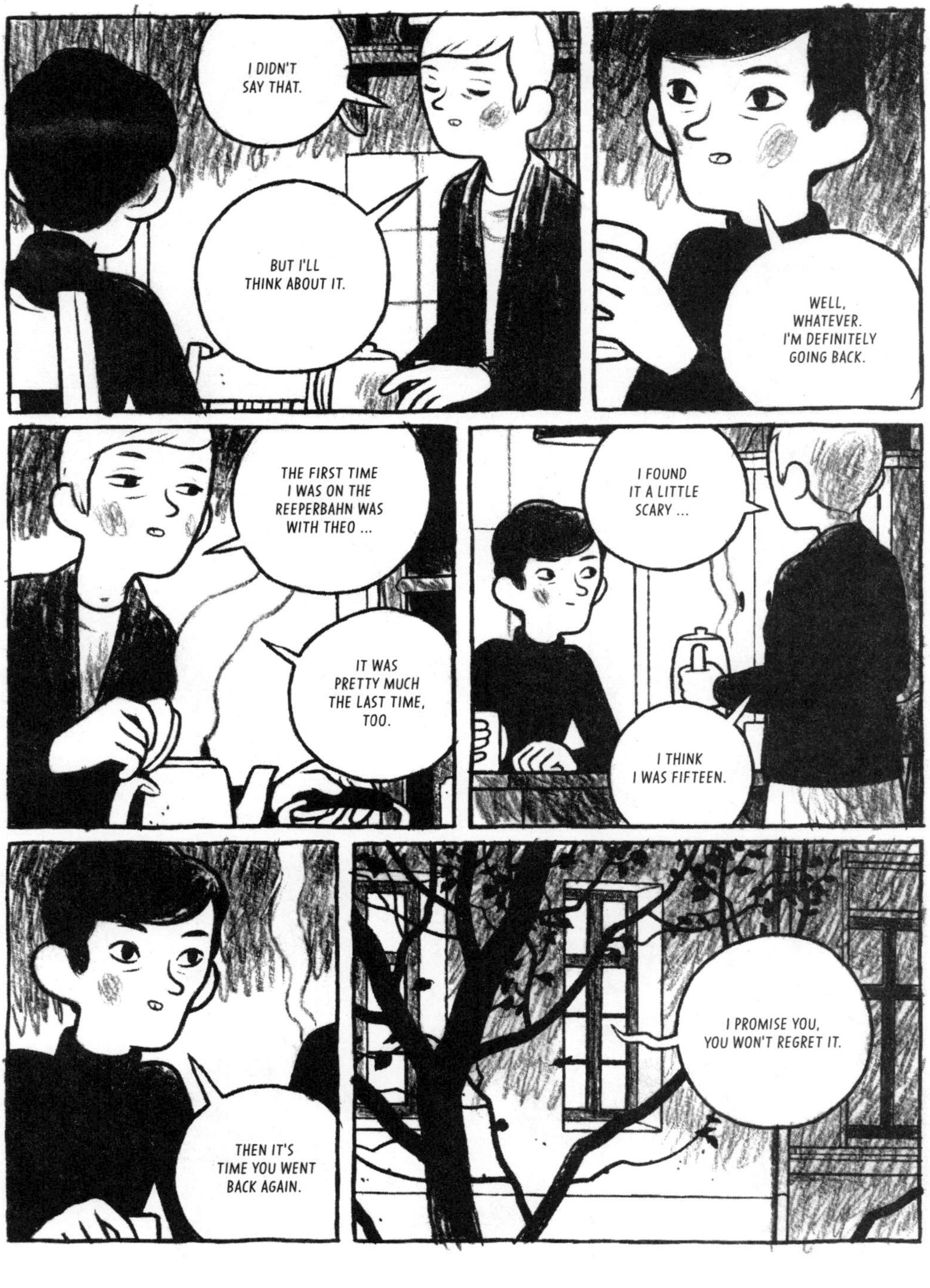
I DIDN'T SAY THAT.
BUT I'LL THINK ABOUT IT.
WELL, WHATEVER. I'M DEFINITELY GOING BACK.
THE FIRST TIME I WAS ON THE REEPERBAHN WAS WITH THEO ...
IT WAS PRETTY MUCH THE LAST TIME, TOO.
I FOUND IT A LITTLE SCARY ...
I THINK I WAS FIFTEEN.
THEN IT'S TIME YOU WENT BACK AGAIN.
I PROMISE YOU, YOU WON'T REGRET IT.

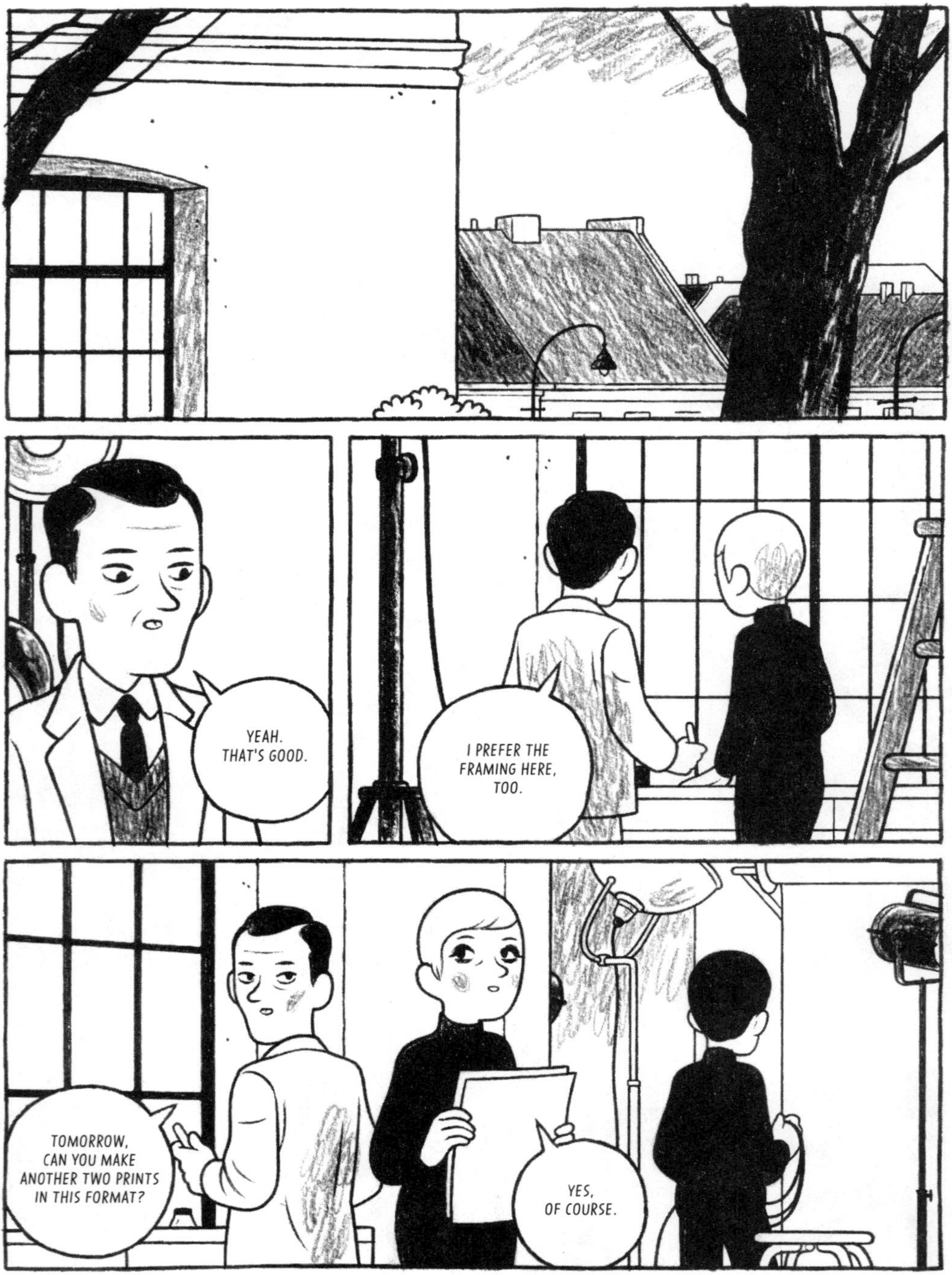
YEAH. THAT'S GOOD.
I PREFER THE FRAMING HERE, TOO.
TOMORROW, CAN YOU MAKE ANOTHER TWO PRINTS IN THIS FORMAT?
YES, OF COURSE.

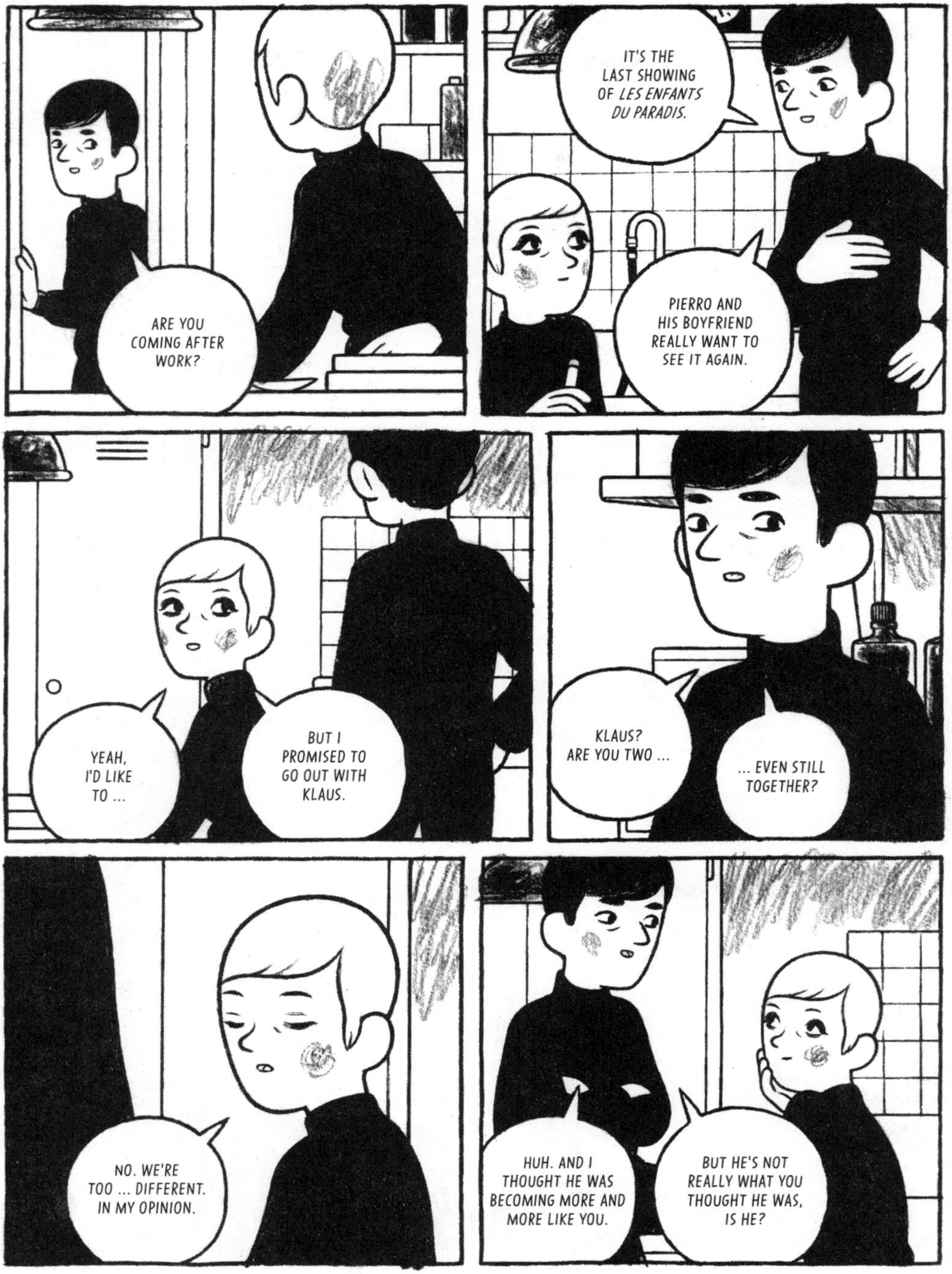
ARE YOU COMING AFTER WORK?
IT'S THE LAST SHOWING OF *LES ENFANTS DU PARADIS*.
PIERRO AND HIS BOYFRIEND REALLY WANT TO SEE IT AGAIN.
YEAH, I'D LIKE TO ...
BUT I PROMISED TO GO OUT WITH KLAUS.
KLAUS? ARE YOU TWO ...
... EVEN STILL TOGETHER?
NO. WE'RE TOO ... DIFFERENT. IN MY OPINION.
HUH. AND I THOUGHT HE WAS BECOMING MORE AND MORE LIKE YOU.
BUT HE'S NOT REALLY WHAT YOU THOUGHT HE WAS, IS HE?

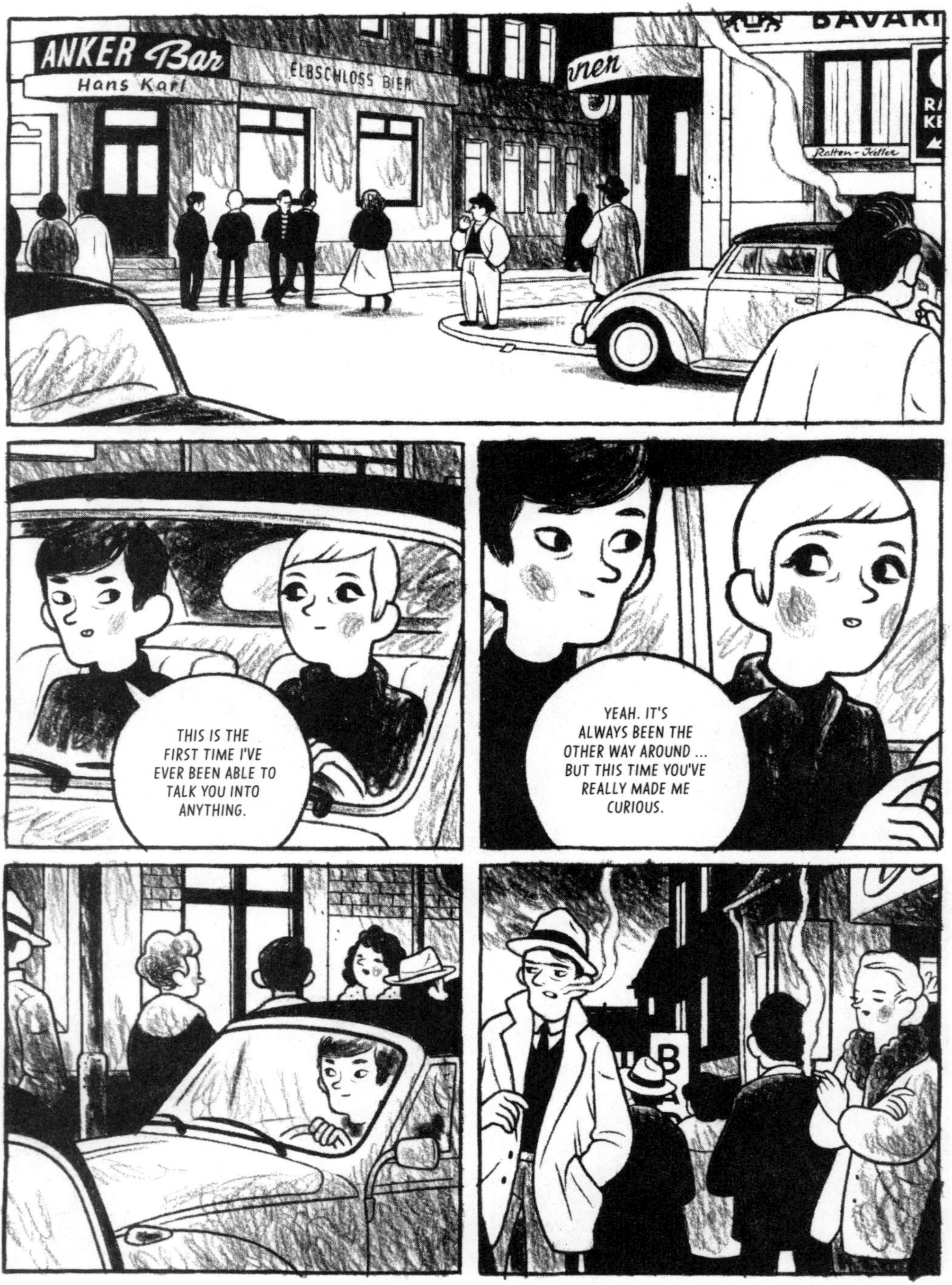
ANKER Bar
Hans Karl
ELBSCHLOSS BIER
BAVARI
Ratten-Keller
THIS IS THE FIRST TIME I'VE EVER BEEN ABLE TO TALK YOU INTO ANYTHING.
YEAH. IT'S ALWAYS BEEN THE OTHER WAY AROUND ... BUT THIS TIME YOU'VE REALLY MADE ME CURIOUS.

IT'S THERE ON THE CORNER.
SERKELLER
FANS
ORIGINAL
HIS HURICAN
ENGLAND-LIVERPOOL
RORY STORM?
... AND THE BEATLES. THAT'S THEM!
I THINK RORY STORM'S ALWAYS ON FIRST.
THEN THEY TAKE TURNS PLAYING.
OH ... HELLO!

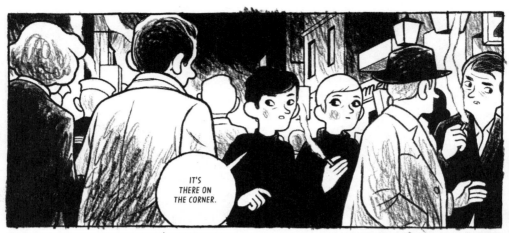

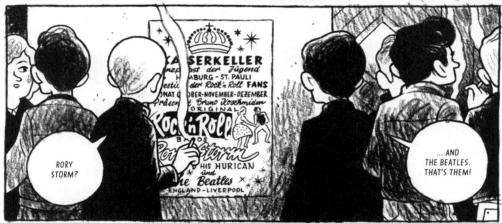

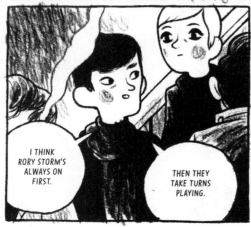

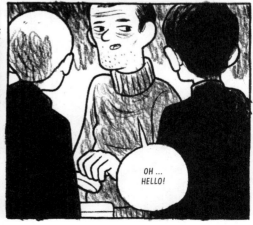

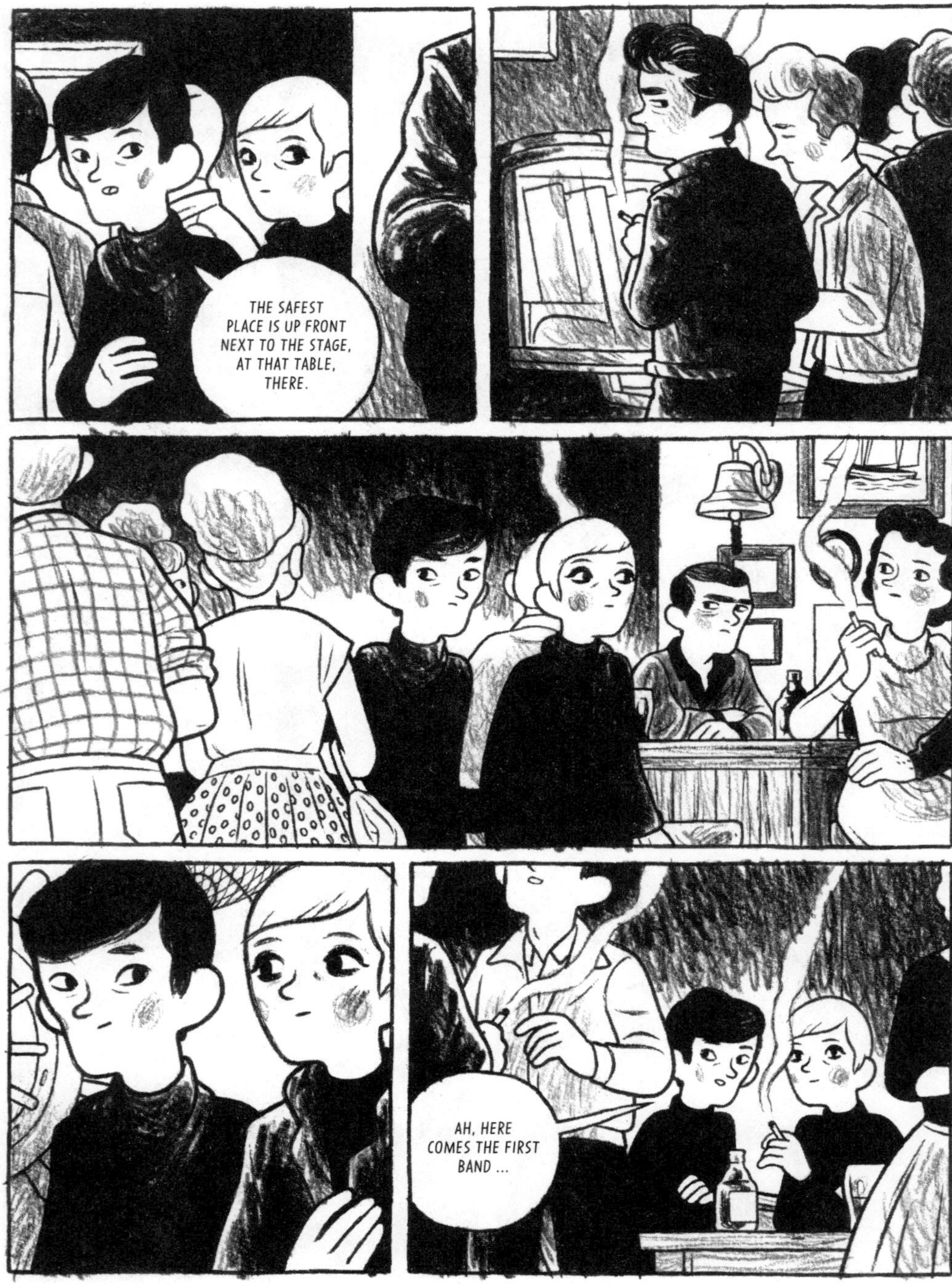
THE SAFEST PLACE IS UP FRONT NEXT TO THE STAGE, AT THAT TABLE, THERE.
AH, HERE COMES THE FIRST BAND ...

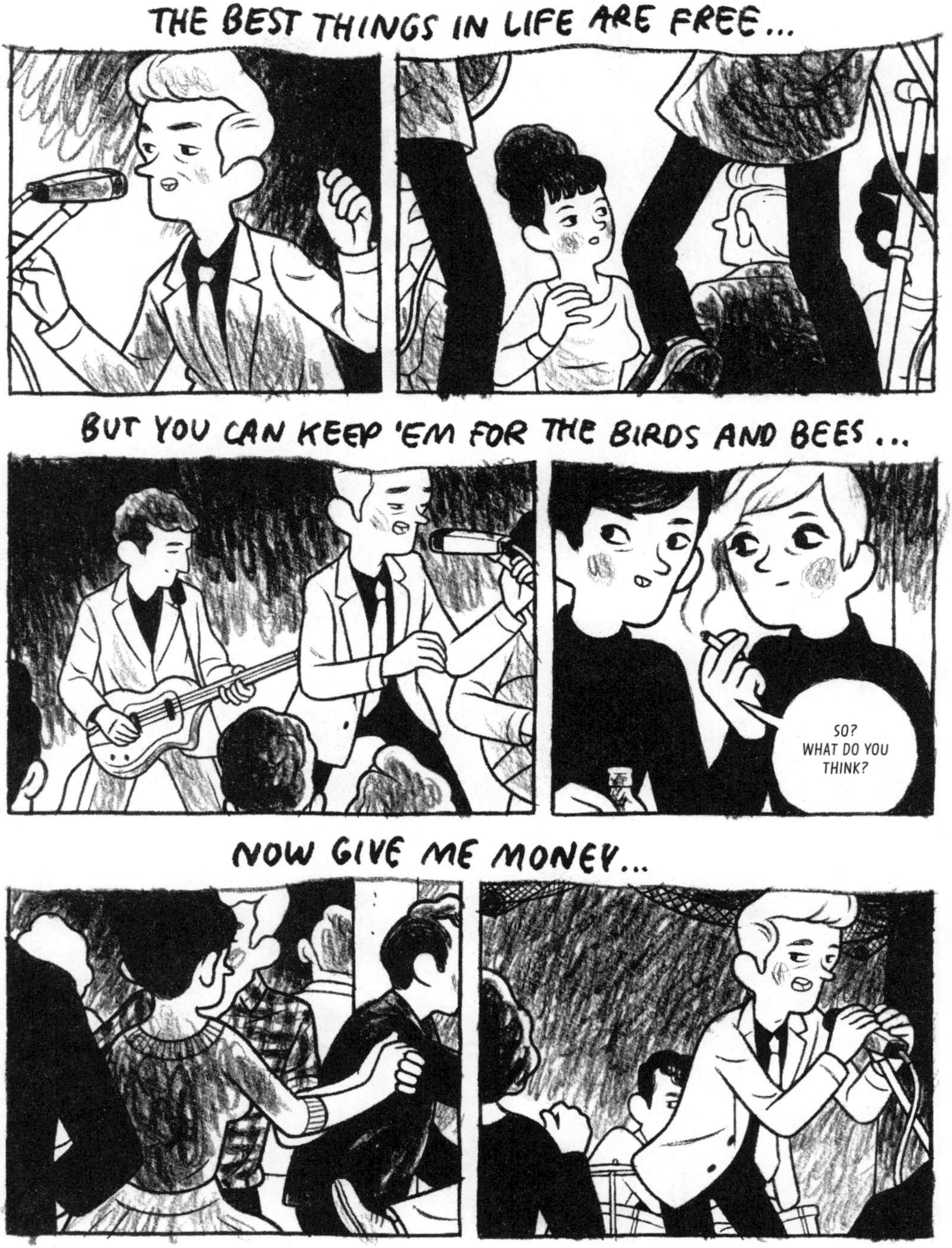
THE BEST THINGS IN LIFE ARE FREE...
BUT YOU CAN KEEP 'EM FOR THE BIRDS AND BEES...
SO? WHAT DO YOU THINK?
NOW GIVE ME MONEY...

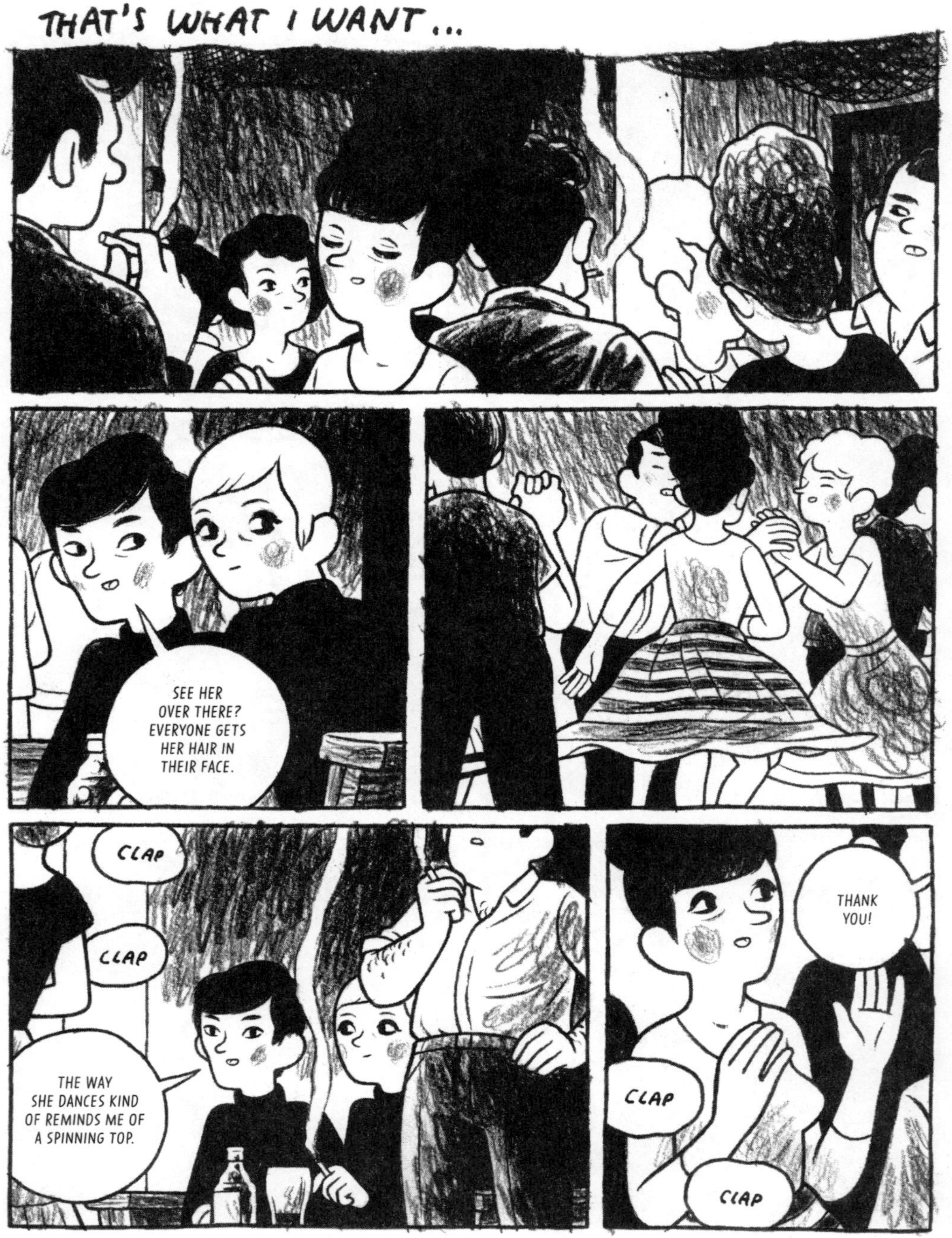
THAT'S WHAT I WANT...
SEE HER OVER THERE? EVERYONE GETS HER HAIR IN THEIR FACE.
CLAP
CLAP
THE WAY SHE DANCES KIND OF REMINDS ME OF A SPINNING TOP.
THANK YOU!
CLAP
CLAP

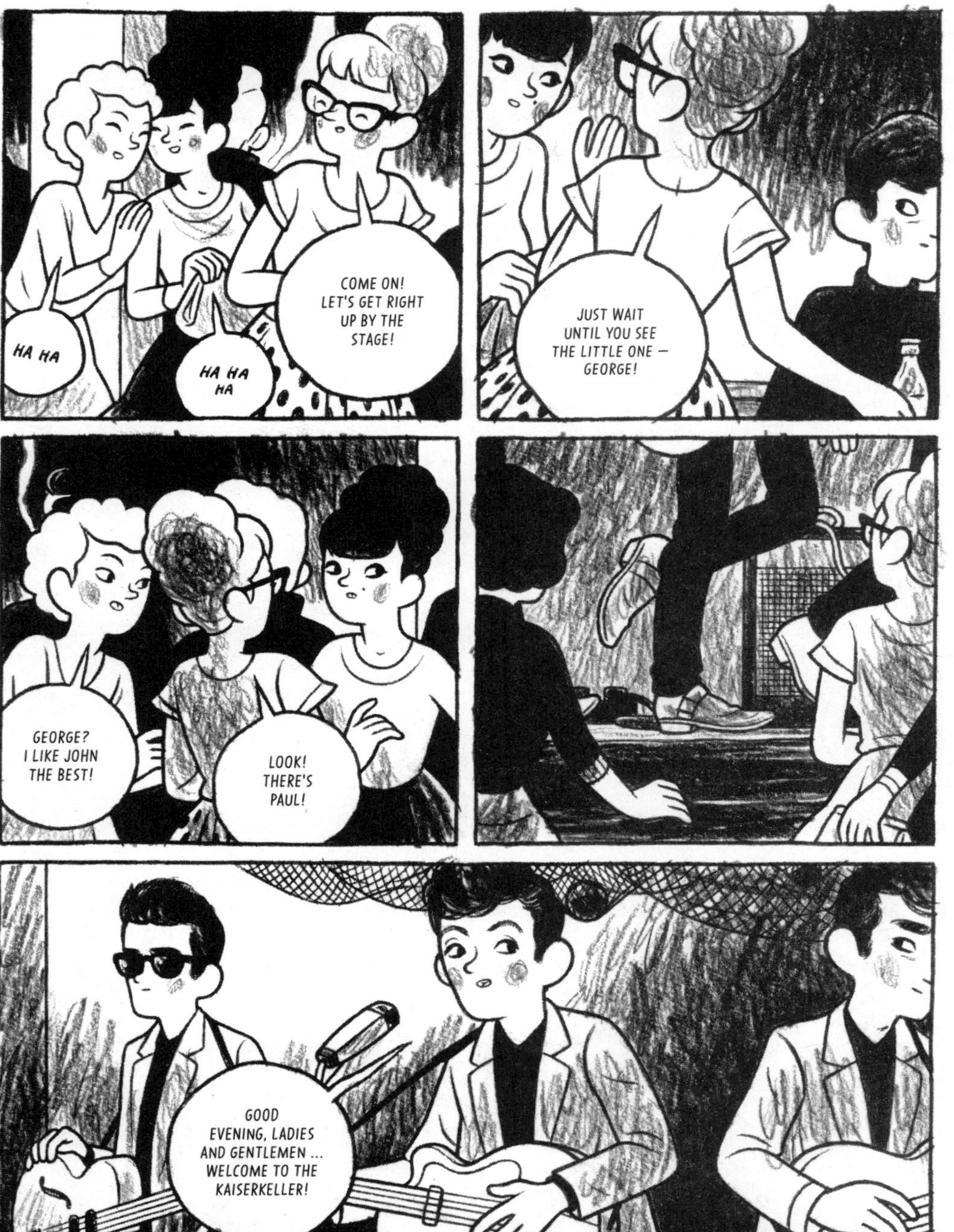
HA HA
HA HA HA
COME ON! LET'S GET RIGHT UP BY THE STAGE!
JUST WAIT UNTIL YOU SEE THE LITTLE ONE — GEORGE!
GEORGE? I LIKE JOHN THE BEST!
LOOK! THERE'S PAUL!
GOOD EVENING, LADIES AND GENTLEMEN ... WELCOME TO THE KAISERKELLER!

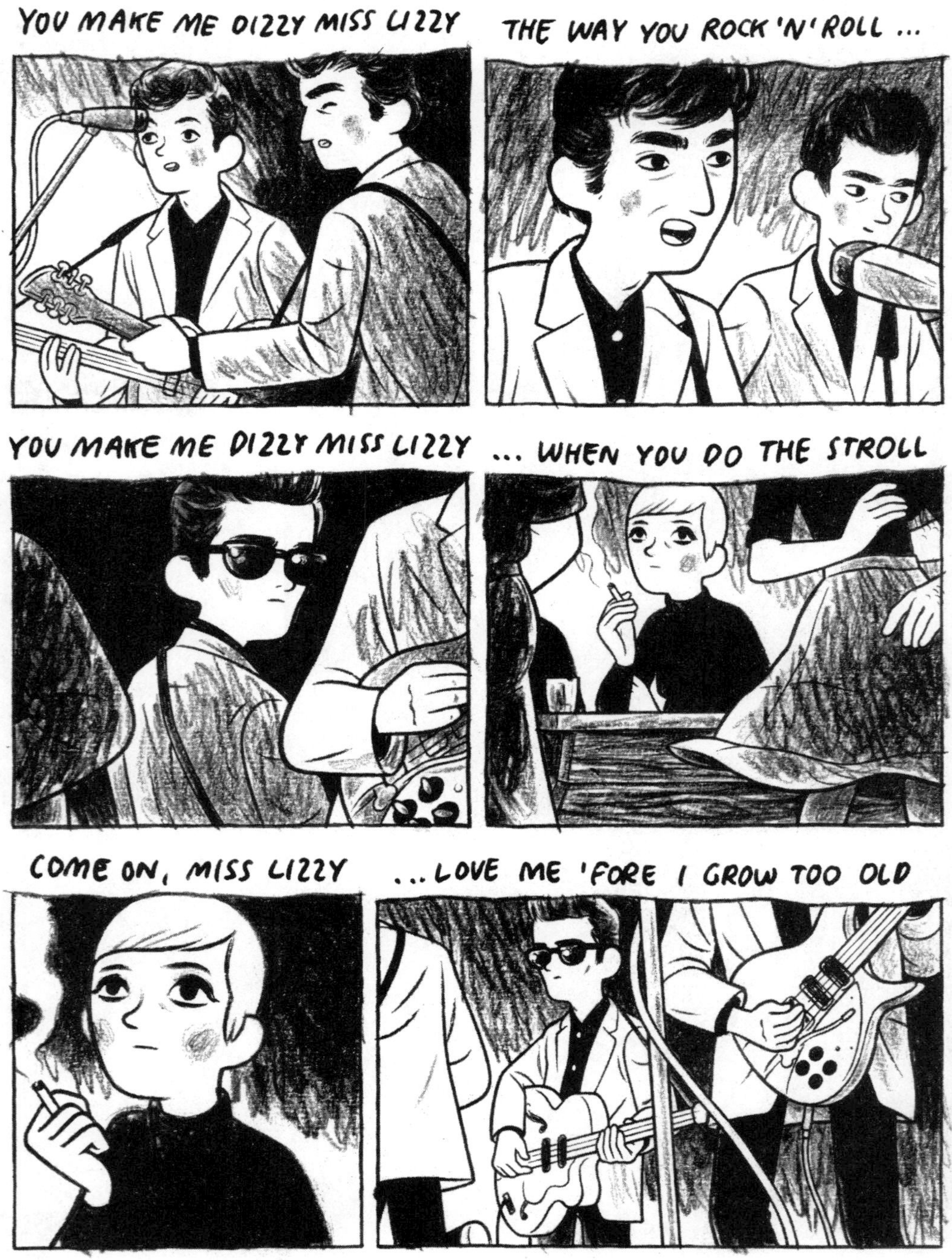
YOU MAKE ME DIZZY MISS LIZZY
THE WAY YOU ROCK 'N' ROLL ...
YOU MAKE ME DIZZY MISS LIZZY
... WHEN YOU DO THE STROLL
COME ON, MISS LIZZY
... LOVE ME 'FORE I GROW TOO OLD

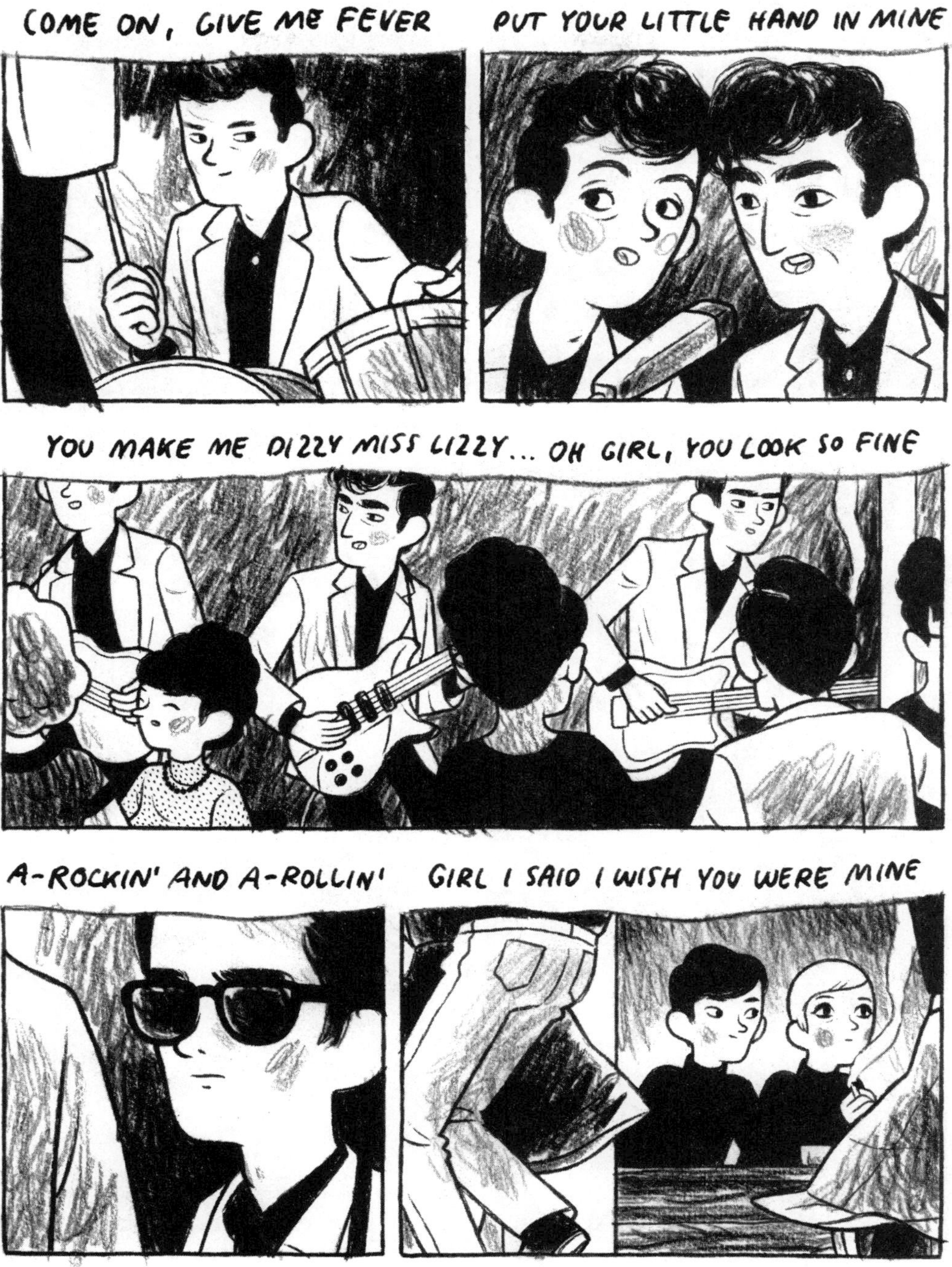
COME ON, GIVE ME FEVER
PUT YOUR LITTLE HAND IN MINE
YOU MAKE ME DIZZY MISS LIZZY... OH GIRL, YOU LOOK SO FINE
A-ROCKIN' AND A-ROLLIN'
GIRL I SAID I WISH YOU WERE MINE

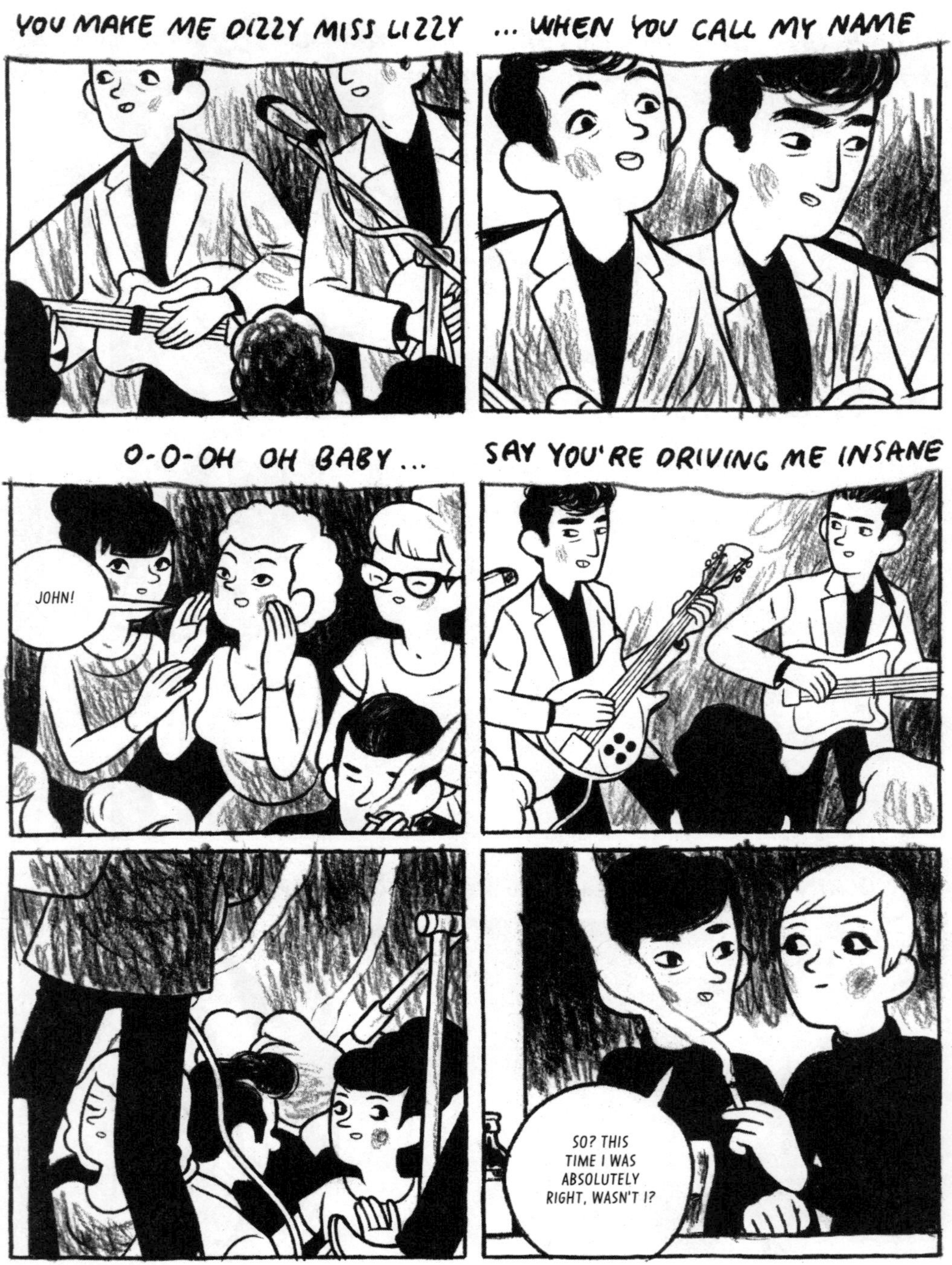
YOU MAKE ME DIZZY MISS LIZZY
... WHEN YOU CALL MY NAME
O-O-OH OH BABY ...
JOHN!
SAY YOU'RE DRIVING ME INSANE
SO? THIS TIME I WAS ABSOLUTELY RIGHT, WASN'T I?

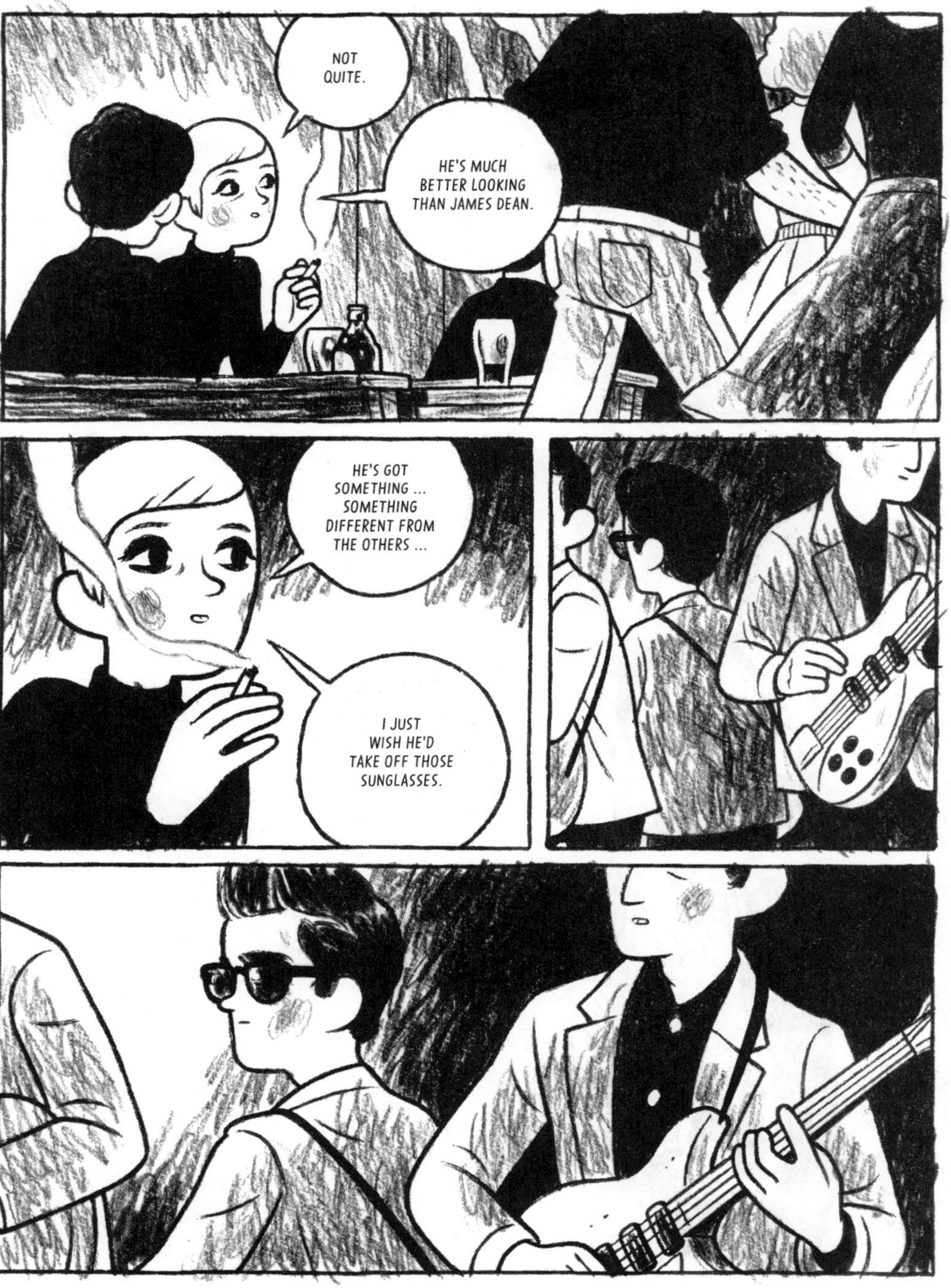
NOT QUITE.
HE'S MUCH BETTER LOOKING THAN JAMES DEAN.
HE'S GOT SOMETHING ... SOMETHING DIFFERENT FROM THE OTHERS ...
I JUST WISH HE'D TAKE OFF THOSE SUNGLASSES.

»My favorite color«

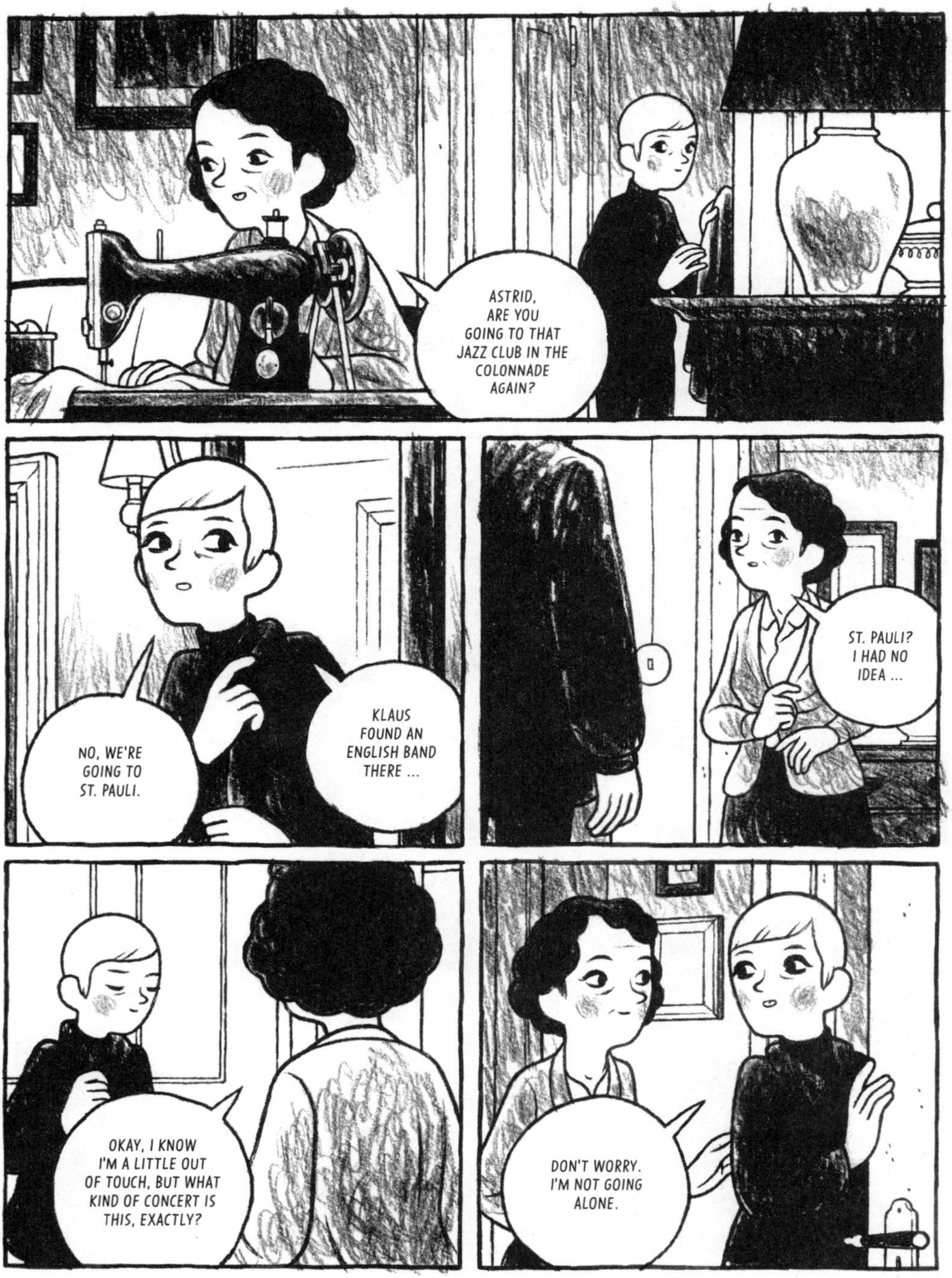
ASTRID, ARE YOU GOING TO THAT JAZZ CLUB IN THE COLONNADE AGAIN?
NO, WE'RE GOING TO ST. PAULI.
KLAUS FOUND AN ENGLISH BAND THERE ...
ST. PAULI? I HAD NO IDEA ...
OKAY, I KNOW I'M A LITTLE OUT OF TOUCH, BUT WHAT KIND OF CONCERT IS THIS, EXACTLY?
DON'T WORRY. I'M NOT GOING ALONE.

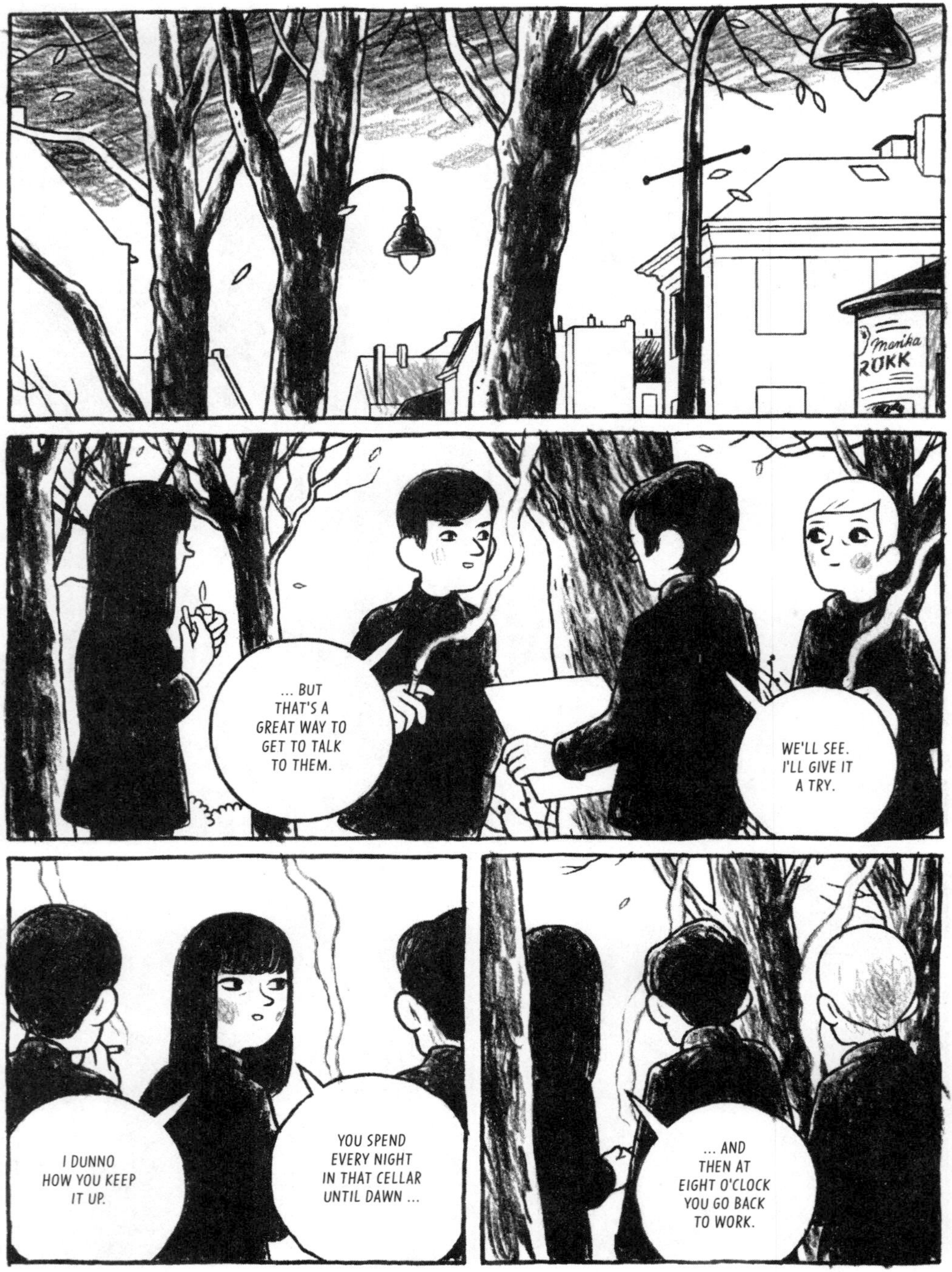
Monika
... BUT THAT'S A GREAT WAY TO GET TO TALK TO THEM.
WE'LL SEE. I'LL GIVE IT A TRY.
I DUNNO HOW YOU KEEP IT UP.
YOU SPEND EVERY NIGHT IN THAT CELLAR UNTIL DAWN ...
... AND THEN AT EIGHT O'CLOCK YOU GO BACK TO WORK.

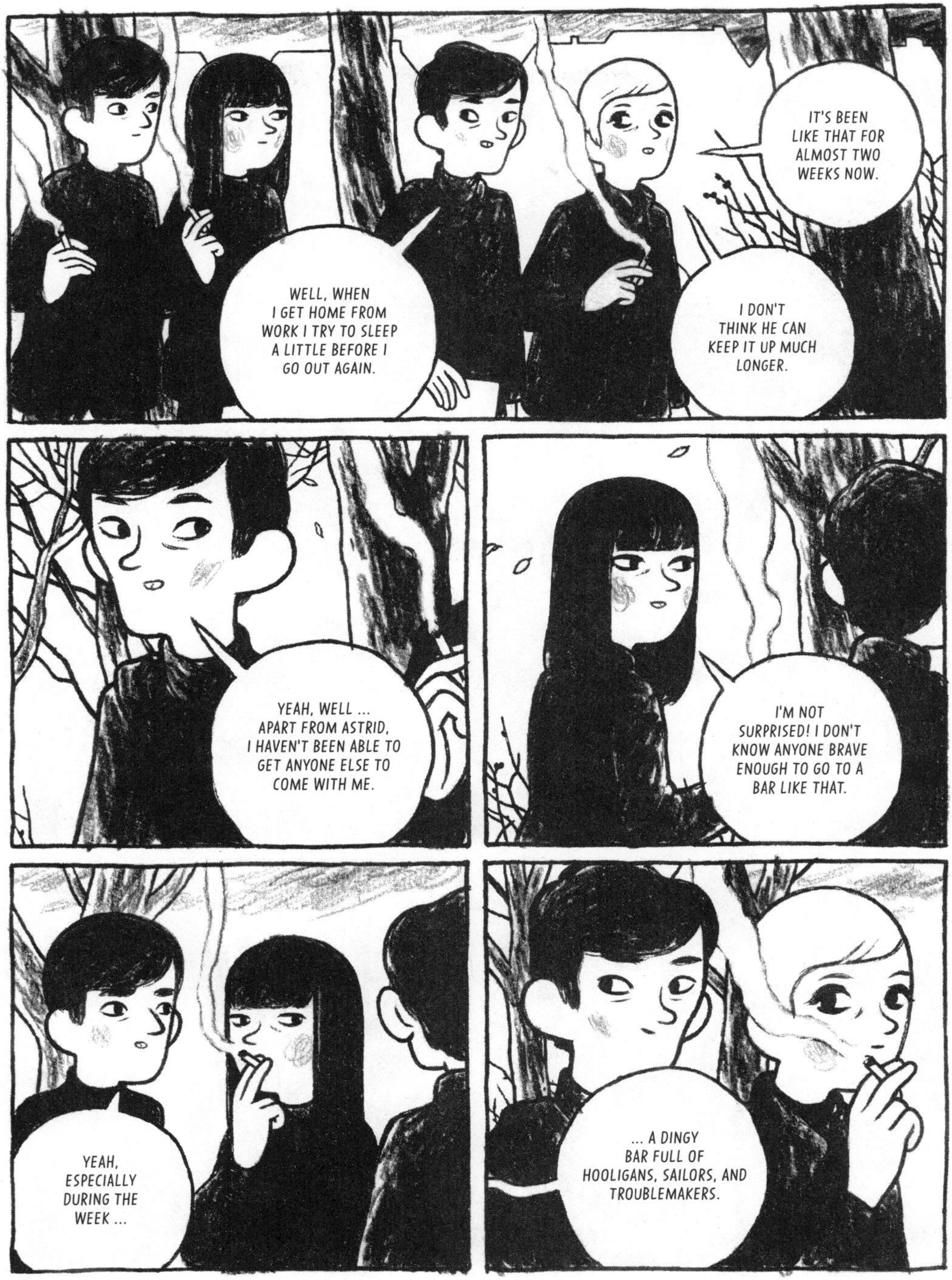
IT'S BEEN LIKE THAT FOR ALMOST TWO WEEKS NOW.
WELL, WHEN I GET HOME FROM WORK I TRY TO SLEEP A LITTLE BEFORE I GO OUT AGAIN.
I DON'T THINK HE CAN KEEP IT UP MUCH LONGER.
YEAH, WELL ... APART FROM ASTRID, I HAVEN'T BEEN ABLE TO GET ANYONE ELSE TO COME WITH ME.
I'M NOT SURPRISED! I DON'T KNOW ANYONE BRAVE ENOUGH TO GO TO A BAR LIKE THAT.
YEAH, ESPECIALLY DURING THE WEEK ...
... A DINGY BAR FULL OF HOOLIGANS, SAILORS, AND TROUBLEMAKERS.

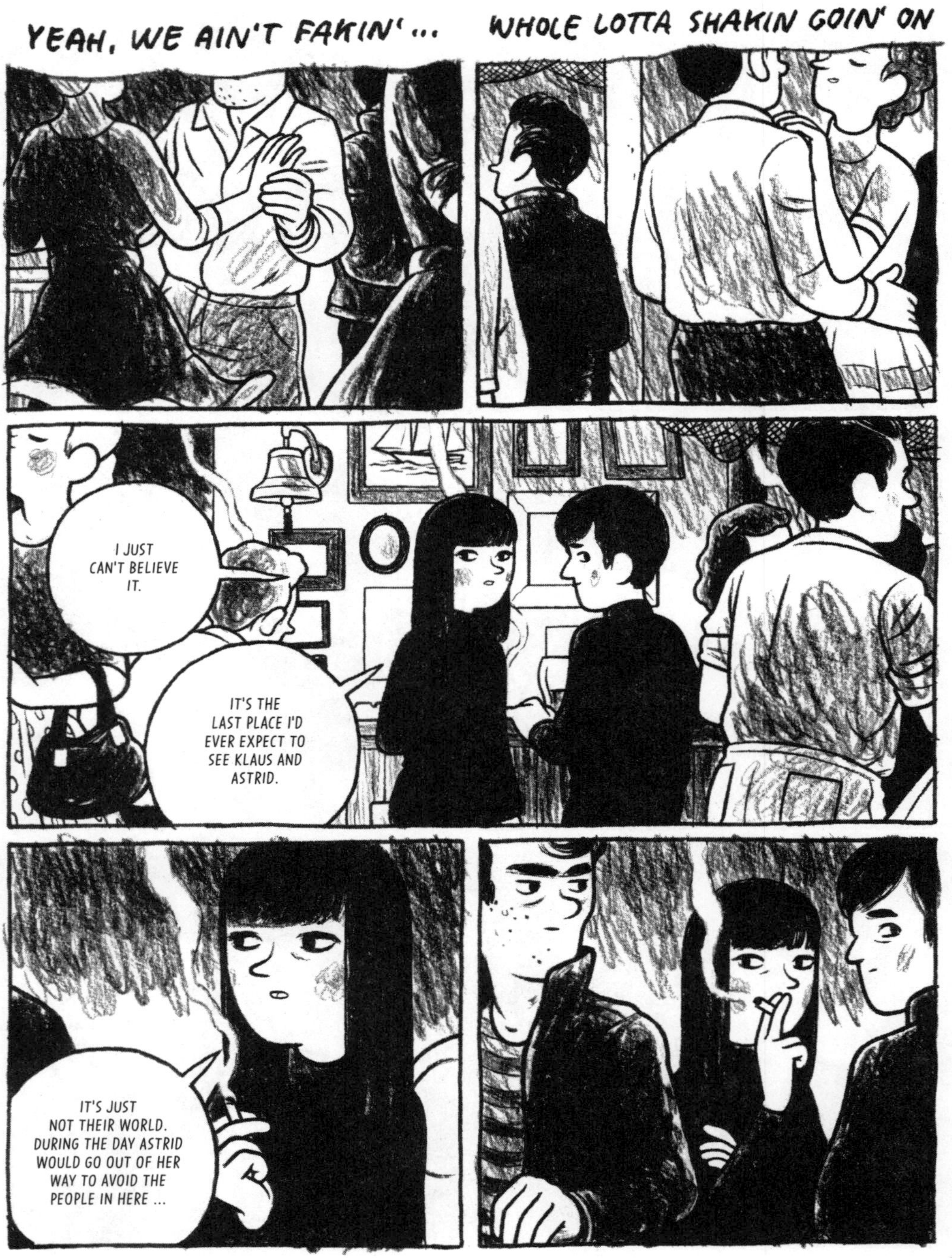
YEAH, WE AIN'T FAKIN' ... WHOLE LOTTA SHAKIN GOIN' ON
I JUST CAN'T BELIEVE IT.
IT'S THE LAST PLACE I'D EVER EXPECT TO SEE KLAUS AND ASTRID.
IT'S JUST NOT THEIR WORLD. DURING THE DAY ASTRID WOULD GO OUT OF HER WAY TO AVOID THE PEOPLE IN HERE ...

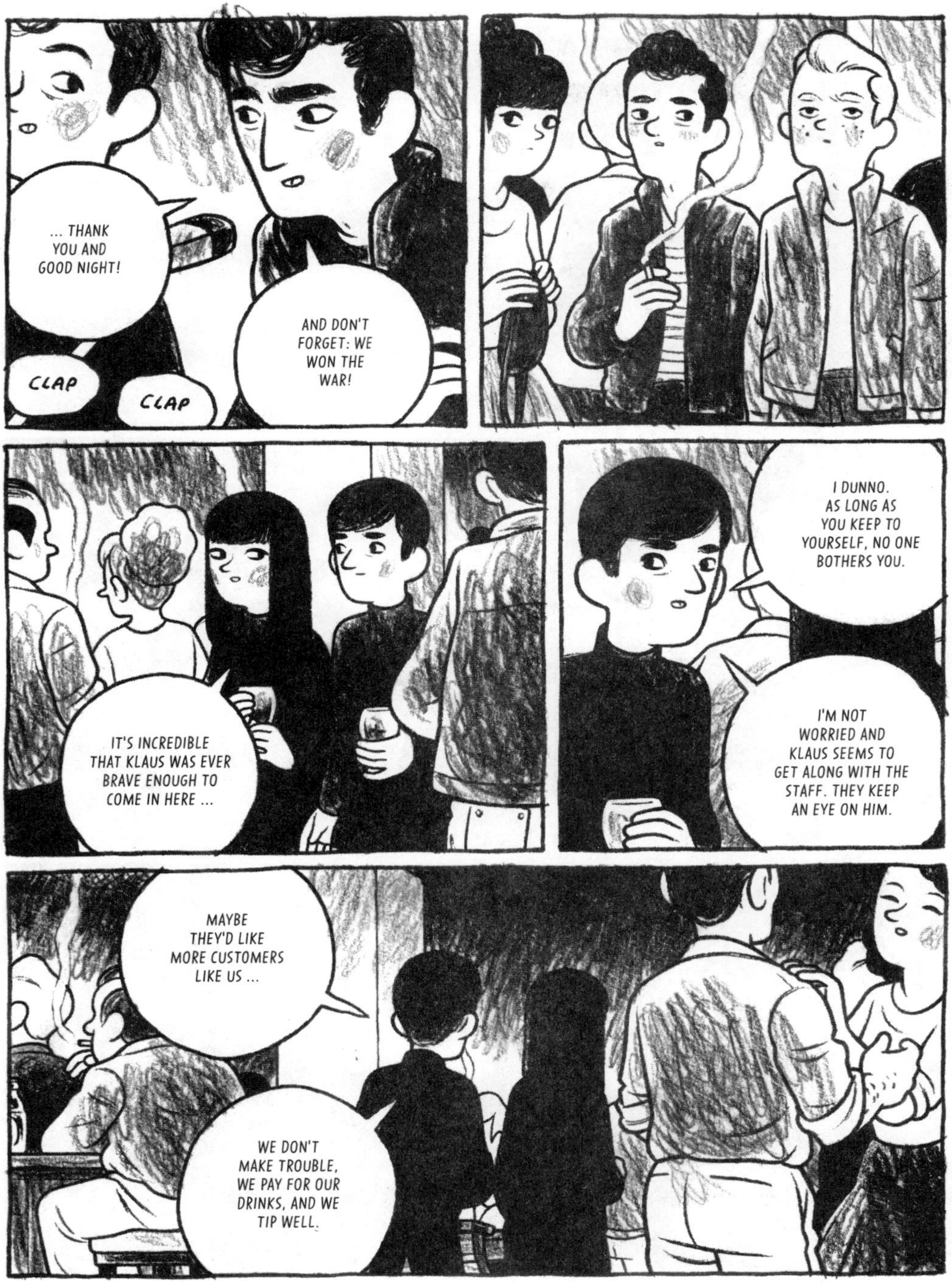
... THANK YOU AND GOOD NIGHT!
AND DON'T FORGET: WE WON THE WAR!
CLAP
CLAP
IT'S INCREDIBLE THAT KLAUS WAS EVER BRAVE ENOUGH TO COME IN HERE ...
I DUNNO. AS LONG AS YOU KEEP TO YOURSELF, NO ONE BOTHERS YOU.
I'M NOT WORRIED AND KLAUS SEEMS TO GET ALONG WITH THE STAFF. THEY KEEP AN EYE ON HIM.
MAYBE THEY'D LIKE MORE CUSTOMERS LIKE US ...
WE DON'T MAKE TROUBLE, WE PAY FOR OUR DRINKS, AND WE TIP WELL.

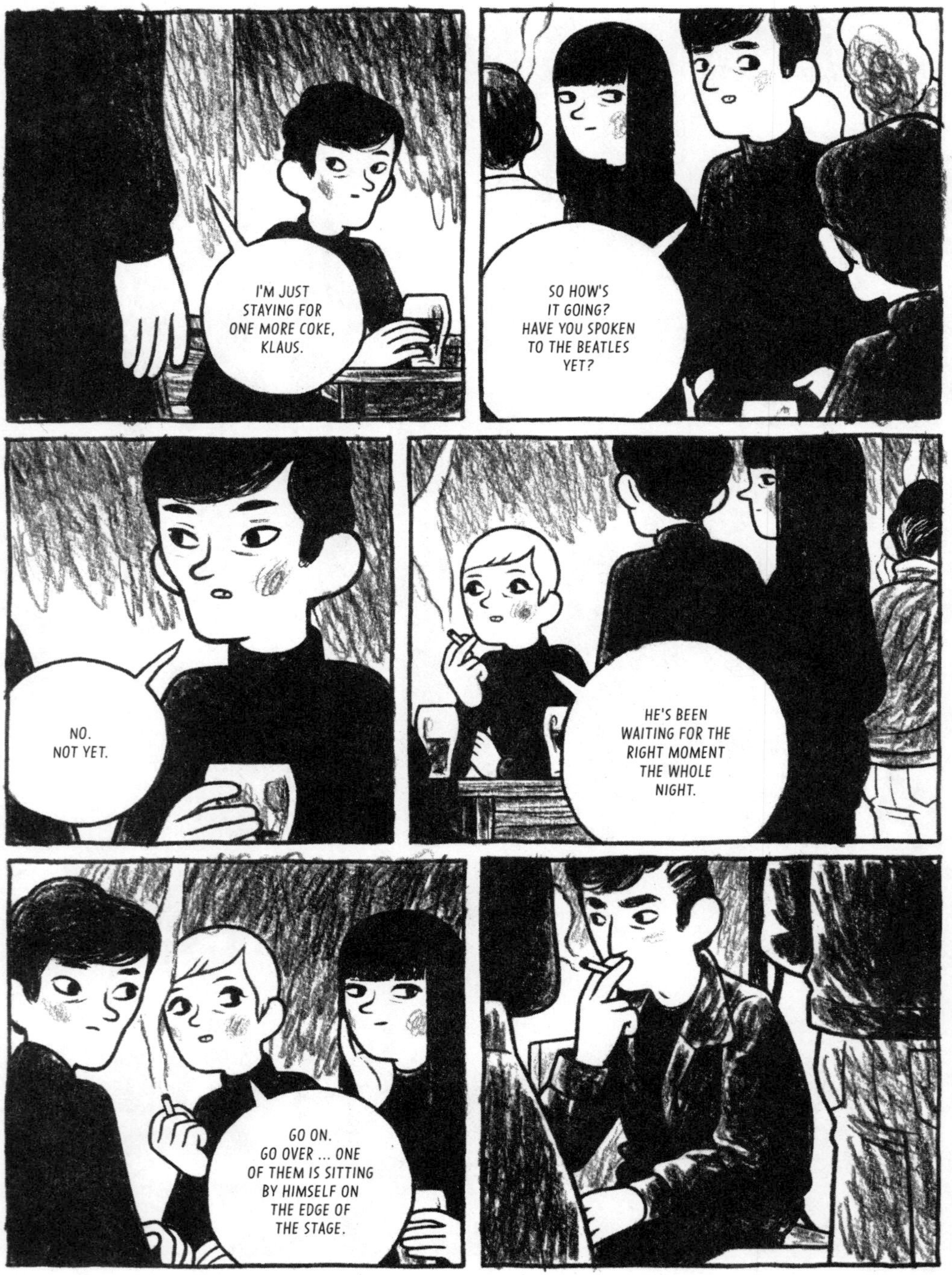
I'M JUST STAYING FOR ONE MORE COKE, KLAUS.
SO HOW'S IT GOING? HAVE YOU SPOKEN TO THE BEATLES YET?
NO. NOT YET.
HE'S BEEN WAITING FOR THE RIGHT MOMENT THE WHOLE NIGHT.
GO ON. GO OVER ... ONE OF THEM IS SITTING BY HIMSELF ON THE EDGE OF THE STAGE.

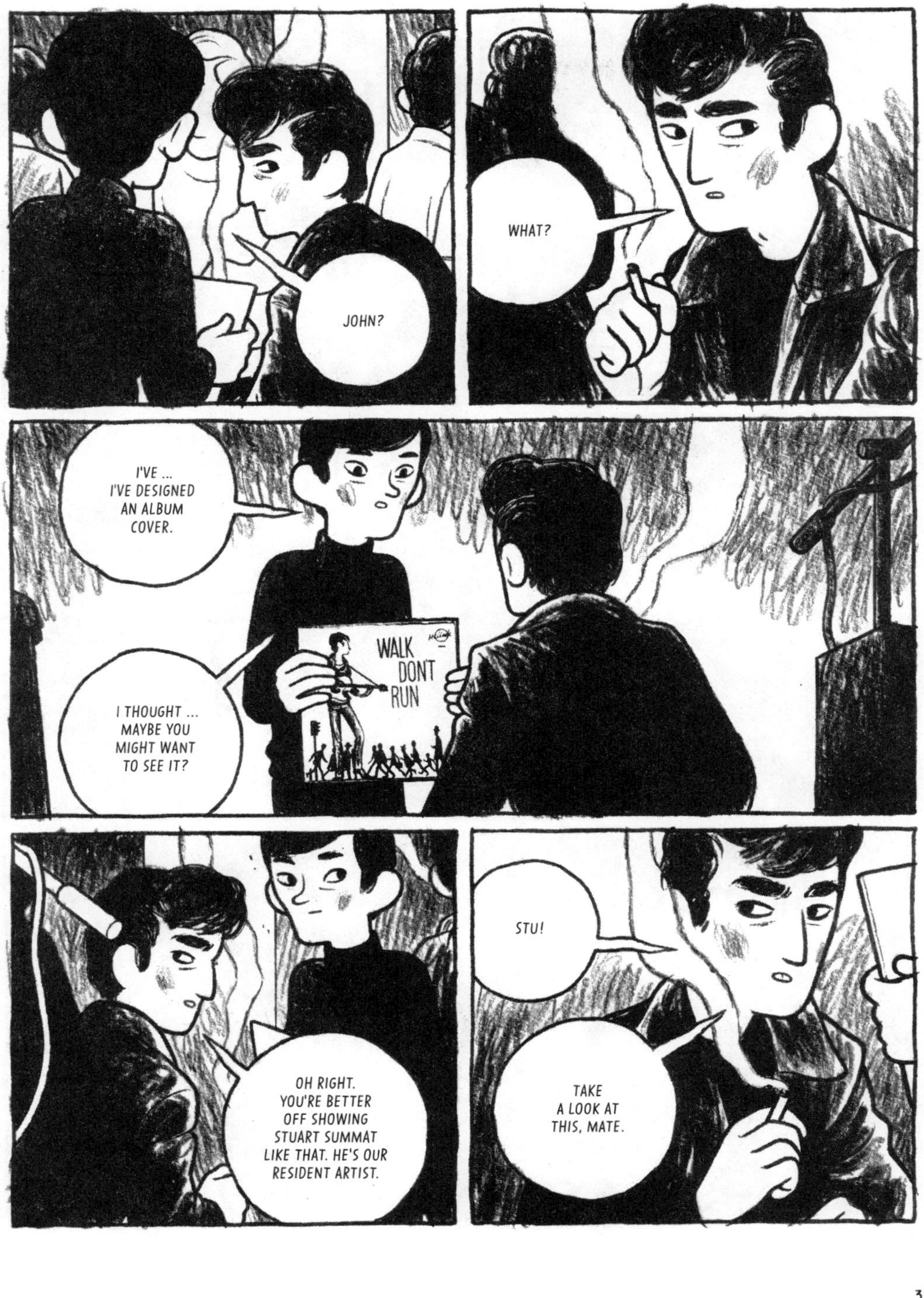
JOHN?
WHAT?
I'VE ... I'VE DESIGNED AN ALBUM COVER.
WALK DON'T RUN
I THOUGHT ... MAYBE YOU MIGHT WANT TO SEE IT?
OH RIGHT. YOU'RE BETTER OFF SHOWING STUART SUMMAT LIKE THAT. HE'S OUR RESIDENT ARTIST.
STU!
TAKE A LOOK AT THIS, MATE.

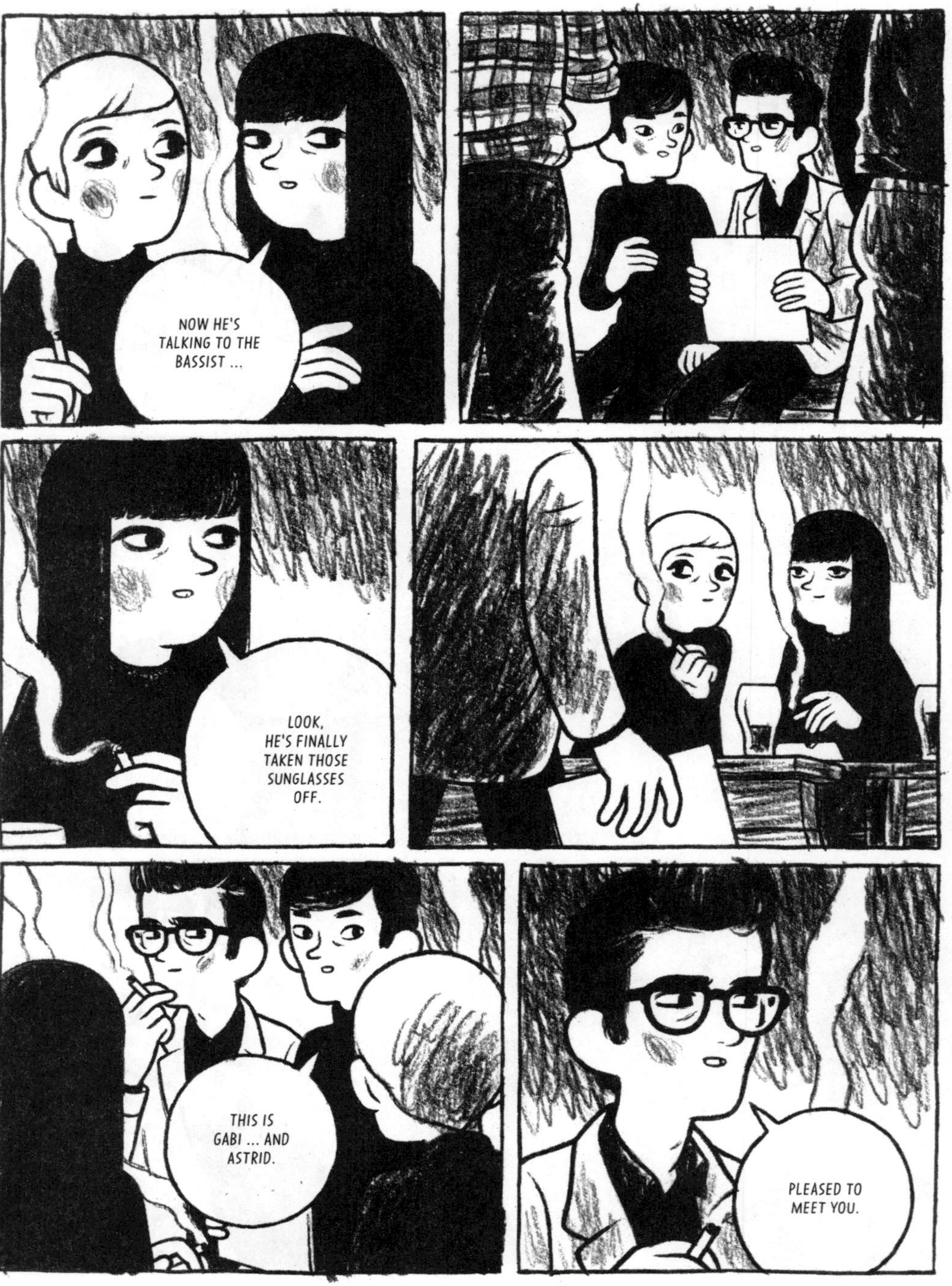
NOW HE'S TALKING TO THE BASSIST ...
LOOK, HE'S FINALLY TAKEN THOSE SUNGLASSES OFF.
THIS IS GABI ... AND ASTRID.
PLEASED TO MEET YOU.

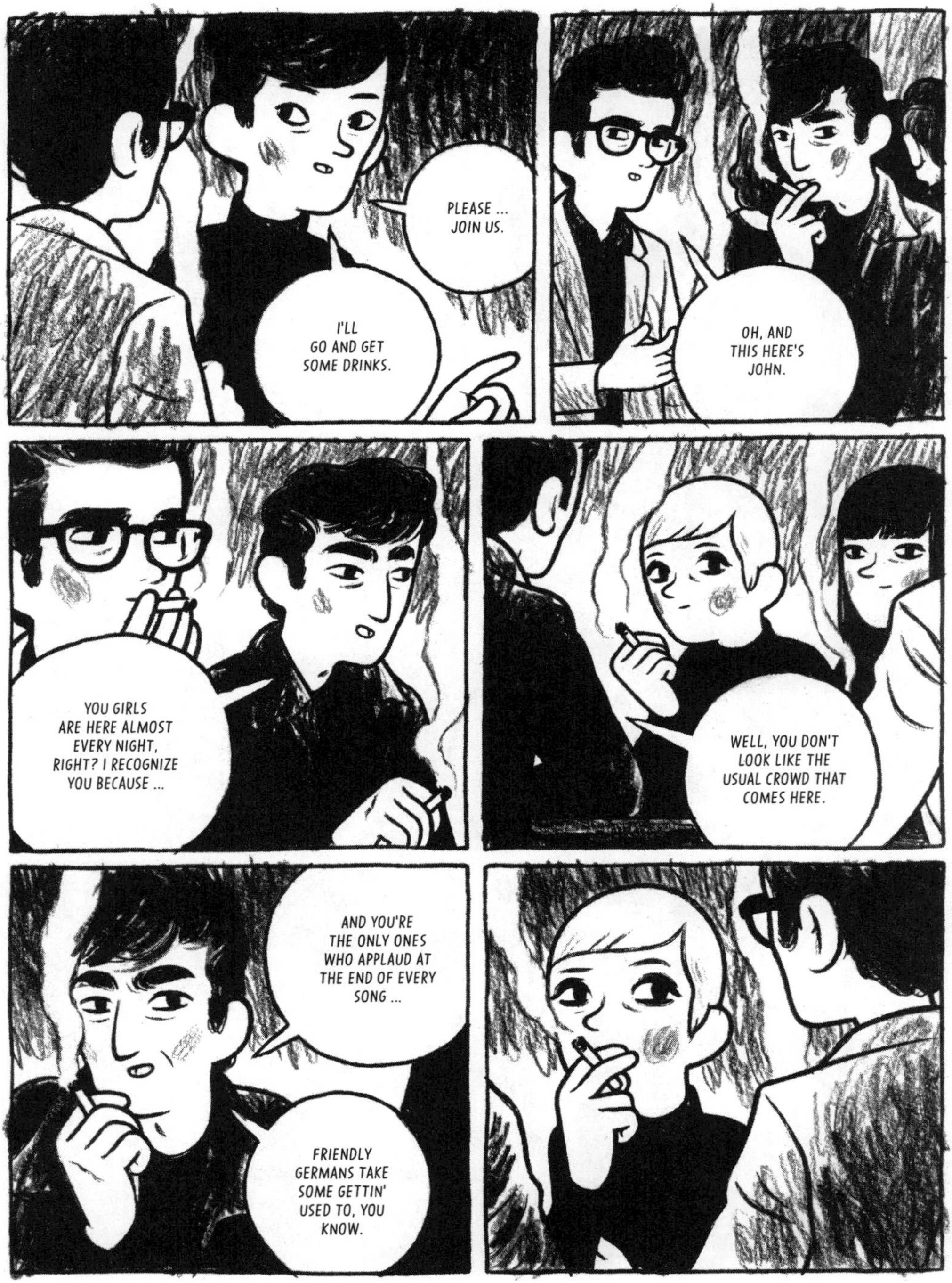
PLEASE ... JOIN US.
I'LL GO AND GET SOME DRINKS.
OH, AND THIS HERE'S JOHN.
YOU GIRLS ARE HERE ALMOST EVERY NIGHT, RIGHT? I RECOGNIZE YOU BECAUSE ...
WELL, YOU DON'T LOOK LIKE THE USUAL CROWD THAT COMES HERE.
AND YOU'RE THE ONLY ONES WHO APPLAUD AT THE END OF EVERY SONG ...
FRIENDLY GERMANS TAKE SOME GETTIN' USED TO, YOU KNOW.

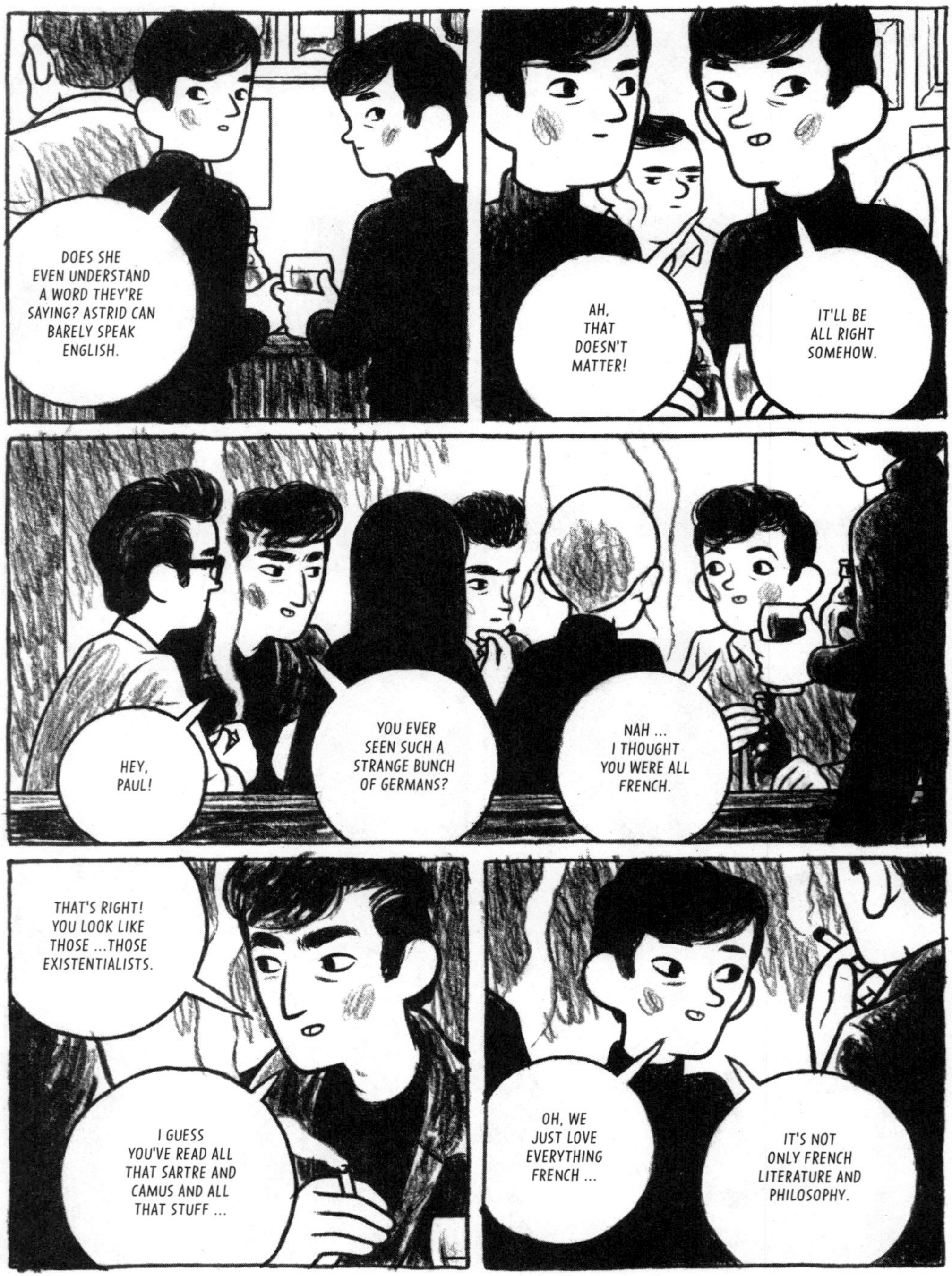
DOES SHE EVEN UNDERSTAND A WORD THEY'RE SAYING? ASTRID CAN BARELY SPEAK ENGLISH.
AH, THAT DOESN'T MATTER!
IT'LL BE ALL RIGHT SOMEHOW.
HEY, PAUL!
YOU EVER SEEN SUCH A STRANGE BUNCH OF GERMANS?
NAH ... I THOUGHT YOU WERE ALL FRENCH.
THAT'S RIGHT! YOU LOOK LIKE THOSE ...THOSE EXISTENTIALISTS.
I GUESS YOU'VE READ ALL THAT SARTRE AND CAMUS AND ALL THAT STUFF ...
OH, WE JUST LOVE EVERYTHING FRENCH ...
IT'S NOT ONLY FRENCH LITERATURE AND PHILOSOPHY.

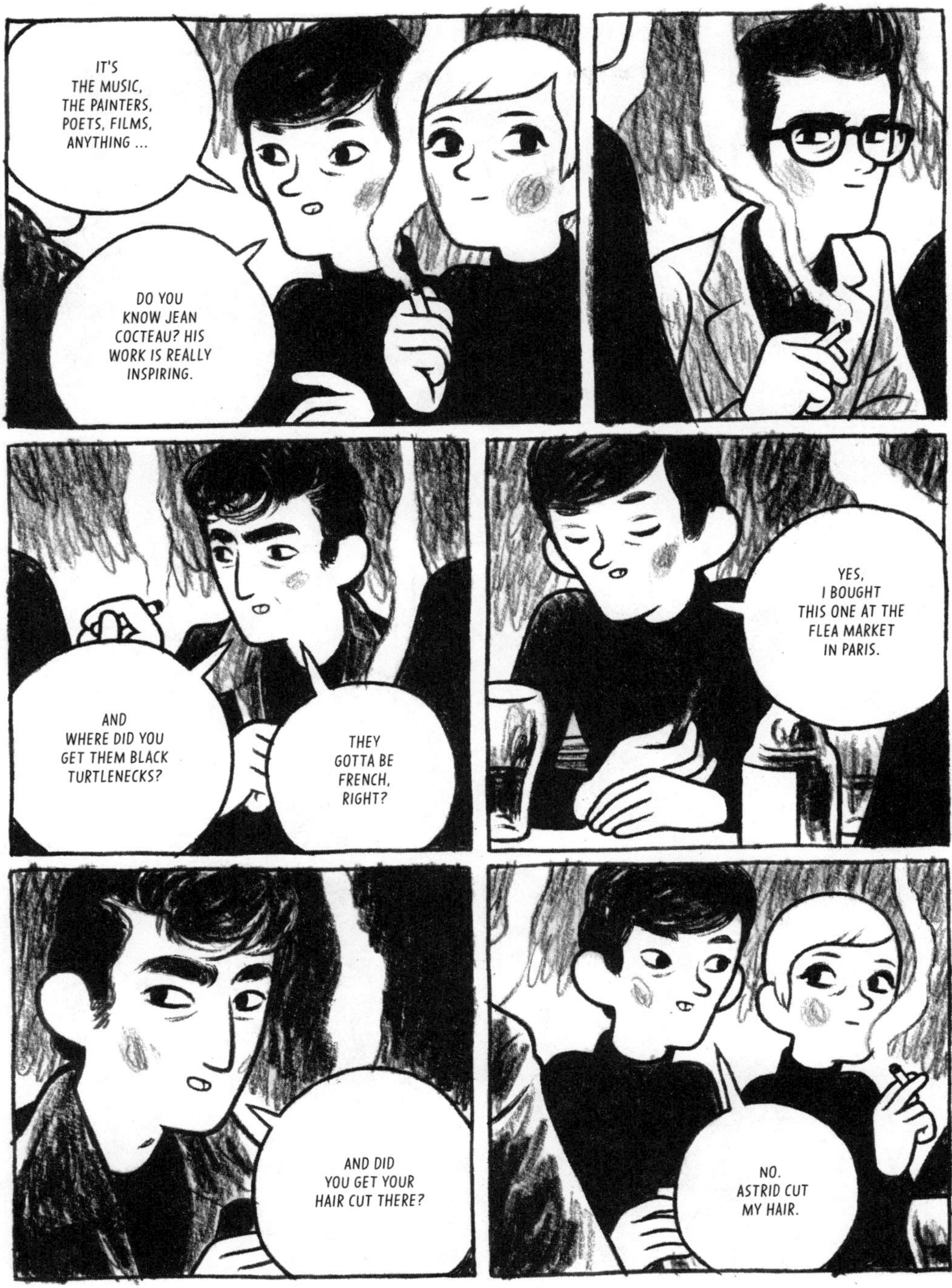
IT'S THE MUSIC, THE PAINTERS, POETS, FILMS, ANYTHING ...
DO YOU KNOW JEAN COCTEAU? HIS WORK IS REALLY INSPIRING.
AND WHERE DID YOU GET THEM BLACK TURTLENECKS?
THEY GOTTA BE FRENCH, RIGHT?
YES, I BOUGHT THIS ONE AT THE FLEA MARKET IN PARIS.
AND DID YOU GET YOUR HAIR CUT THERE?
NO. ASTRID CUT MY HAIR.

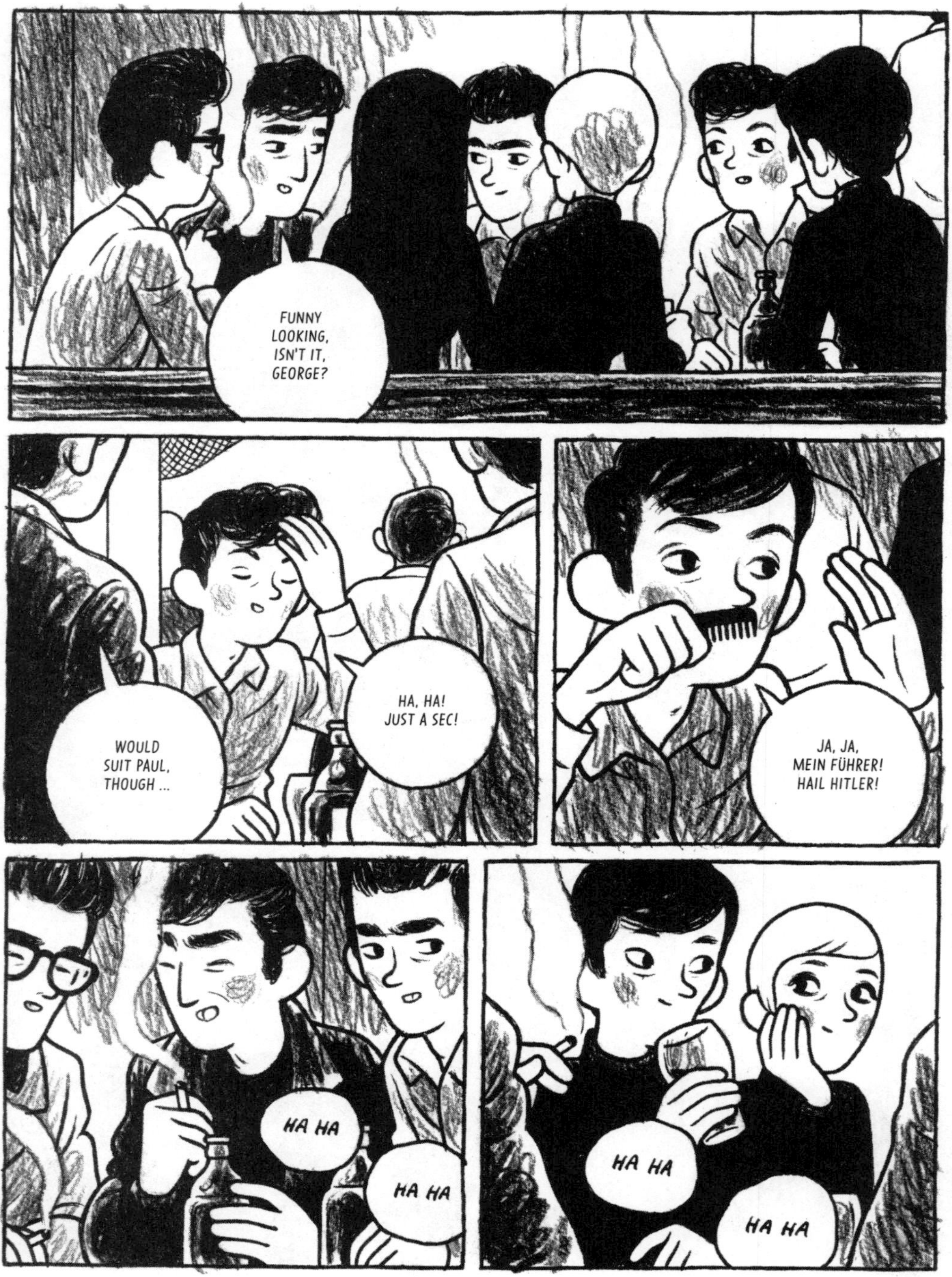
FUNNY LOOKING, ISN'T IT, GEORGE?
WOULD SUIT PAUL, THOUGH ...
HA, HA! JUST A SEC!
JA, JA, MEIN FÜHRER! HAIL HITLER!
HA HA
HA HA
HA HA
HA HA

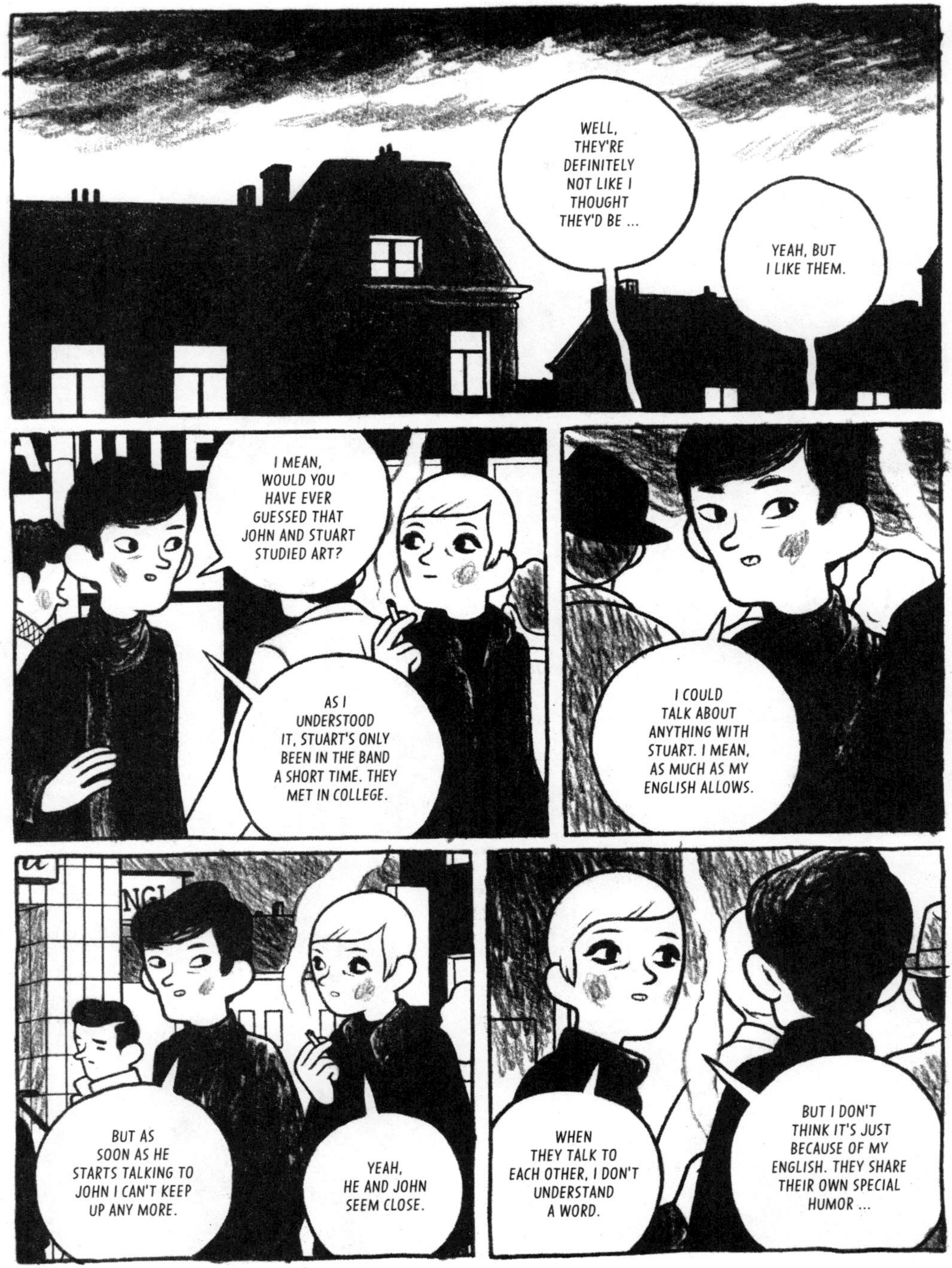
WELL, THEY'RE DEFINITELY NOT LIKE I THOUGHT THEY'D BE ...
YEAH, BUT I LIKE THEM.
I MEAN, WOULD YOU HAVE EVER GUESSED THAT JOHN AND STUART STUDIED ART?
AS I UNDERSTOOD IT, STUART'S ONLY BEEN IN THE BAND A SHORT TIME. THEY MET IN COLLEGE.
I COULD TALK ABOUT ANYTHING WITH STUART. I MEAN, AS MUCH AS MY ENGLISH ALLOWS.
BUT AS SOON AS HE STARTS TALKING TO JOHN I CAN'T KEEP UP ANY MORE.
YEAH, HE AND JOHN SEEM CLOSE.
WHEN THEY TALK TO EACH OTHER, I DON'T UNDERSTAND A WORD.
BUT I DON'T THINK IT'S JUST BECAUSE OF MY ENGLISH. THEY SHARE THEIR OWN SPECIAL HUMOR ...

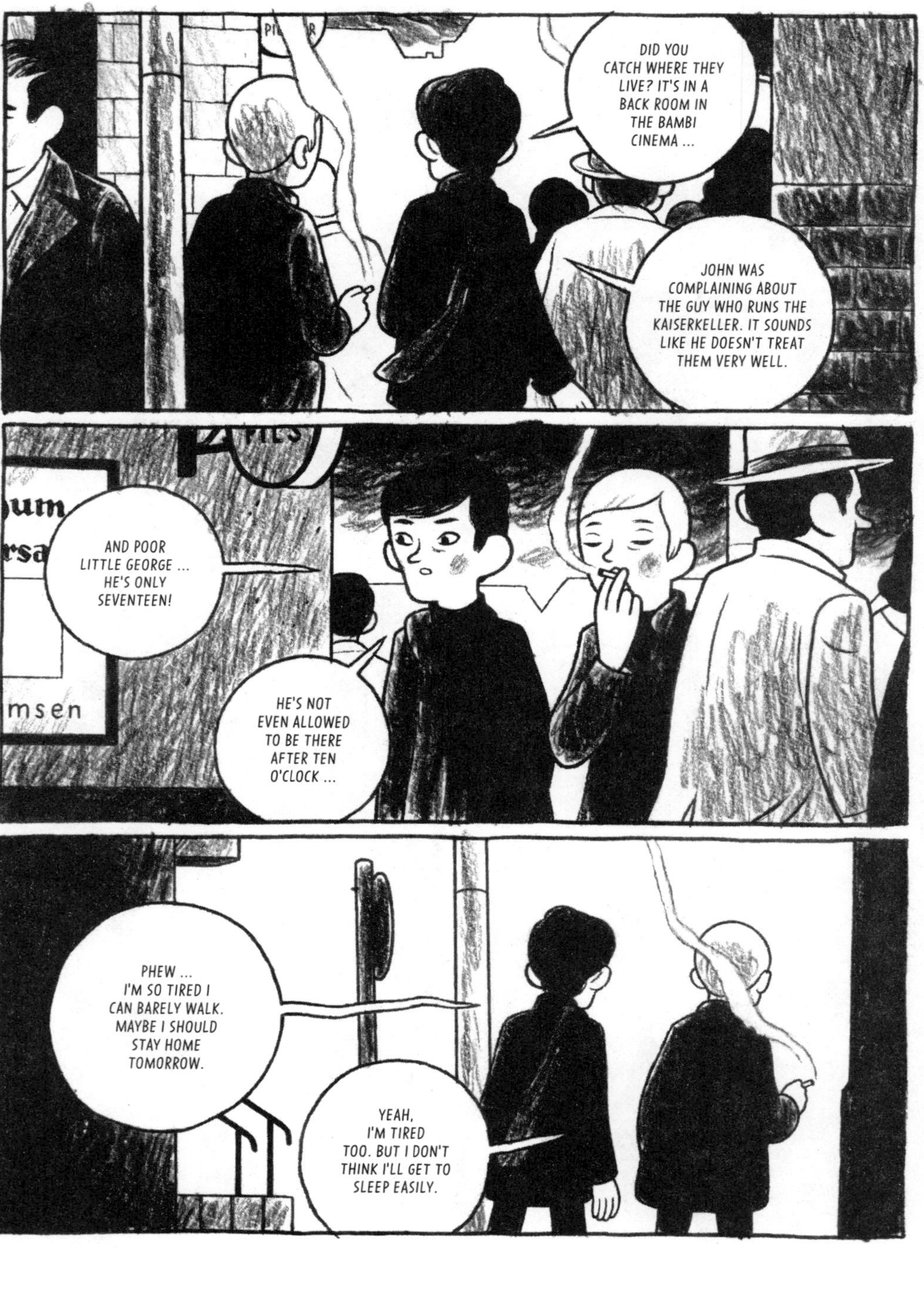
DID YOU CATCH WHERE THEY LIVE? IT'S IN A BACK ROOM IN THE BAMBI CINEMA ...
JOHN WAS COMPLAINING ABOUT THE GUY WHO RUNS THE KAISERKELLER. IT SOUNDS LIKE HE DOESN'T TREAT THEM VERY WELL.
AND POOR LITTLE GEORGE ... HE'S ONLY SEVENTEEN!
HE'S NOT EVEN ALLOWED TO BE THERE AFTER TEN O'CLOCK ...
PHEW ... I'M SO TIRED I CAN BARELY WALK. MAYBE I SHOULD STAY HOME TOMORROW.
YEAH, I'M TIRED TOO. BUT I DON'T THINK I'LL GET TO SLEEP EASILY.

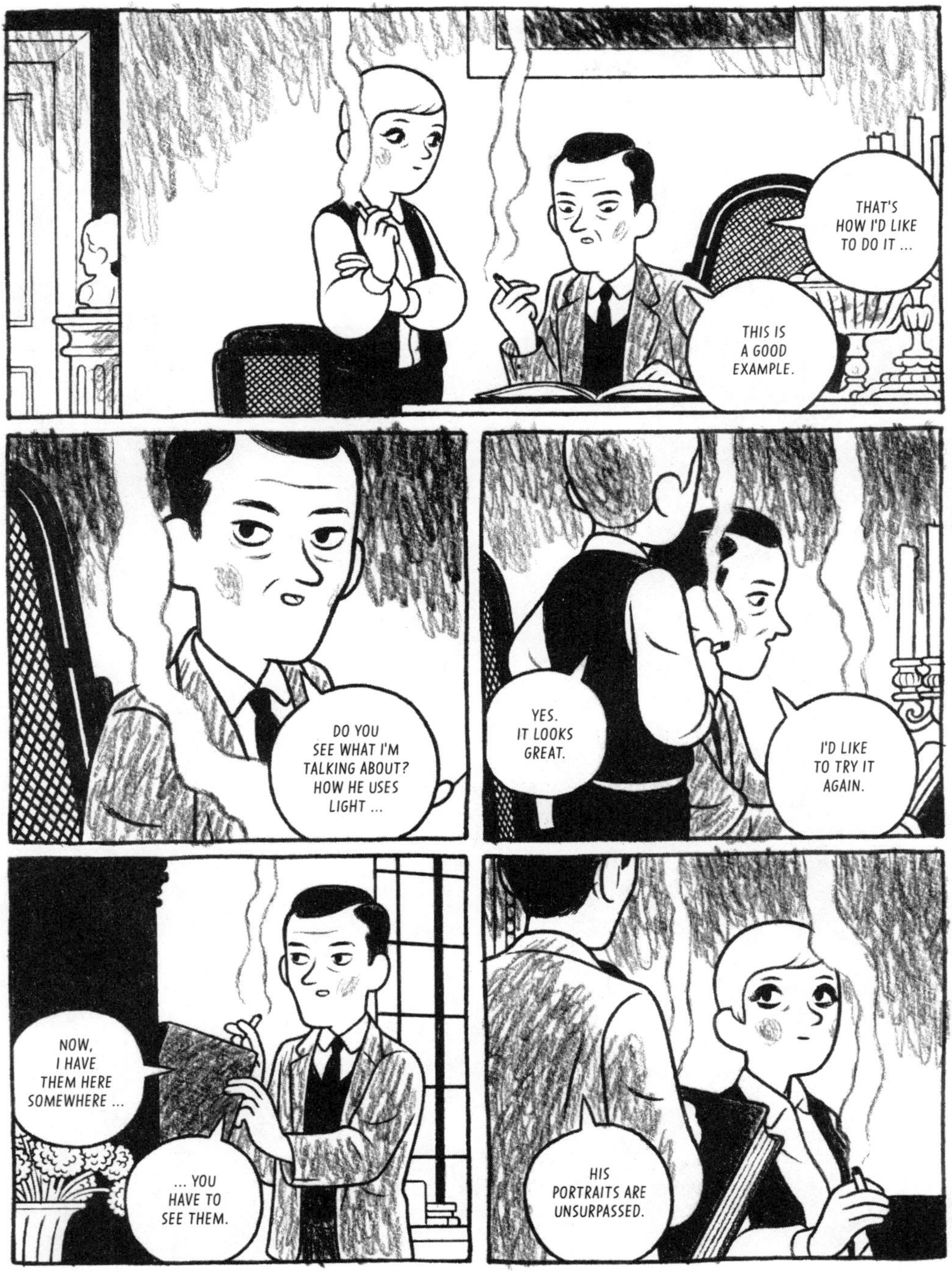
THAT'S HOW I'D LIKE TO DO IT ...
THIS IS A GOOD EXAMPLE.
DO YOU SEE WHAT I'M TALKING ABOUT? HOW HE USES LIGHT ...
YES. IT LOOKS GREAT.
I'D LIKE TO TRY IT AGAIN.
NOW, I HAVE THEM HERE SOMEWHERE ...
... YOU HAVE TO SEE THEM.
HIS PORTRAITS ARE UNSURPASSED.

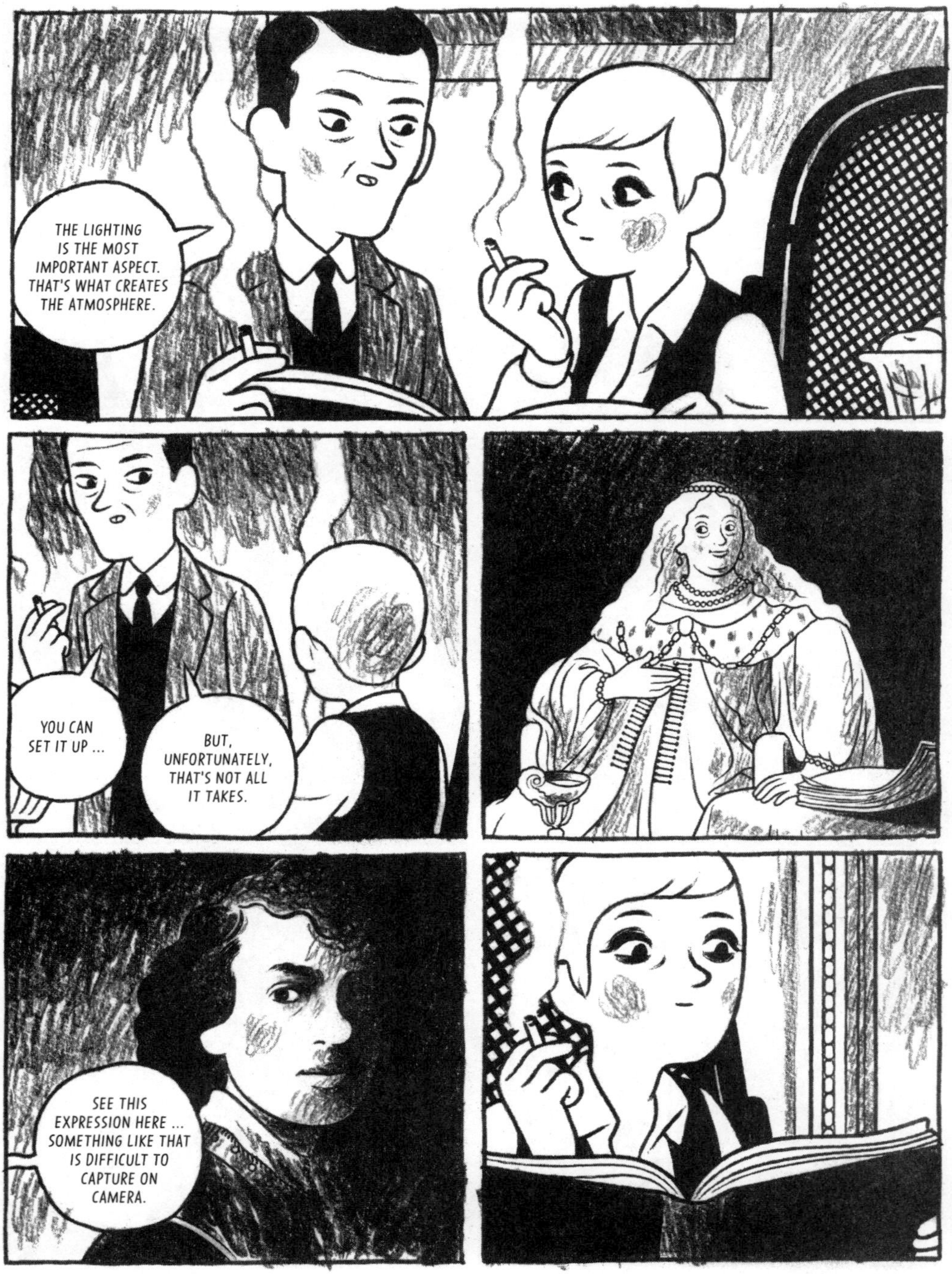
THE LIGHTING IS THE MOST IMPORTANT ASPECT. THAT'S WHAT CREATES THE ATMOSPHERE.
YOU CAN SET IT UP ...
BUT, UNFORTUNATELY, THAT'S NOT ALL IT TAKES.
SEE THIS EXPRESSION HERE ... SOMETHING LIKE THAT IS DIFFICULT TO CAPTURE ON CAMERA.

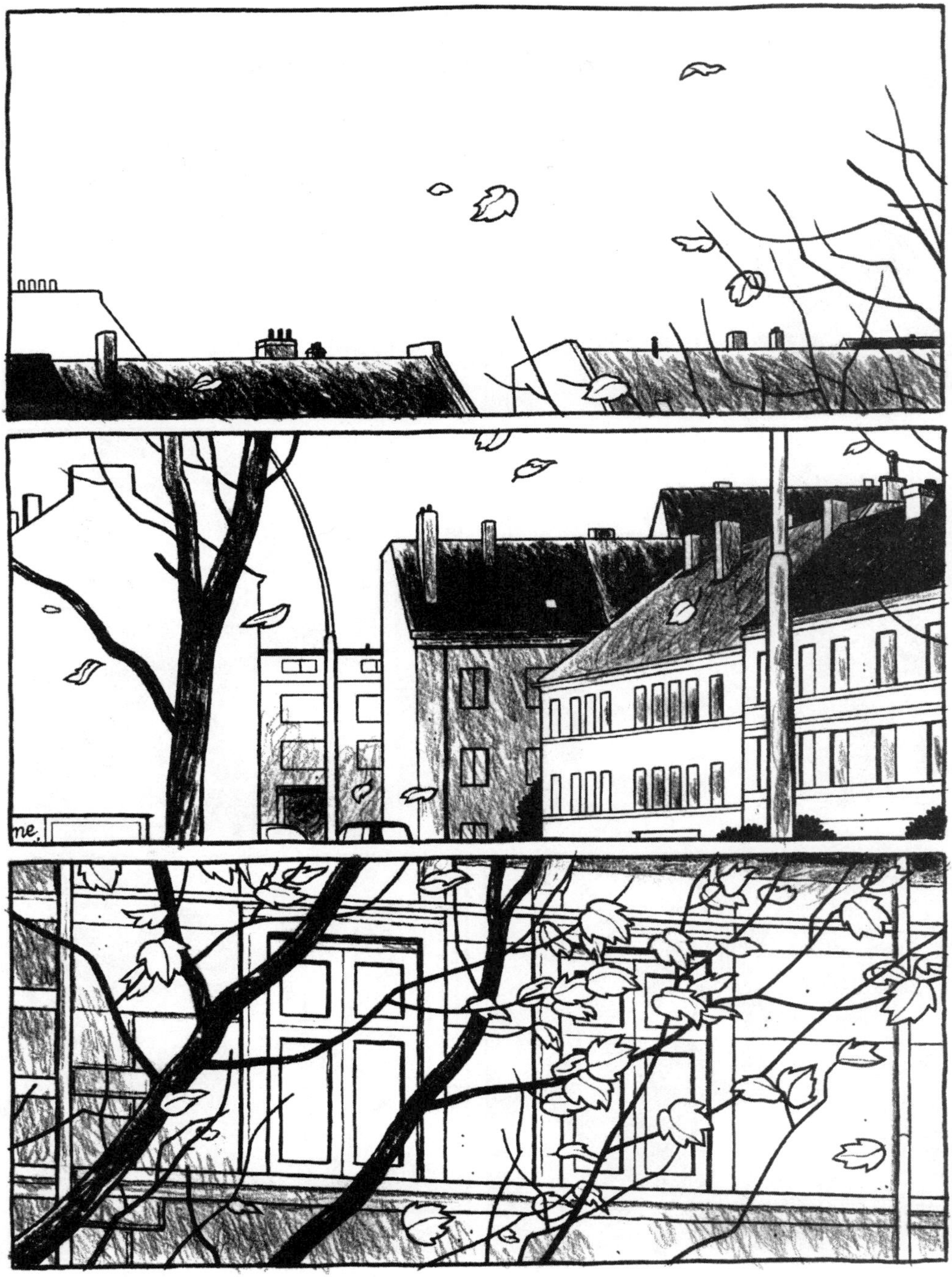

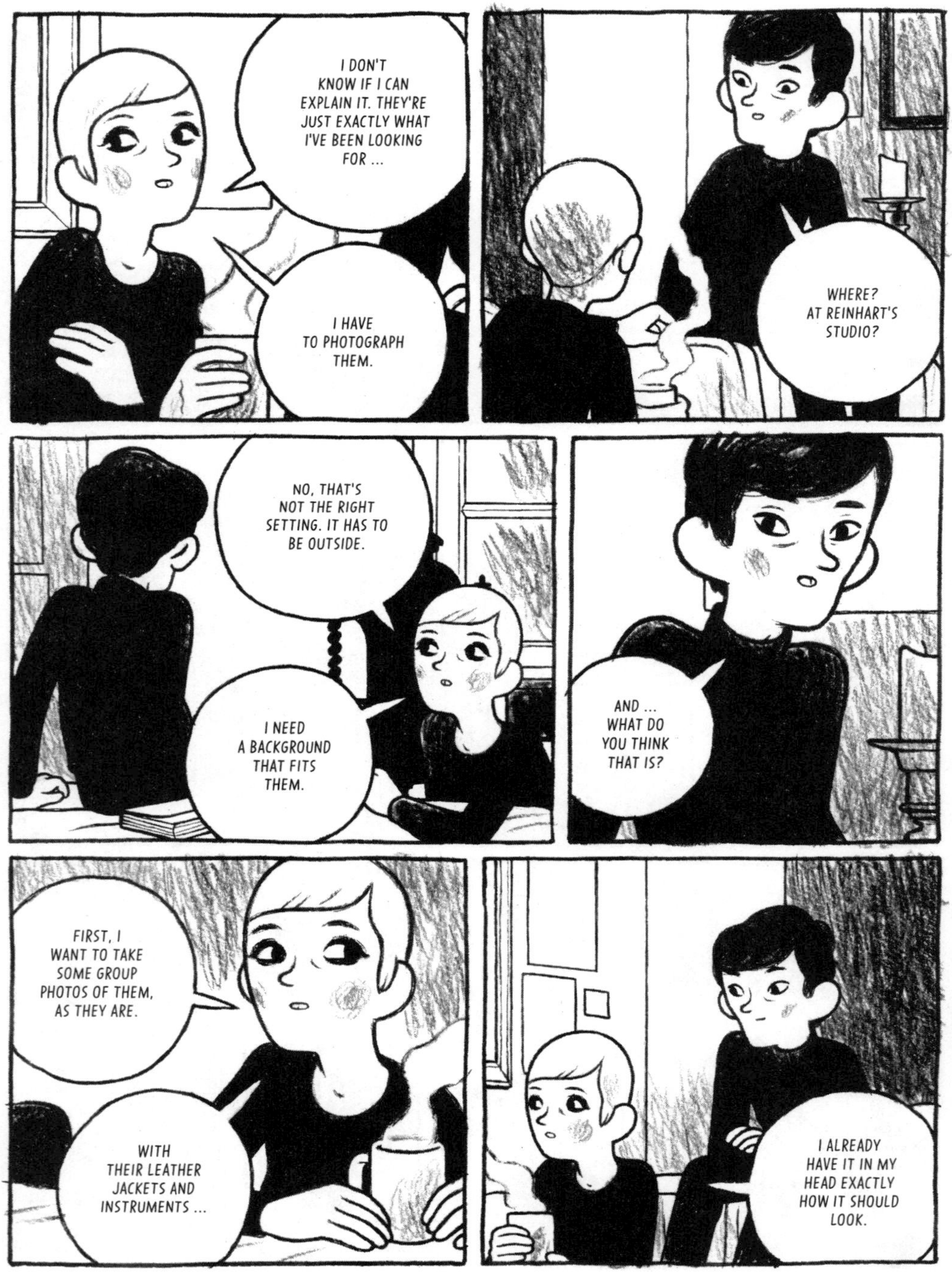
I DON'T KNOW IF I CAN EXPLAIN IT. THEY'RE JUST EXACTLY WHAT I'VE BEEN LOOKING FOR ...
I HAVE TO PHOTOGRAPH THEM.
WHERE? AT REINHART'S STUDIO?
NO, THAT'S NOT THE RIGHT SETTING. IT HAS TO BE OUTSIDE.
I NEED A BACKGROUND THAT FITS THEM.
AND ... WHAT DO YOU THINK THAT IS?
FIRST, I WANT TO TAKE SOME GROUP PHOTOS OF THEM, AS THEY ARE.
WITH THEIR LEATHER JACKETS AND INSTRUMENTS ...
I ALREADY HAVE IT IN MY HEAD EXACTLY HOW IT SHOULD LOOK.

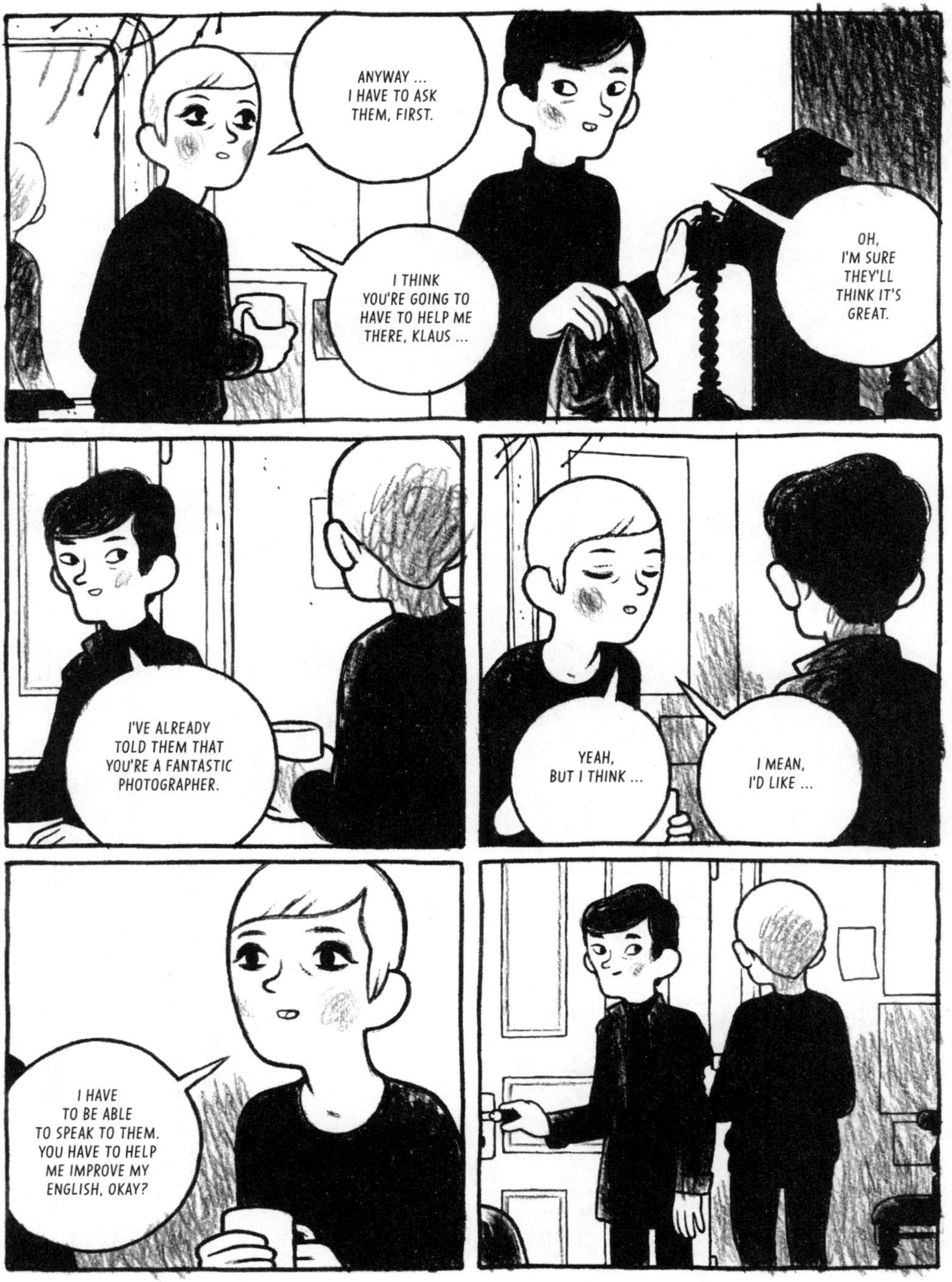
ANYWAY ... I HAVE TO ASK THEM, FIRST.
I THINK YOU'RE GOING TO HAVE TO HELP ME THERE, KLAUS ...
OH, I'M SURE THEY'LL THINK IT'S GREAT.
I'VE ALREADY TOLD THEM THAT YOU'RE A FANTASTIC PHOTOGRAPHER.
YEAH, BUT I THINK ...
I MEAN, I'D LIKE ...
I HAVE TO BE ABLE TO SPEAK TO THEM. YOU HAVE TO HELP ME IMPROVE MY ENGLISH, OKAY?

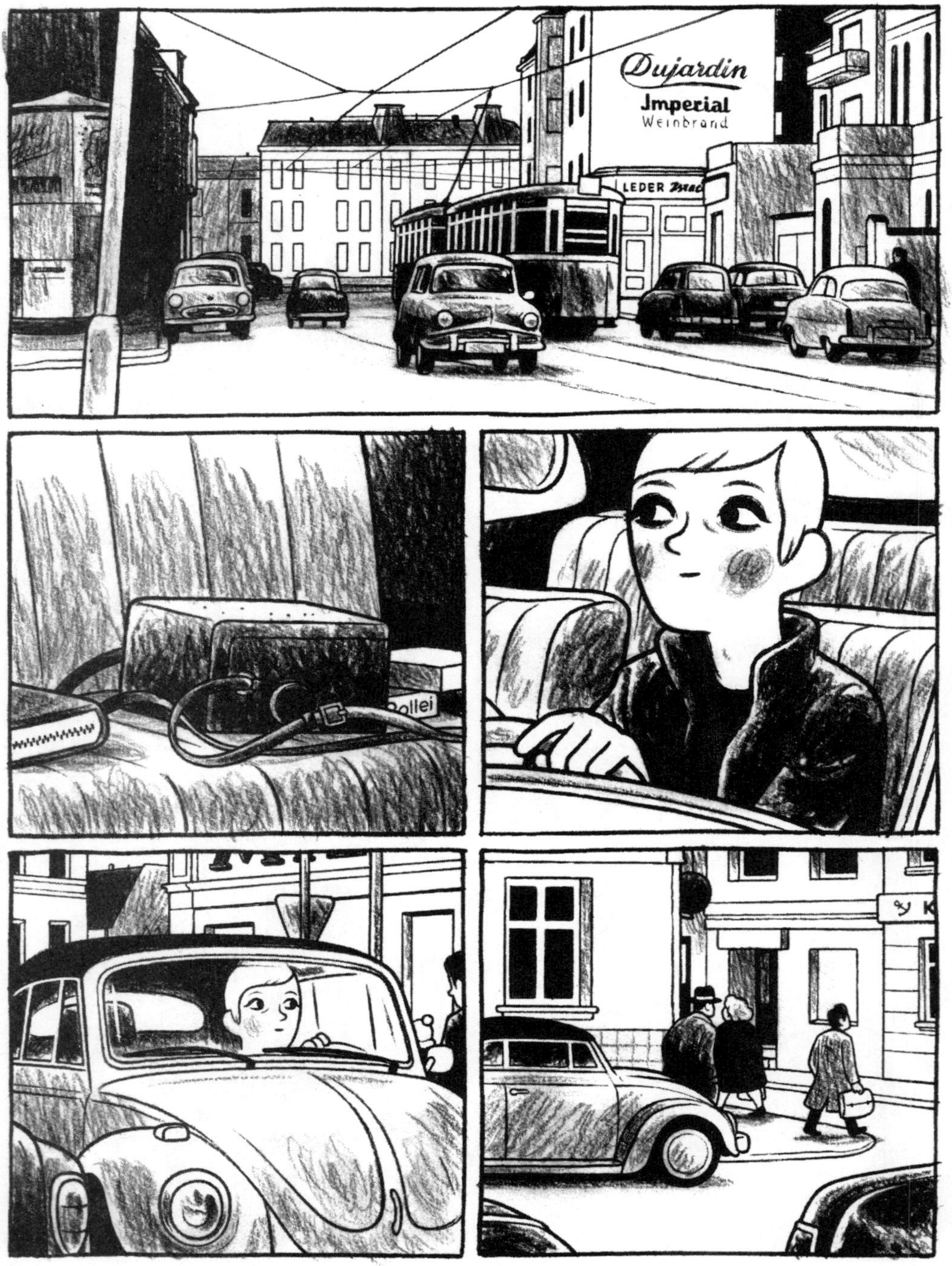
Dujardin
Jmperial
Weinbrand
LEDER
Rollei

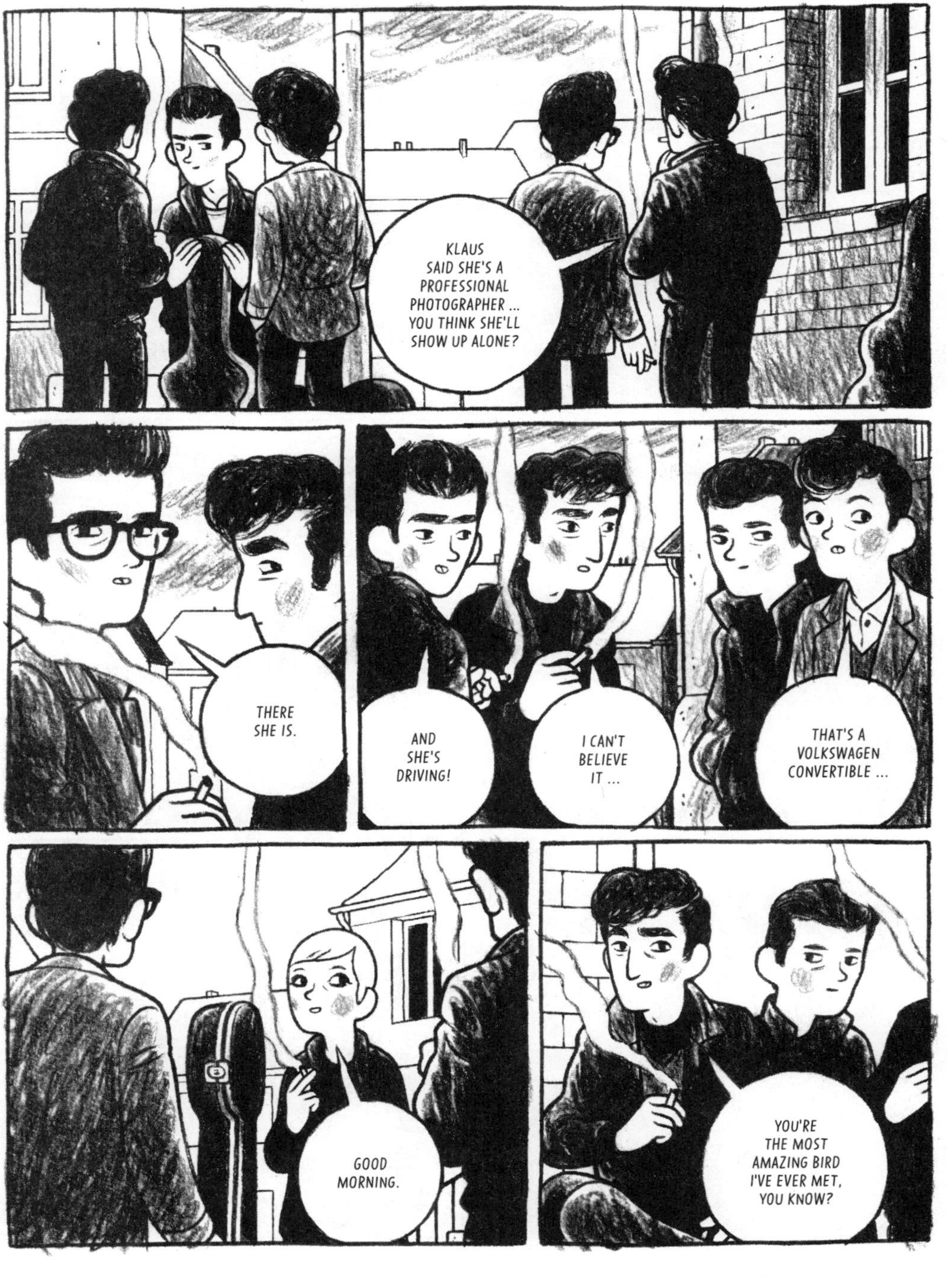
KLAUS SAID SHE'S A PROFESSIONAL PHOTOGRAPHER ... YOU THINK SHE'LL SHOW UP ALONE?
THERE SHE IS.
AND SHE'S DRIVING!
I CAN'T BELIEVE IT ...
THAT'S A VOLKSWAGEN CONVERTIBLE ...
GOOD MORNING.
YOU'RE THE MOST AMAZING BIRD I'VE EVER MET, YOU KNOW?

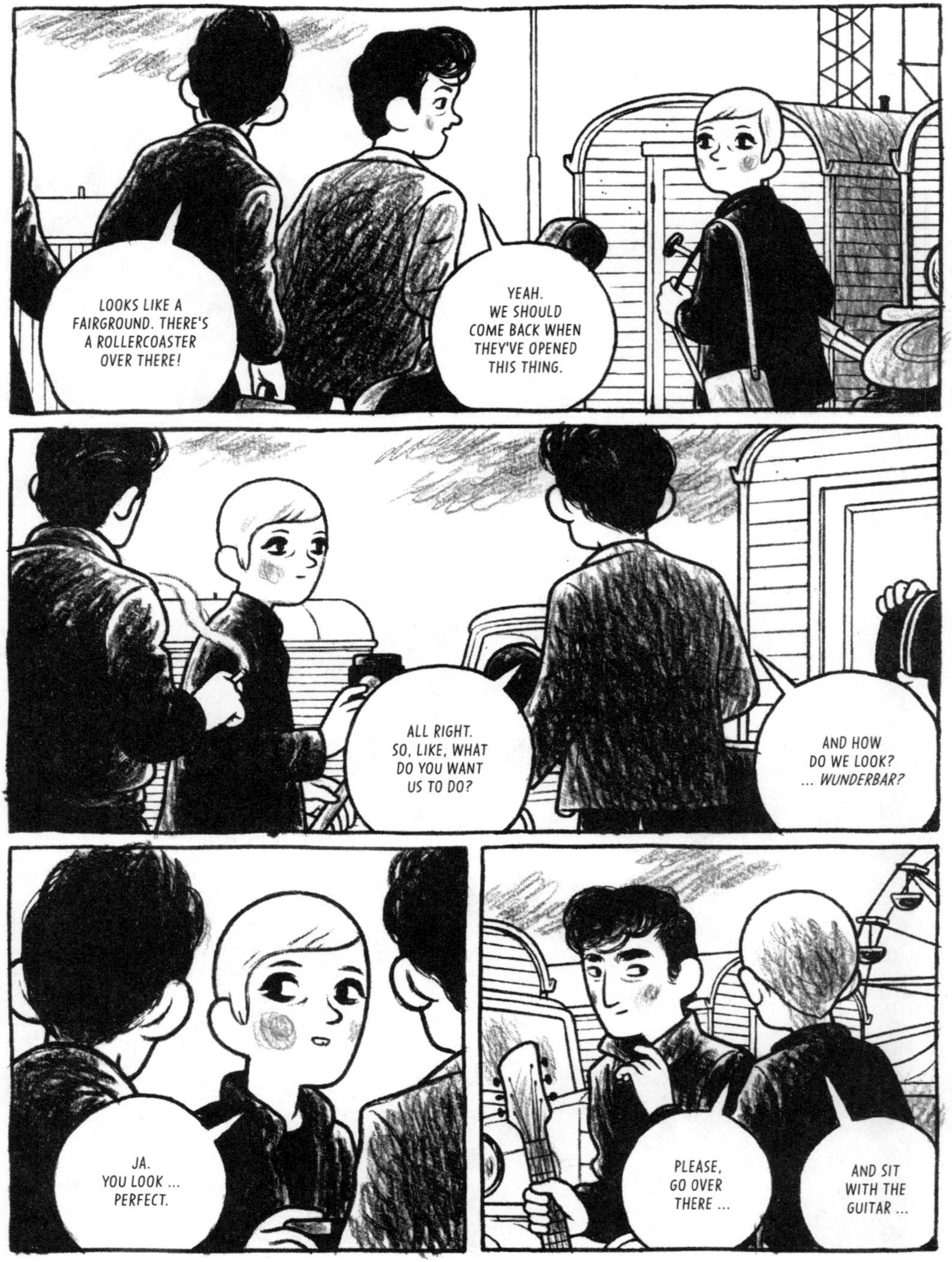
LOOKS LIKE A FAIRGROUND. THERE'S A ROLLERCOASTER OVER THERE!
YEAH. WE SHOULD COME BACK WHEN THEY'VE OPENED THIS THING.
ALL RIGHT. SO, LIKE, WHAT DO YOU WANT US TO DO?
AND HOW DO WE LOOK? ... *WUNDERBAR?*
JA. YOU LOOK ... PERFECT.
PLEASE, GO OVER THERE ...
AND SIT WITH THE GUITAR ...

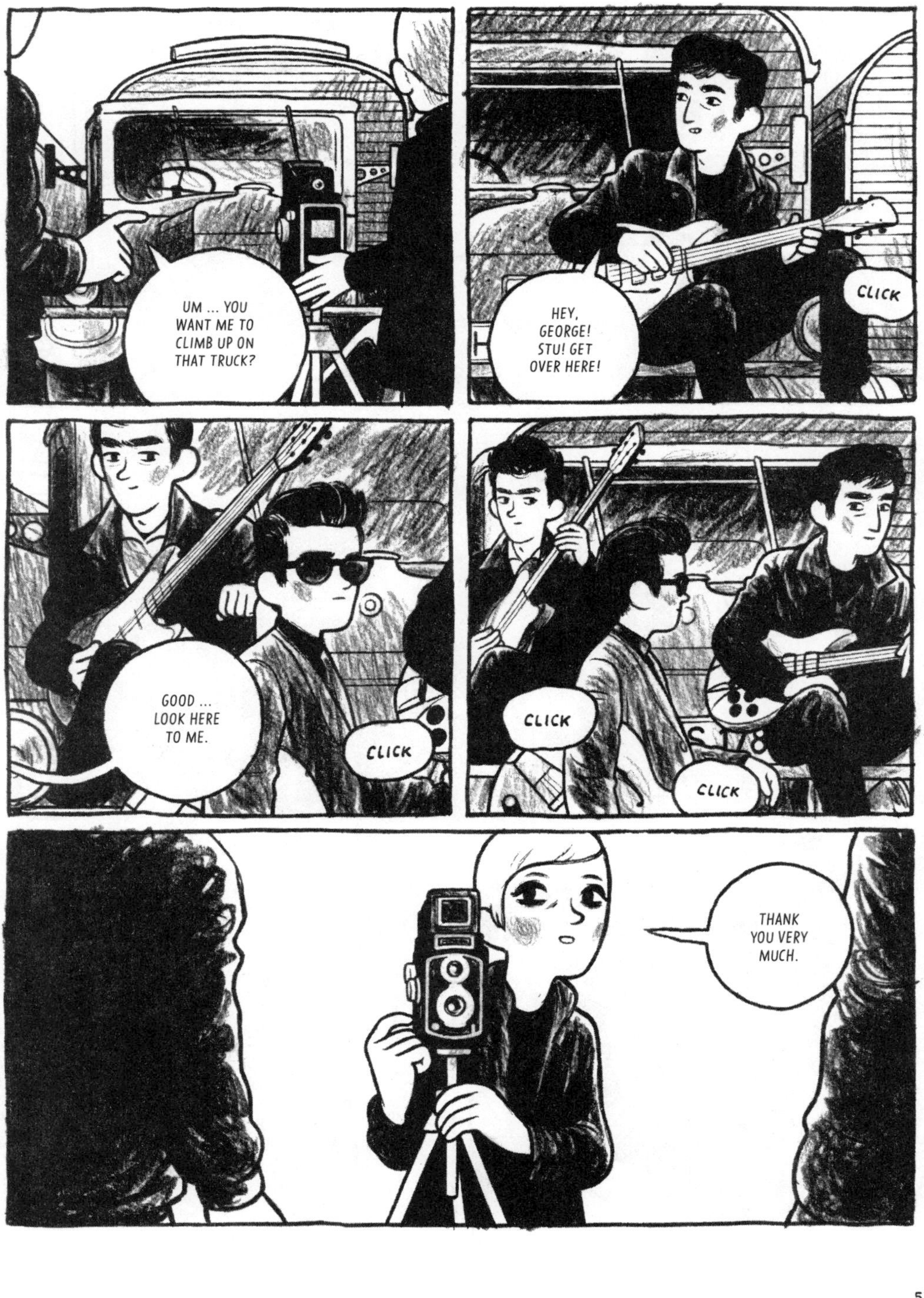
UM ... YOU WANT ME TO CLIMB UP ON THAT TRUCK?
HEY, GEORGE! STU! GET OVER HERE!
CLICK
GOOD ... LOOK HERE TO ME.
CLICK
CLICK
CLICK
THANK YOU VERY MUCH.

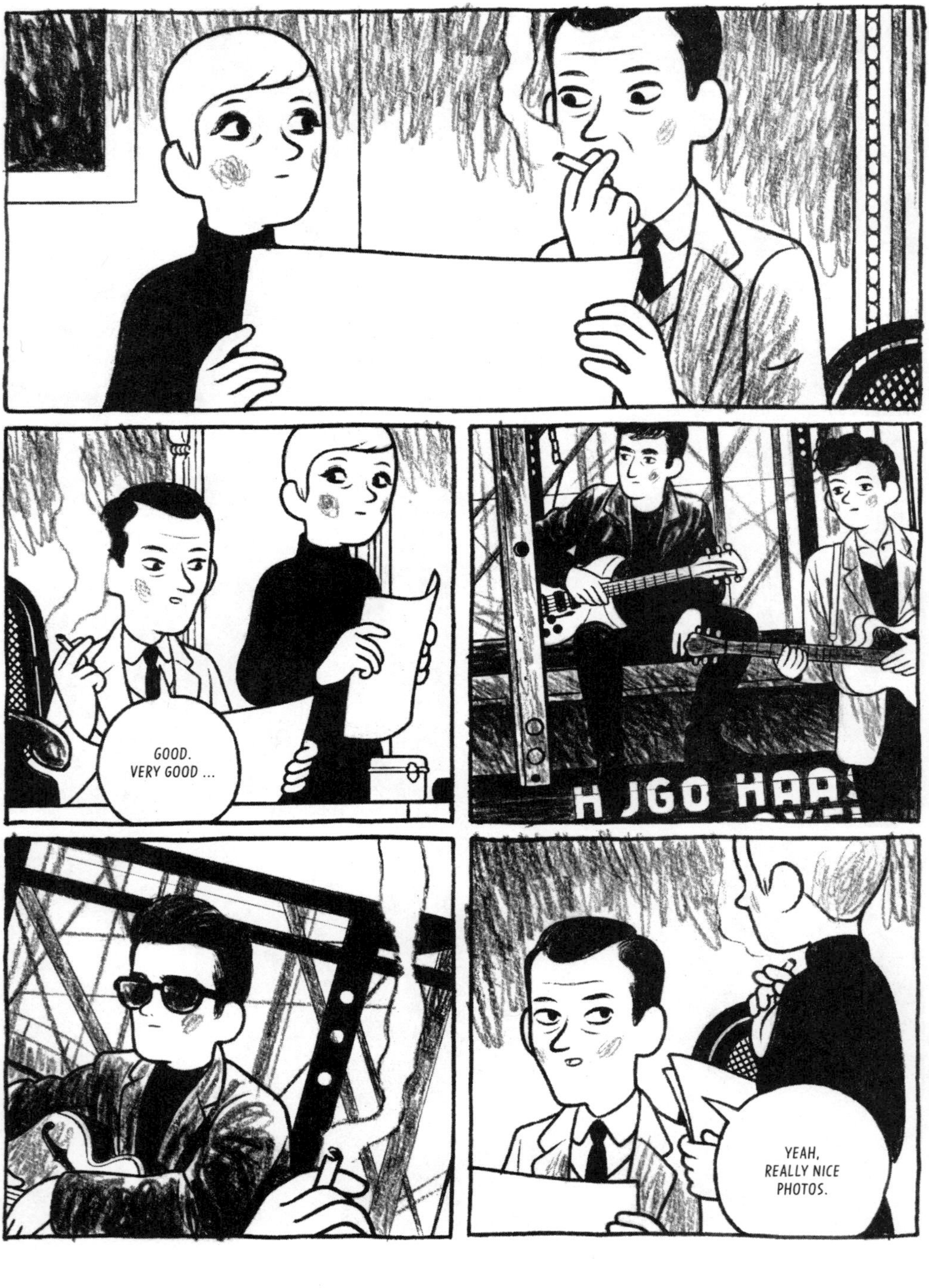
GOOD.
VERY GOOD ...
H JGO HAA
YEAH,
REALLY NICE
PHOTOS.

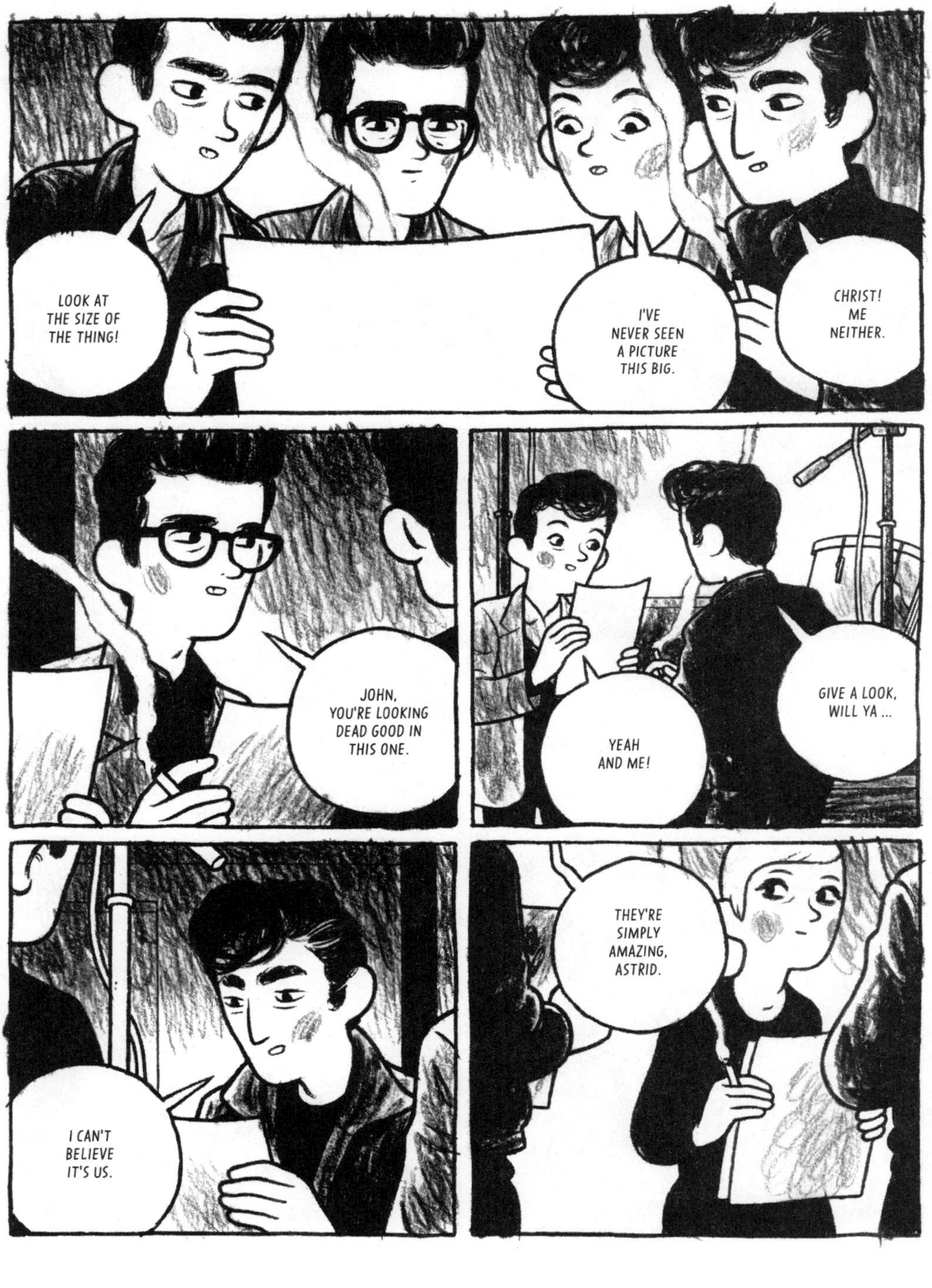
LOOK AT THE SIZE OF THE THING!
I'VE NEVER SEEN A PICTURE THIS BIG.
CHRIST! ME NEITHER.
JOHN, YOU'RE LOOKING DEAD GOOD IN THIS ONE.
GIVE A LOOK, WILL YA ...
YEAH AND ME!
I CAN'T BELIEVE IT'S US.
THEY'RE SIMPLY AMAZING, ASTRID.

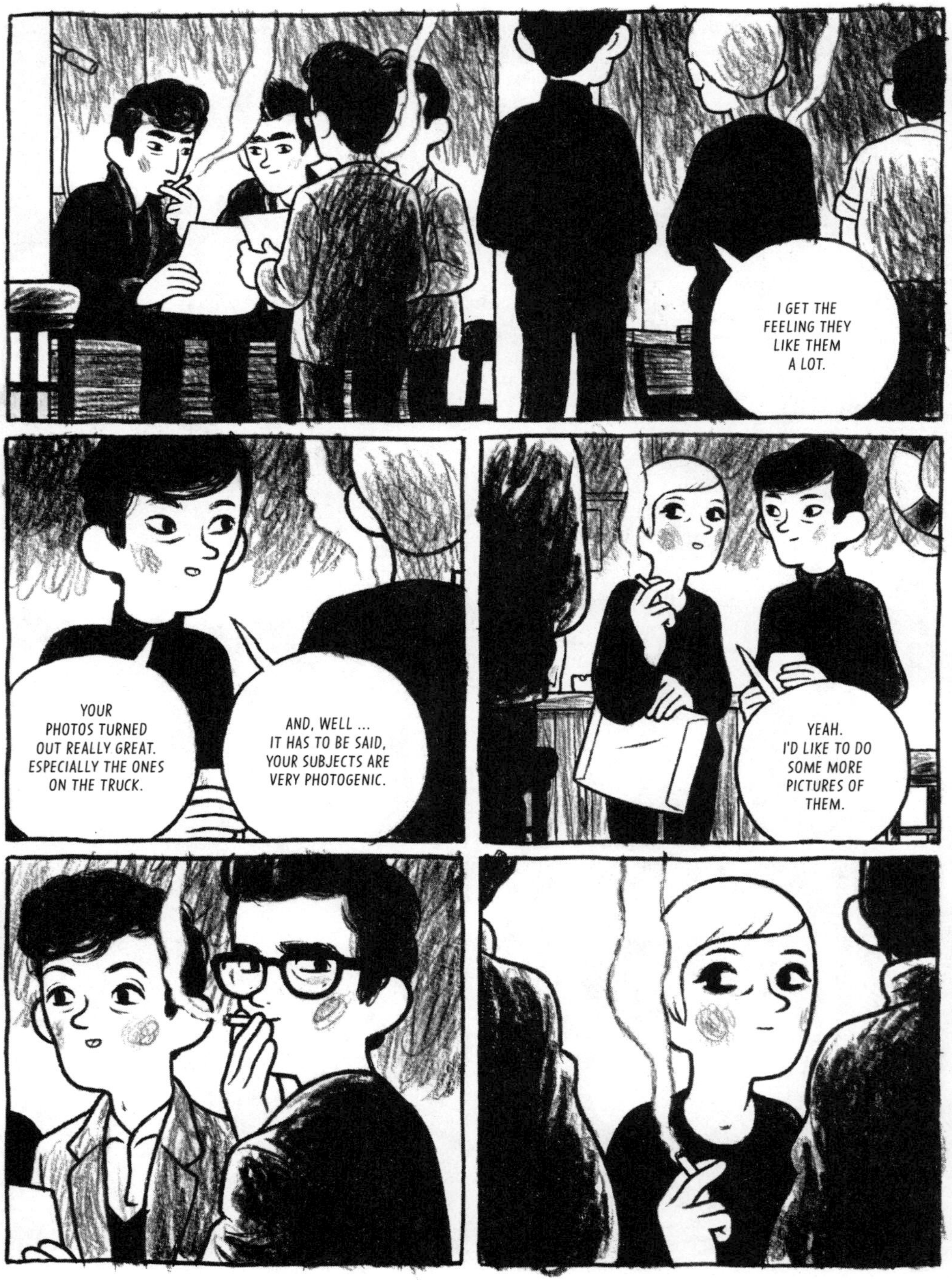
I GET THE FEELING THEY LIKE THEM A LOT.
YOUR PHOTOS TURNED OUT REALLY GREAT. ESPECIALLY THE ONES ON THE TRUCK.
AND, WELL ... IT HAS TO BE SAID, YOUR SUBJECTS ARE VERY PHOTOGENIC.
YEAH. I'D LIKE TO DO SOME MORE PICTURES OF THEM.

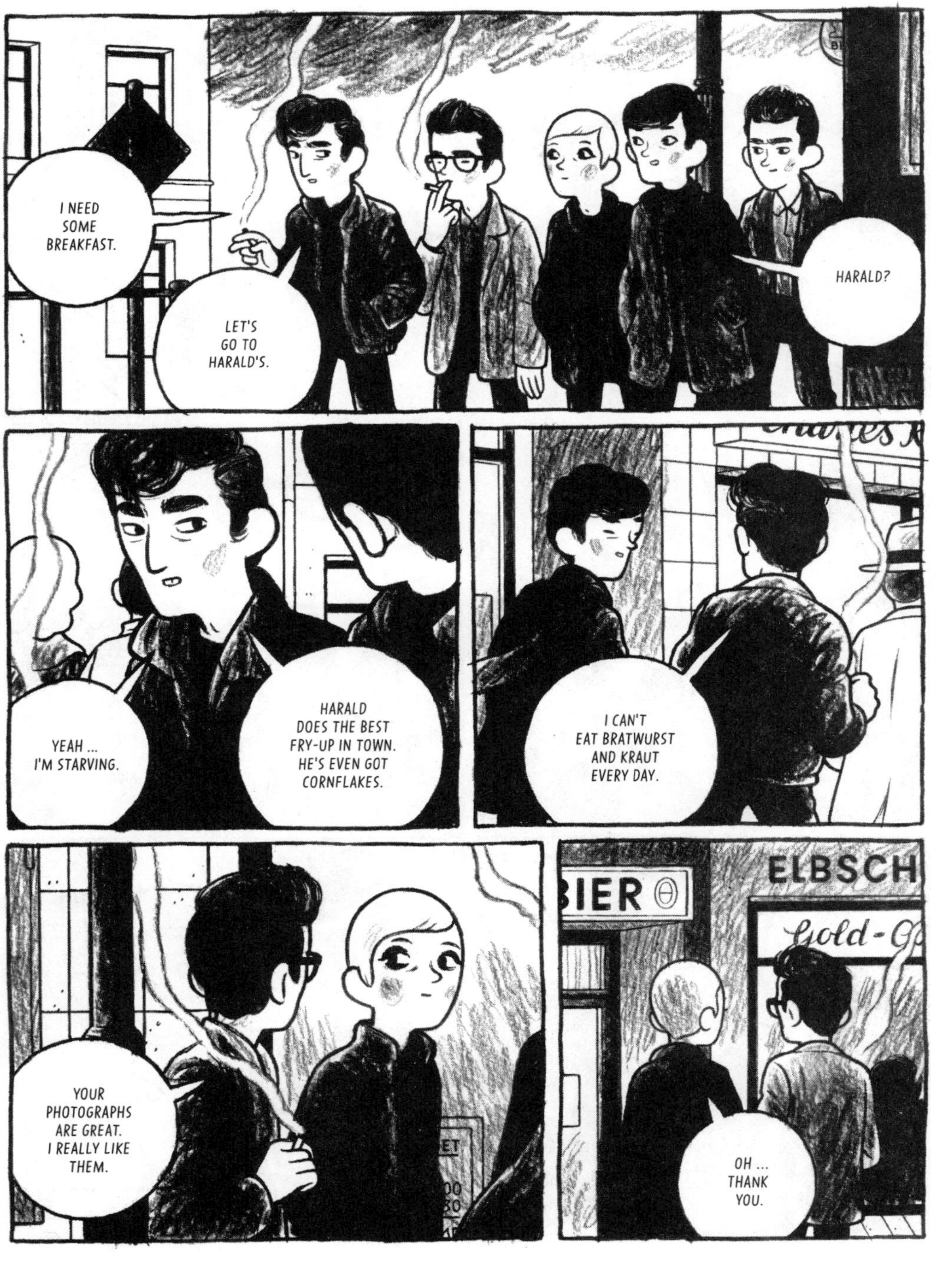
I NEED SOME BREAKFAST.
LET'S GO TO HARALD'S.
HARALD?
YEAH ... I'M STARVING.
HARALD DOES THE BEST FRY-UP IN TOWN. HE'S EVEN GOT CORNFLAKES.
I CAN'T EAT BRATWURST AND KRAUT EVERY DAY.
YOUR PHOTOGRAPHS ARE GREAT. I REALLY LIKE THEM.
BIER
ELBSCH
Gold-G
OH ... THANK YOU.

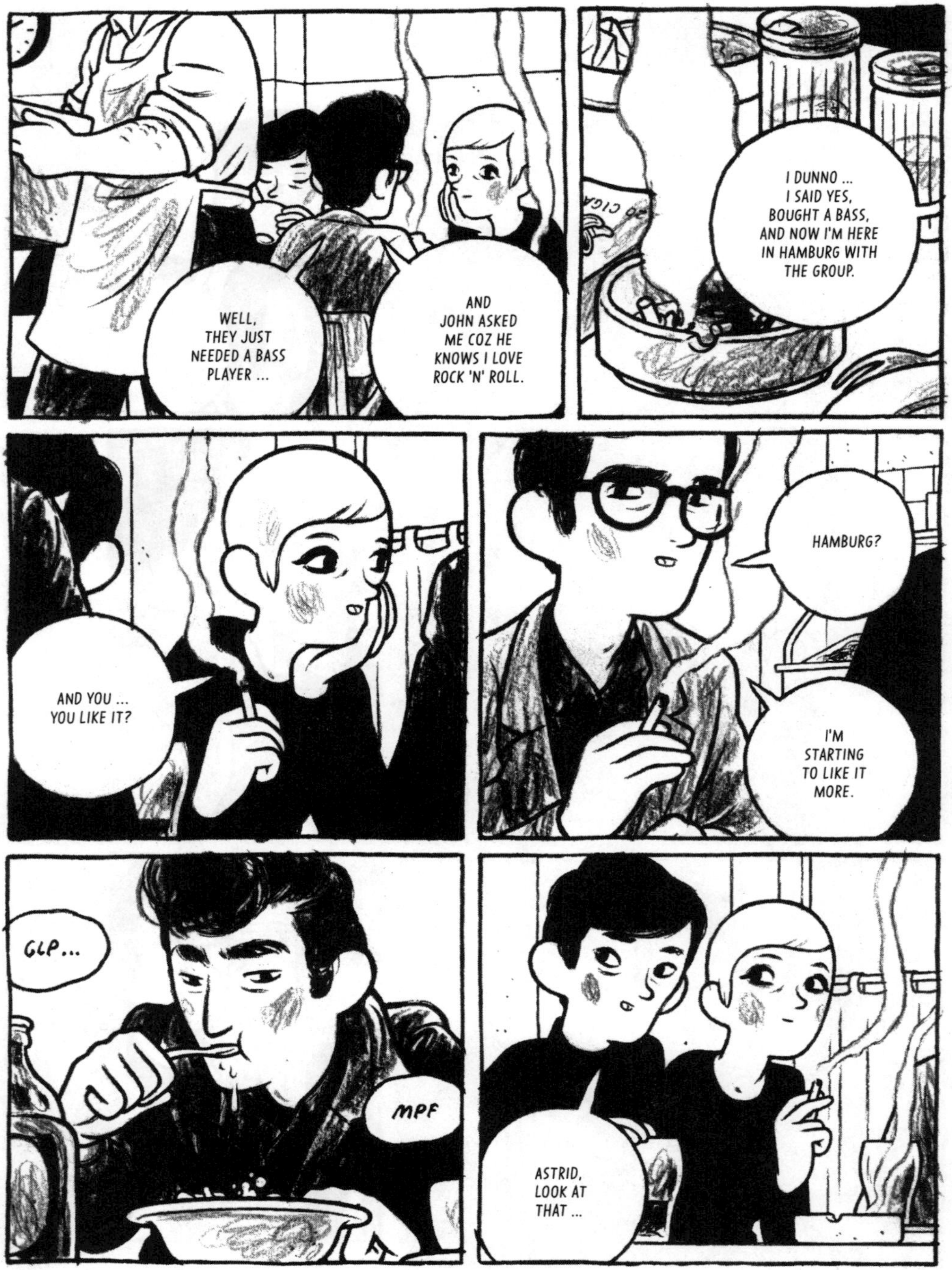
WELL, THEY JUST NEEDED A BASS PLAYER ...
AND JOHN ASKED ME COZ HE KNOWS I LOVE ROCK 'N' ROLL.
I DUNNO ... I SAID YES, BOUGHT A BASS, AND NOW I'M HERE IN HAMBURG WITH THE GROUP.
AND YOU ... YOU LIKE IT?
HAMBURG?
I'M STARTING TO LIKE IT MORE.
GLP...
MPF
ASTRID, LOOK AT THAT ...

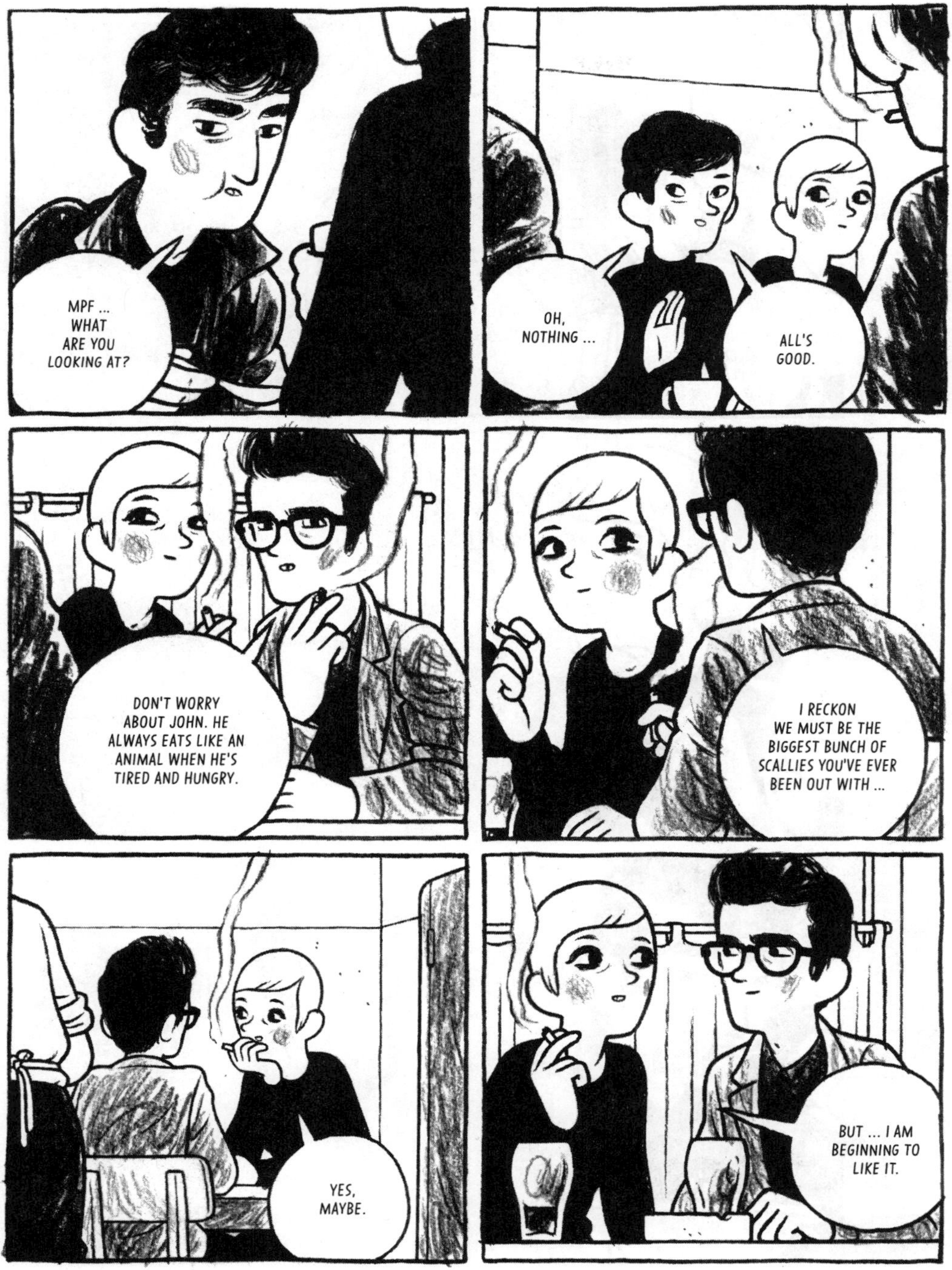
MPF ... WHAT ARE YOU LOOKING AT?
OH, NOTHING ...
ALL'S GOOD.
DON'T WORRY ABOUT JOHN. HE ALWAYS EATS LIKE AN ANIMAL WHEN HE'S TIRED AND HUNGRY.
I RECKON WE MUST BE THE BIGGEST BUNCH OF SCALLIES YOU'VE EVER BEEN OUT WITH ...
YES, MAYBE.
BUT ... I AM BEGINNING TO LIKE IT.

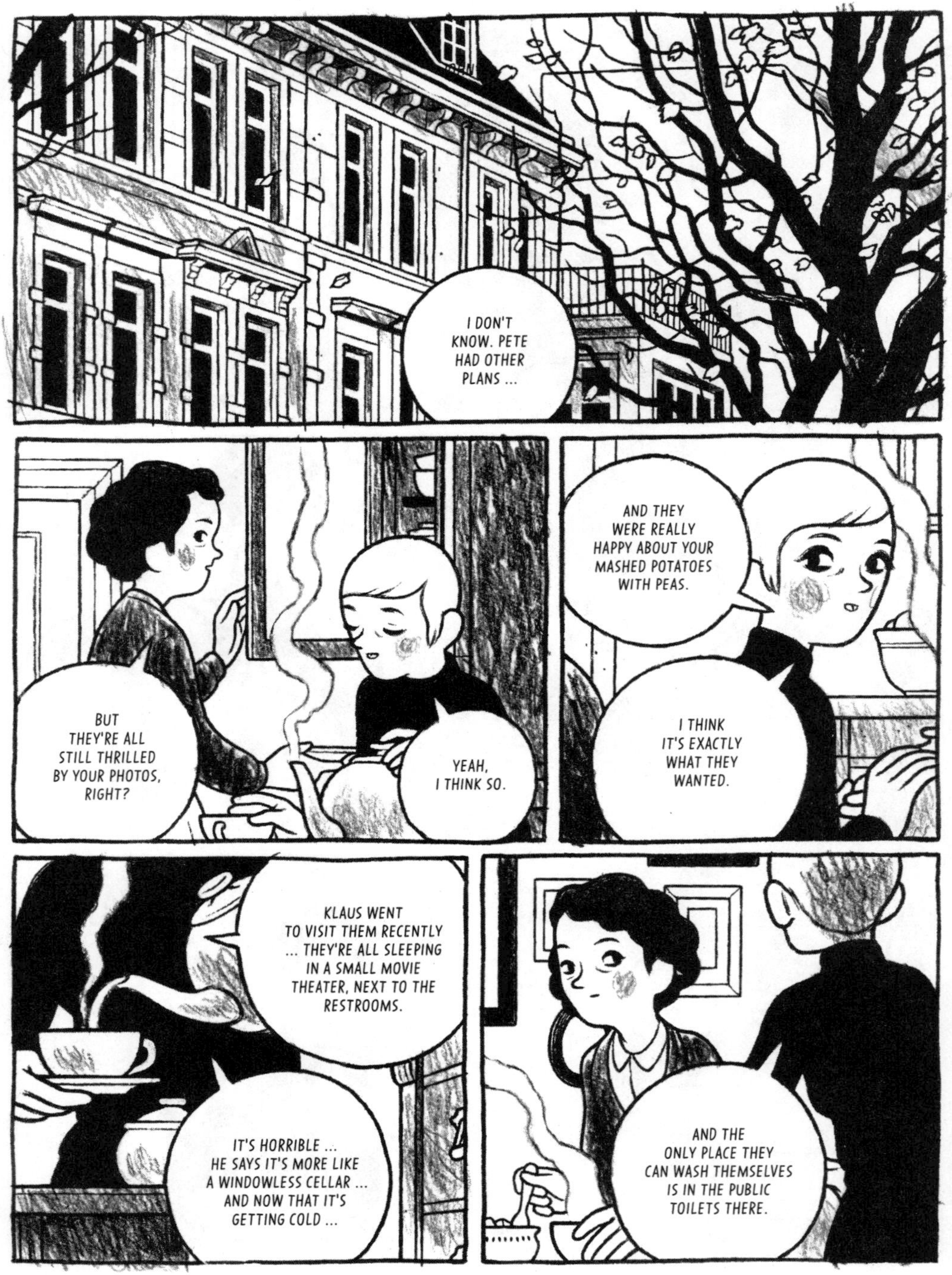
I DON'T KNOW. PETE HAD OTHER PLANS ...
BUT THEY'RE ALL STILL THRILLED BY YOUR PHOTOS, RIGHT?
YEAH, I THINK SO.
AND THEY WERE REALLY HAPPY ABOUT YOUR MASHED POTATOES WITH PEAS.
I THINK IT'S EXACTLY WHAT THEY WANTED.
KLAUS WENT TO VISIT THEM RECENTLY ... THEY'RE ALL SLEEPING IN A SMALL MOVIE THEATER, NEXT TO THE RESTROOMS.
IT'S HORRIBLE ... HE SAYS IT'S MORE LIKE A WINDOWLESS CELLAR ... AND NOW THAT IT'S GETTING COLD ...
AND THE ONLY PLACE THEY CAN WASH THEMSELVES IS IN THE PUBLIC TOILETS THERE.

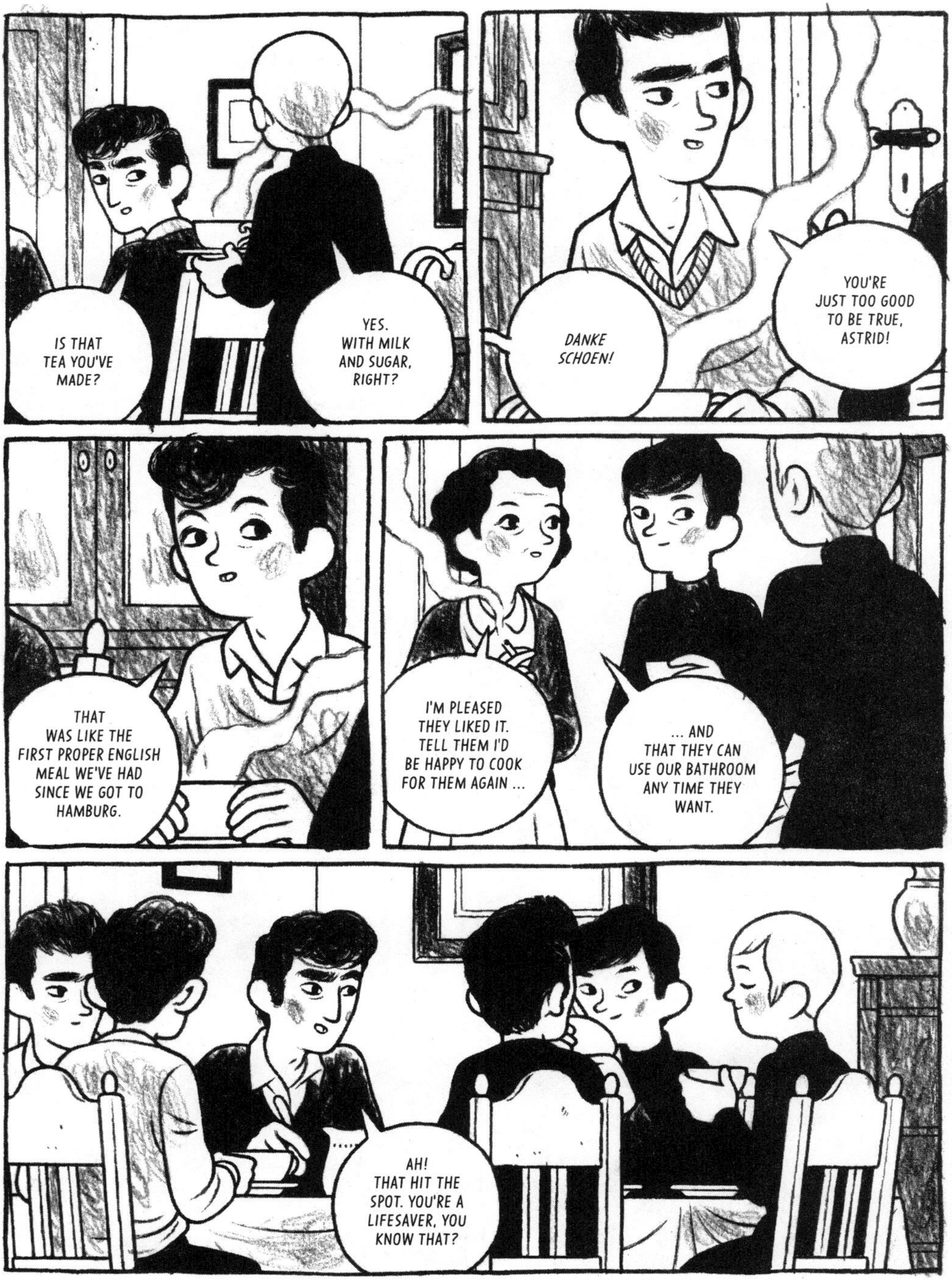
IS THAT TEA YOU'VE MADE?
YES. WITH MILK AND SUGAR, RIGHT?
DANKE SCHOEN!
YOU'RE JUST TOO GOOD TO BE TRUE, ASTRID!
THAT WAS LIKE THE FIRST PROPER ENGLISH MEAL WE'VE HAD SINCE WE GOT TO HAMBURG.
I'M PLEASED THEY LIKED IT. TELL THEM I'D BE HAPPY TO COOK FOR THEM AGAIN ...
... AND THAT THEY CAN USE OUR BATHROOM ANY TIME THEY WANT.
AH! THAT HIT THE SPOT. YOU'RE A LIFESAVER, YOU KNOW THAT?

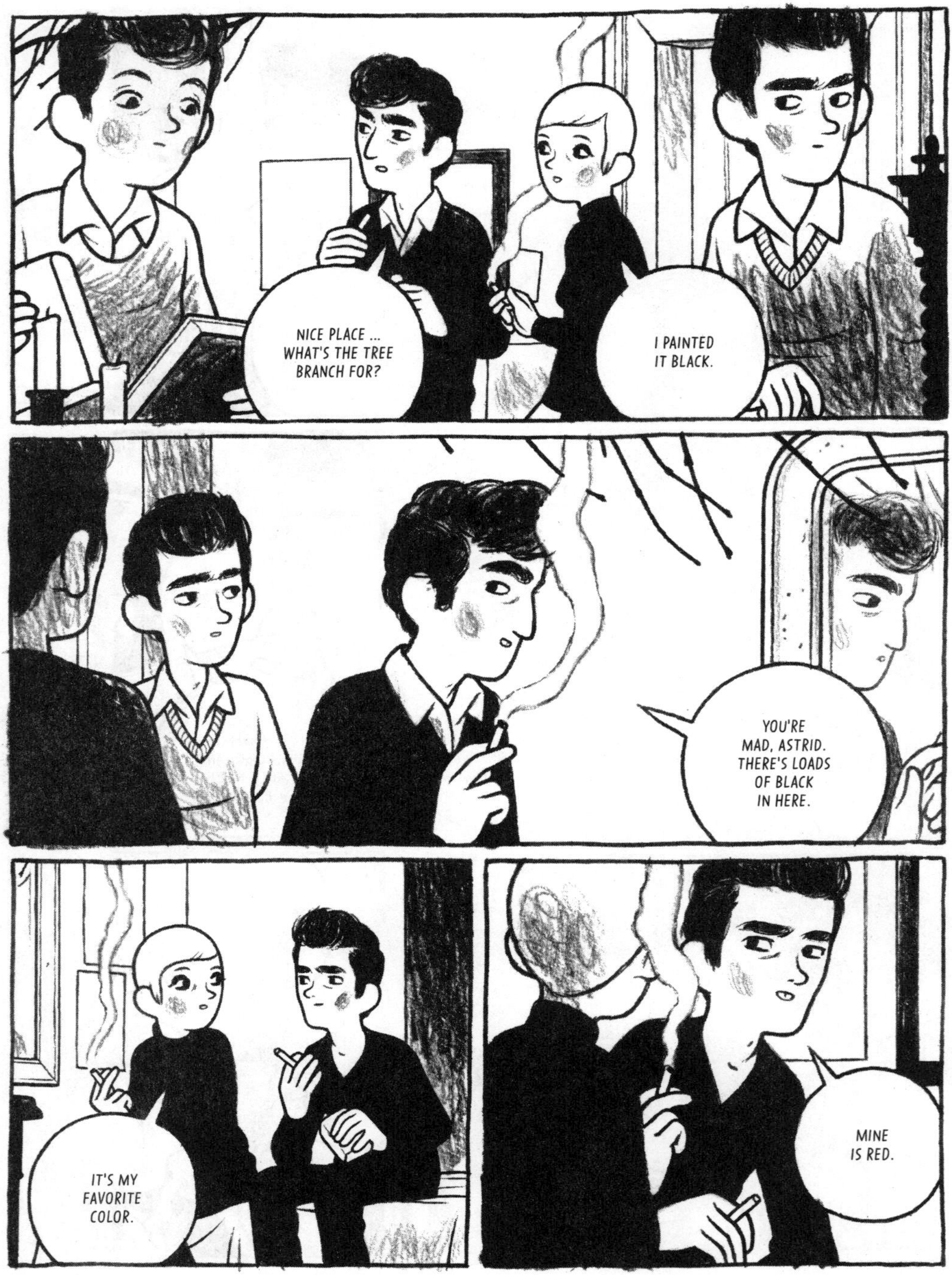
NICE PLACE ... WHAT'S THE TREE BRANCH FOR?
I PAINTED IT BLACK.
YOU'RE MAD, ASTRID. THERE'S LOADS OF BLACK IN HERE.
IT'S MY FAVORITE COLOR.
MINE IS RED.

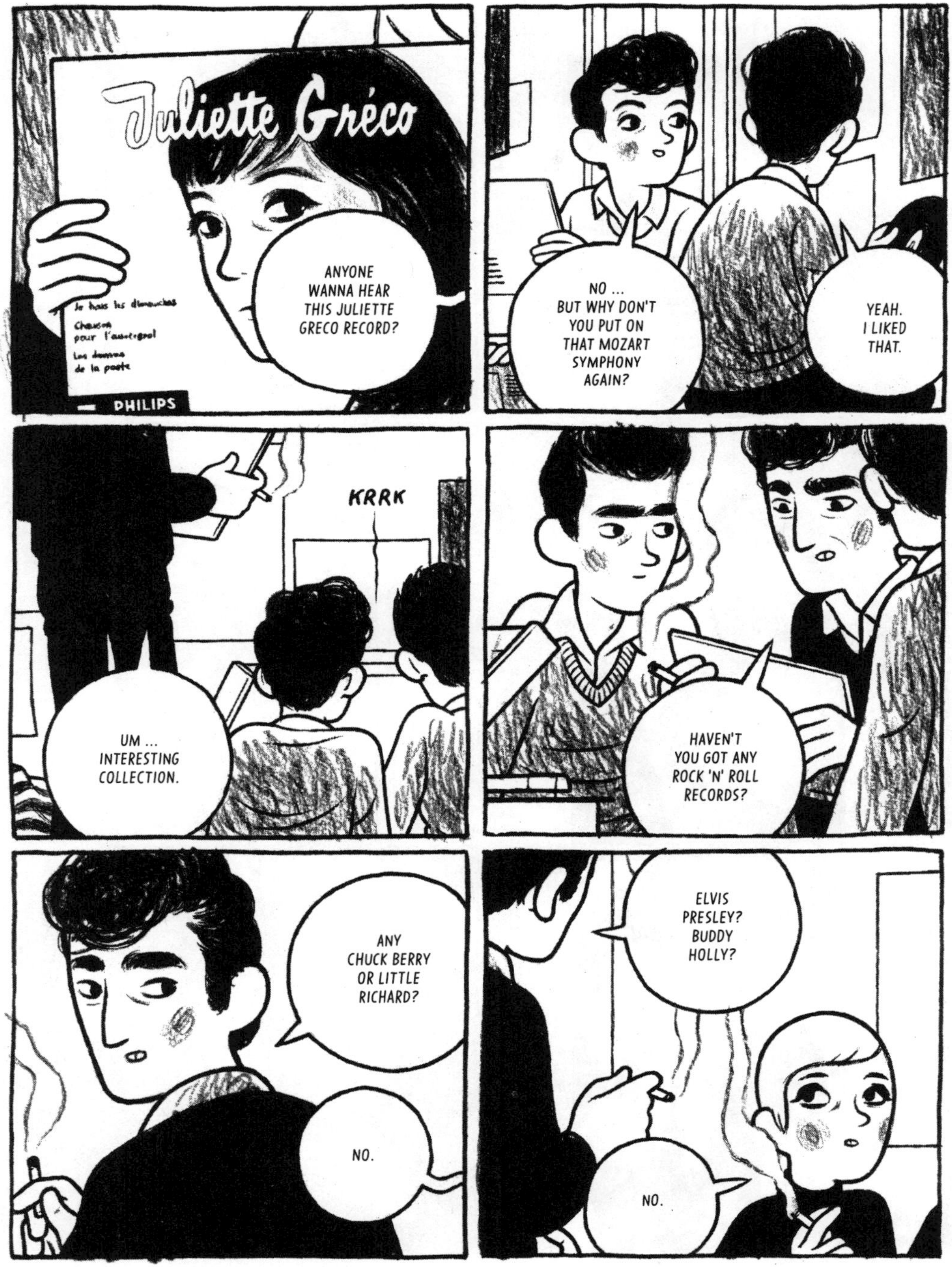
Juliette Gréco
PHILIPS
ANYONE WANNA HEAR THIS JULIETTE GRECO RECORD?
NO ... BUT WHY DON'T YOU PUT ON THAT MOZART SYMPHONY AGAIN?
YEAH. I LIKED THAT.
KRRK
UM ... INTERESTING COLLECTION.
HAVEN'T YOU GOT ANY ROCK 'N' ROLL RECORDS?
ANY CHUCK BERRY OR LITTLE RICHARD?
NO.
ELVIS PRESLEY? BUDDY HOLLY?
NO.

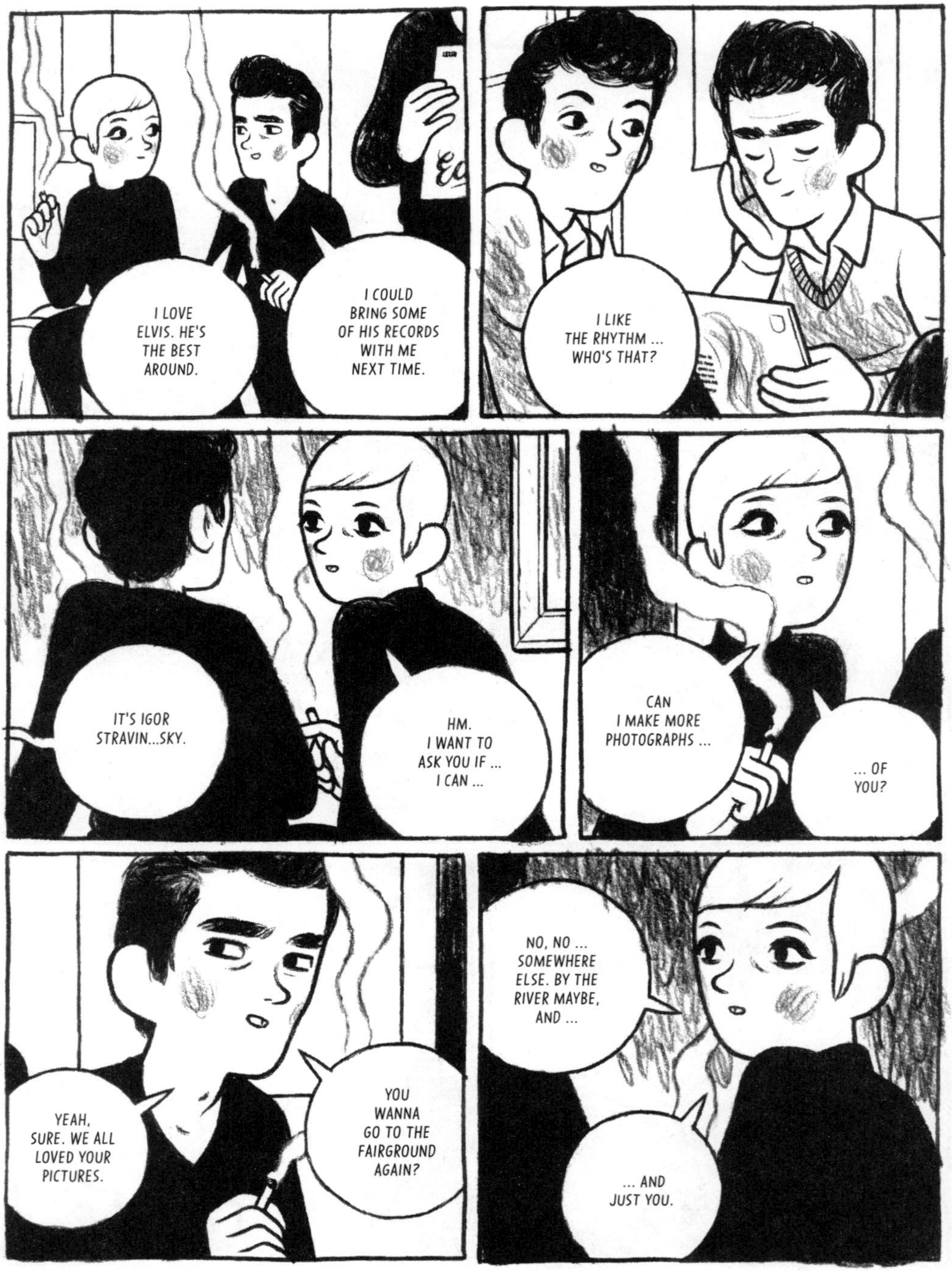
I LOVE ELVIS. HE'S THE BEST AROUND.
I COULD BRING SOME OF HIS RECORDS WITH ME NEXT TIME.
I LIKE THE RHYTHM ... WHO'S THAT?
IT'S IGOR STRAVIN...SKY.
HM. I WANT TO ASK YOU IF ... I CAN ...
CAN I MAKE MORE PHOTOGRAPHS ...
... OF YOU?
YEAH, SURE. WE ALL LOVED YOUR PICTURES.
YOU WANNA GO TO THE FAIRGROUND AGAIN?
NO, NO ... SOMEWHERE ELSE. BY THE RIVER MAYBE, AND ...
... AND JUST YOU.

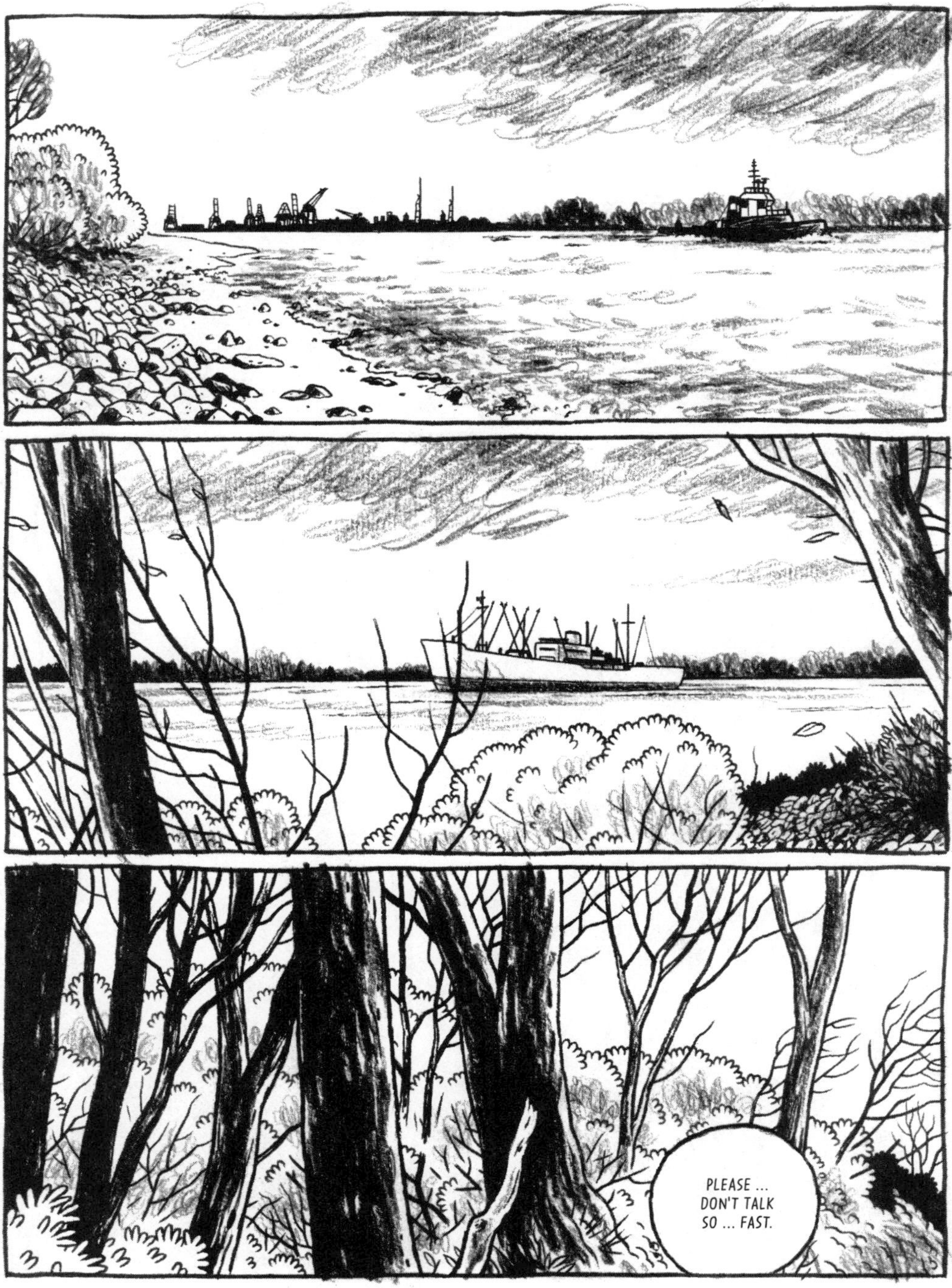
PLEASE ... DON'T TALK SO ... FAST.

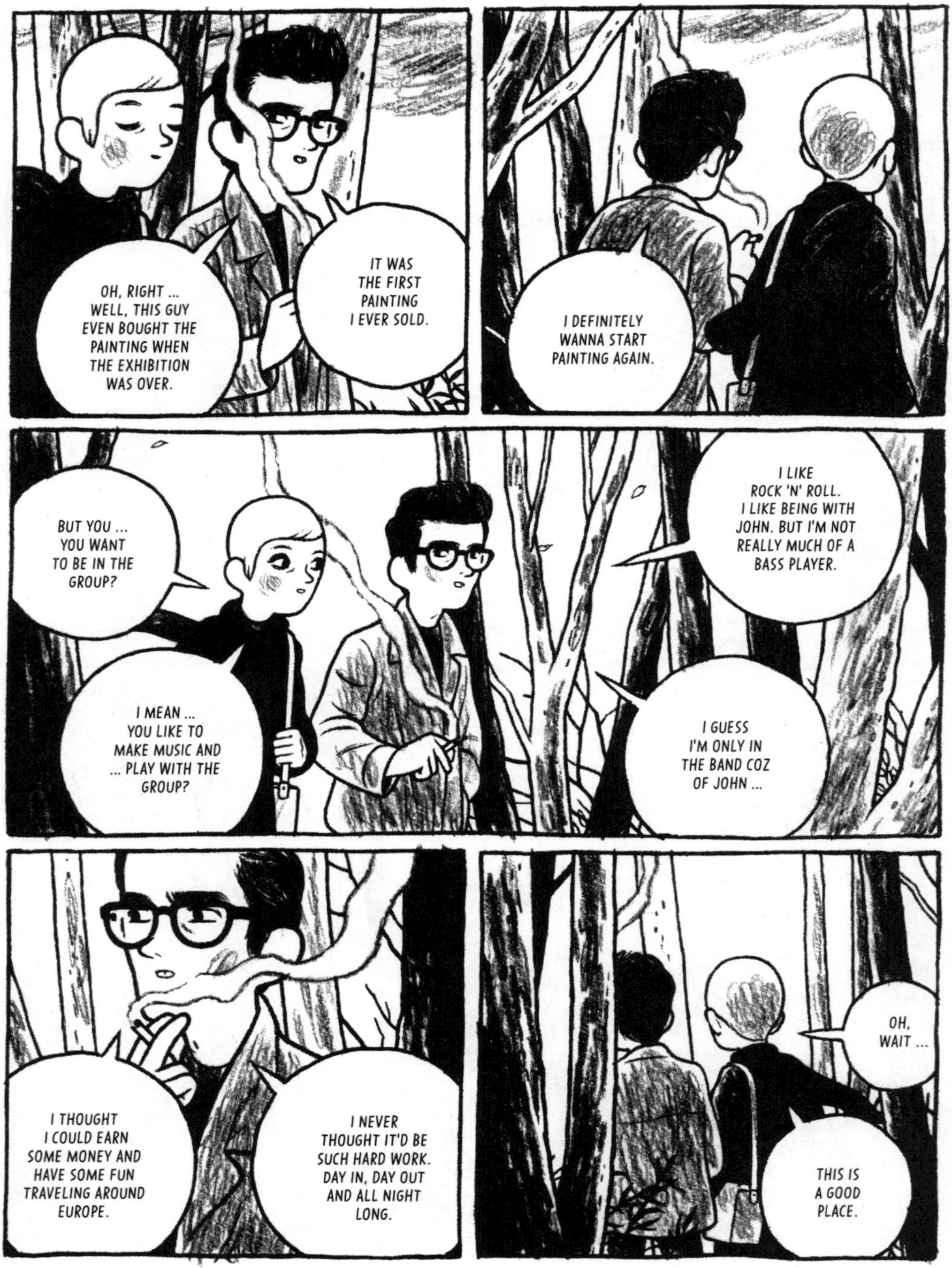
OH, RIGHT ... WELL, THIS GUY EVEN BOUGHT THE PAINTING WHEN THE EXHIBITION WAS OVER.
IT WAS THE FIRST PAINTING I EVER SOLD.
I DEFINITELY WANNA START PAINTING AGAIN.
BUT YOU ... YOU WANT TO BE IN THE GROUP?
I MEAN ... YOU LIKE TO MAKE MUSIC AND ... PLAY WITH THE GROUP?
I LIKE ROCK 'N' ROLL. I LIKE BEING WITH JOHN. BUT I'M NOT REALLY MUCH OF A BASS PLAYER.
I GUESS I'M ONLY IN THE BAND COZ OF JOHN ...
I THOUGHT I COULD EARN SOME MONEY AND HAVE SOME FUN TRAVELING AROUND EUROPE.
I NEVER THOUGHT IT'D BE SUCH HARD WORK. DAY IN, DAY OUT AND ALL NIGHT LONG.
OH, WAIT ...
THIS IS A GOOD PLACE.

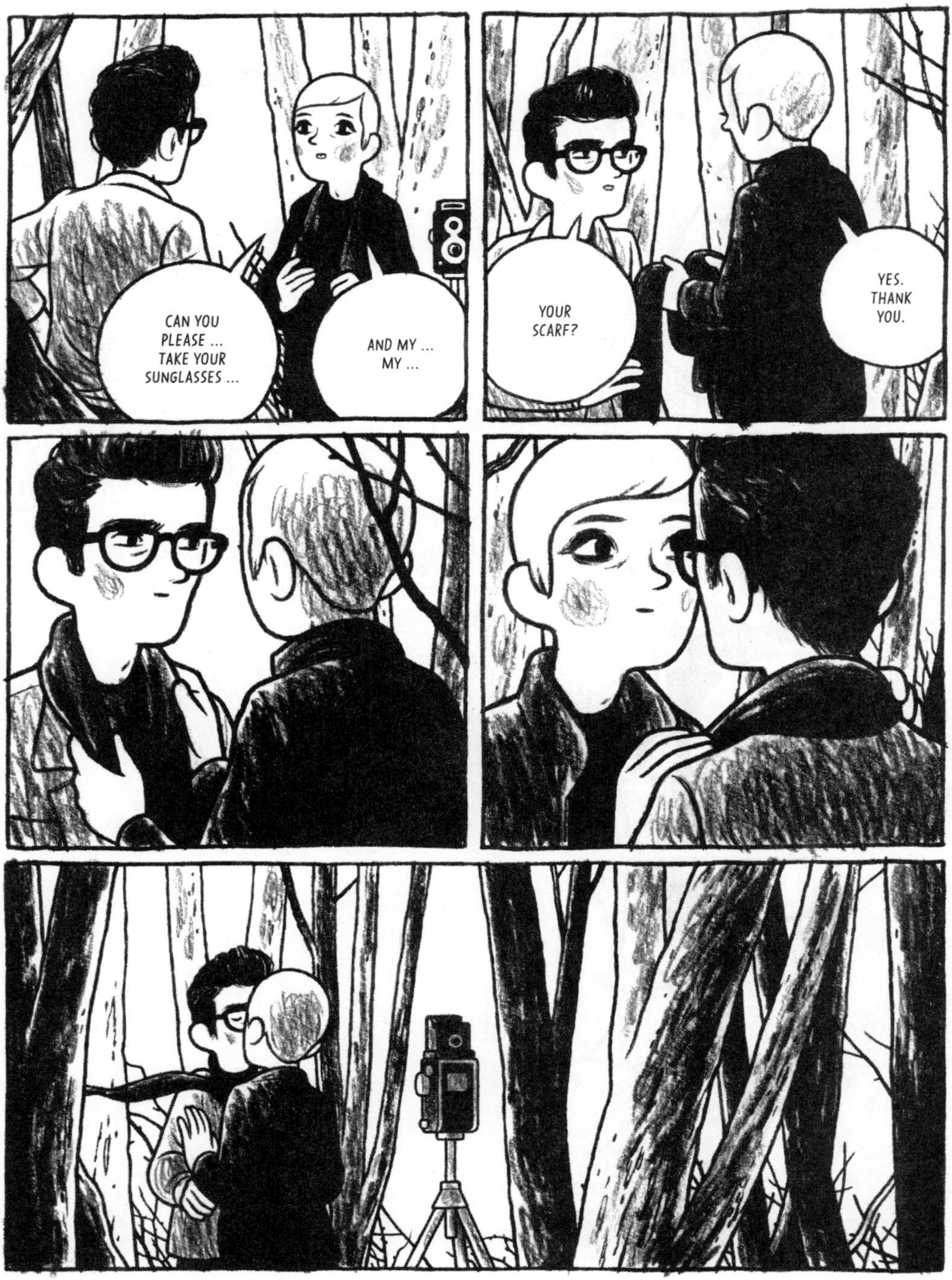
CAN YOU PLEASE ... TAKE YOUR SUNGLASSES ...
AND MY ... MY ...
YOUR SCARF?
YES. THANK YOU.

»Love me tender«

November 1960

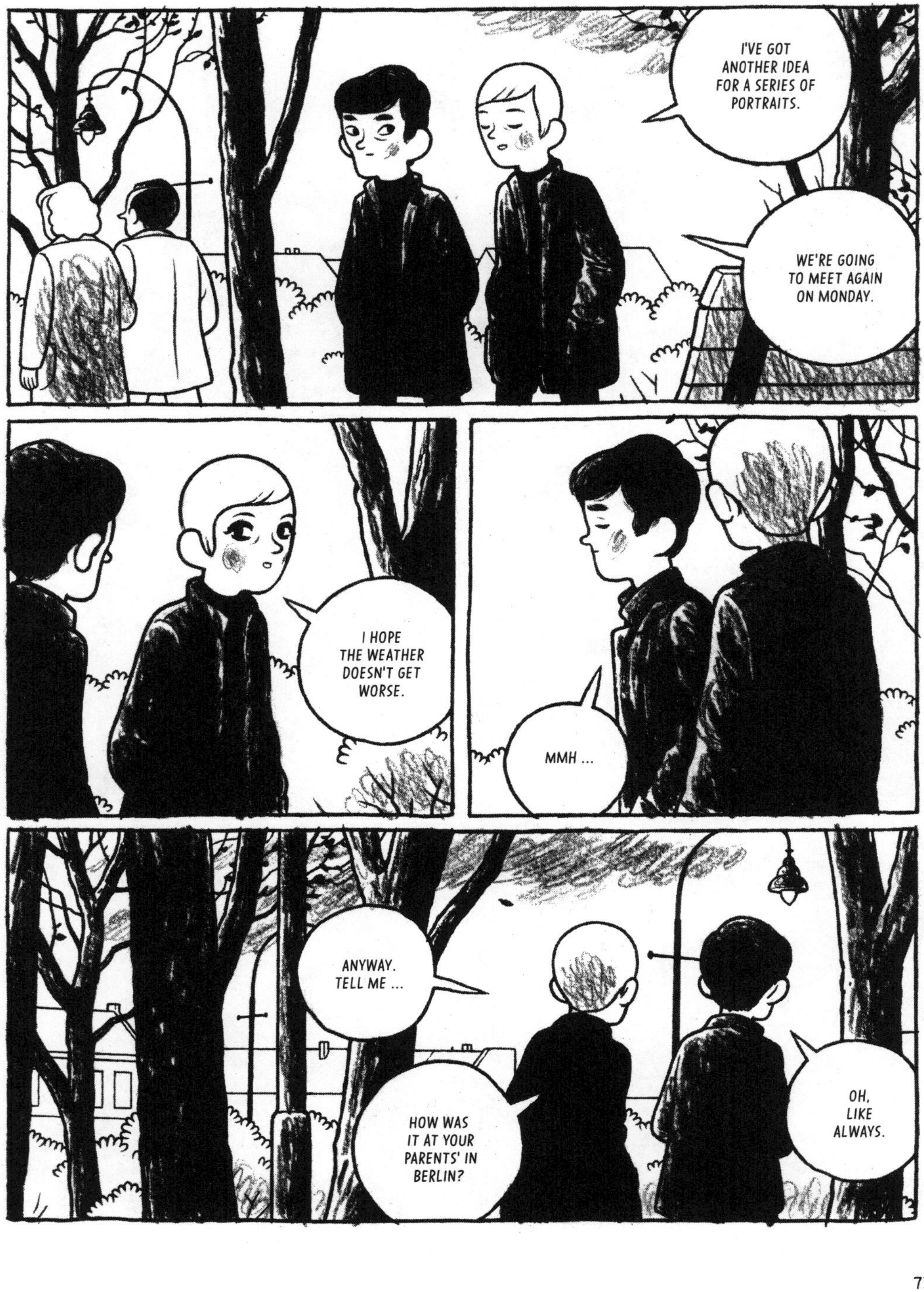
I'VE GOT ANOTHER IDEA FOR A SERIES OF PORTRAITS.
WE'RE GOING TO MEET AGAIN ON MONDAY.
I HOPE THE WEATHER DOESN'T GET WORSE.
MMH ...
ANYWAY. TELL ME ...
HOW WAS IT AT YOUR PARENTS' IN BERLIN?
OH, LIKE ALWAYS.

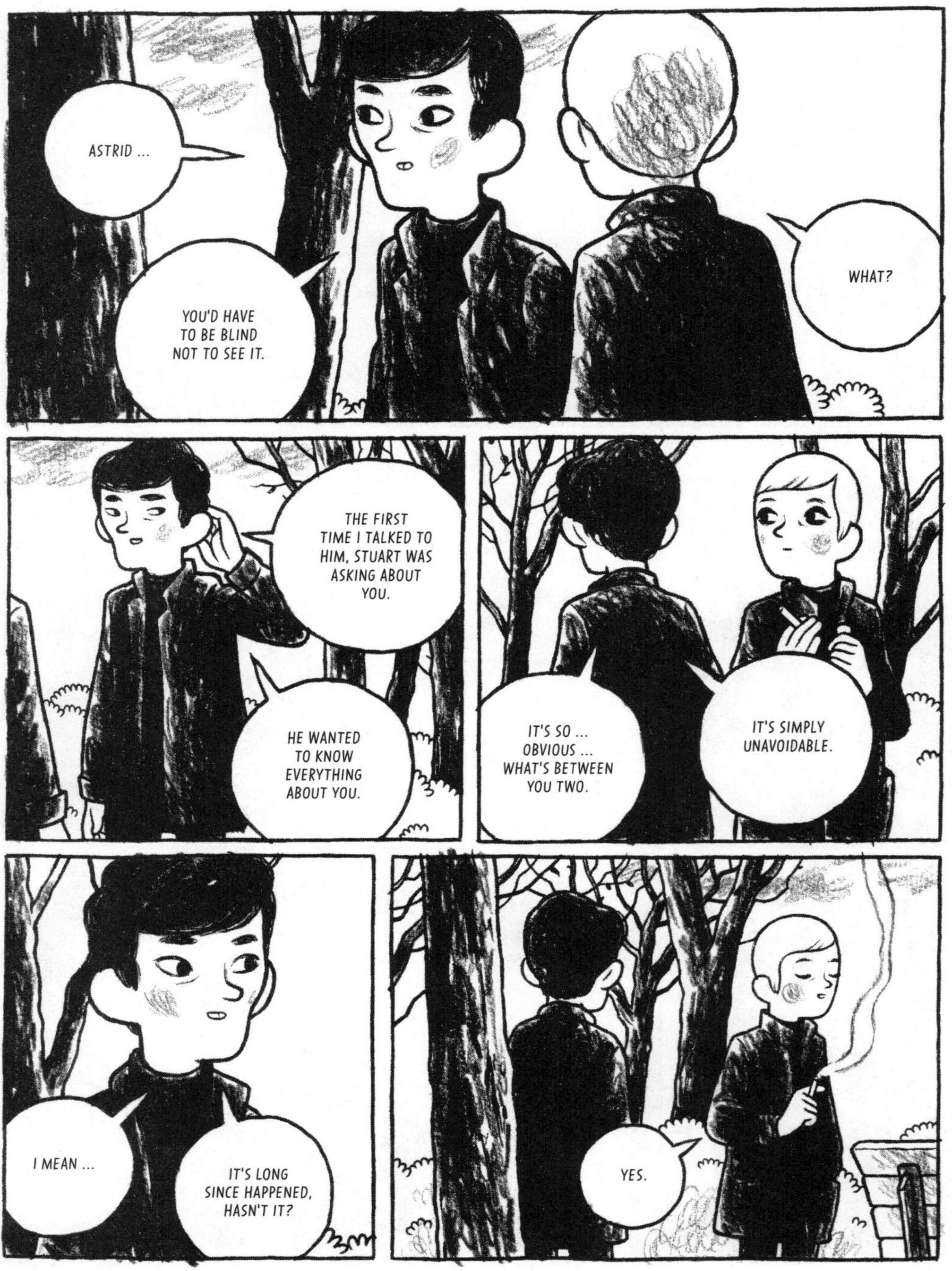
ASTRID ...
YOU'D HAVE TO BE BLIND NOT TO SEE IT.
WHAT?
THE FIRST TIME I TALKED TO HIM, STUART WAS ASKING ABOUT YOU.
HE WANTED TO KNOW EVERYTHING ABOUT YOU.
IT'S SO ... OBVIOUS ... WHAT'S BETWEEN YOU TWO.
IT'S SIMPLY UNAVOIDABLE.
I MEAN ...
IT'S LONG SINCE HAPPENED, HASN'T IT?
YES.

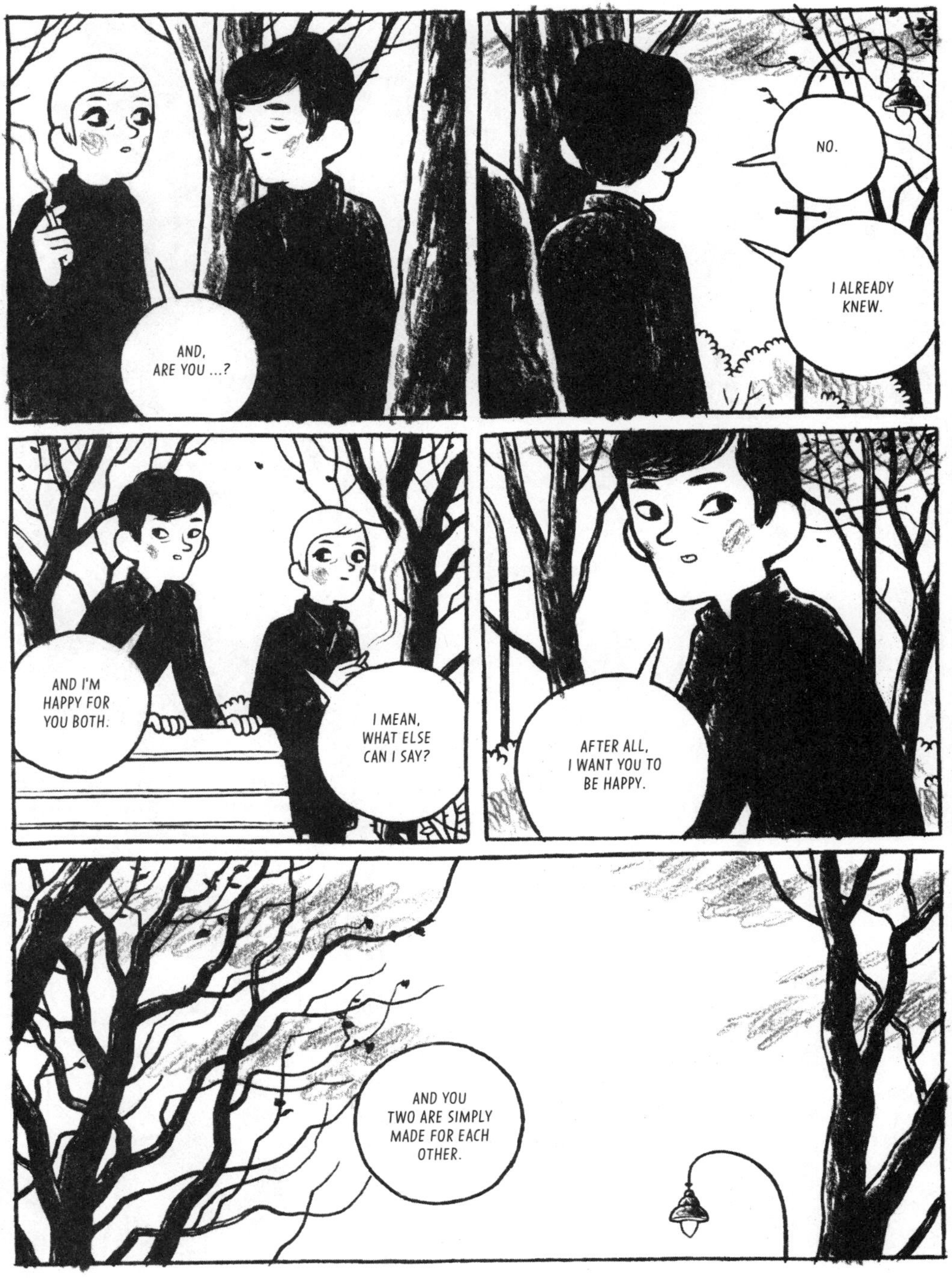
AND, ARE YOU ...?
NO.
I ALREADY KNEW.
AND I'M HAPPY FOR YOU BOTH.
I MEAN, WHAT ELSE CAN I SAY?
AFTER ALL, I WANT YOU TO BE HAPPY.
AND YOU TWO ARE SIMPLY MADE FOR EACH OTHER.

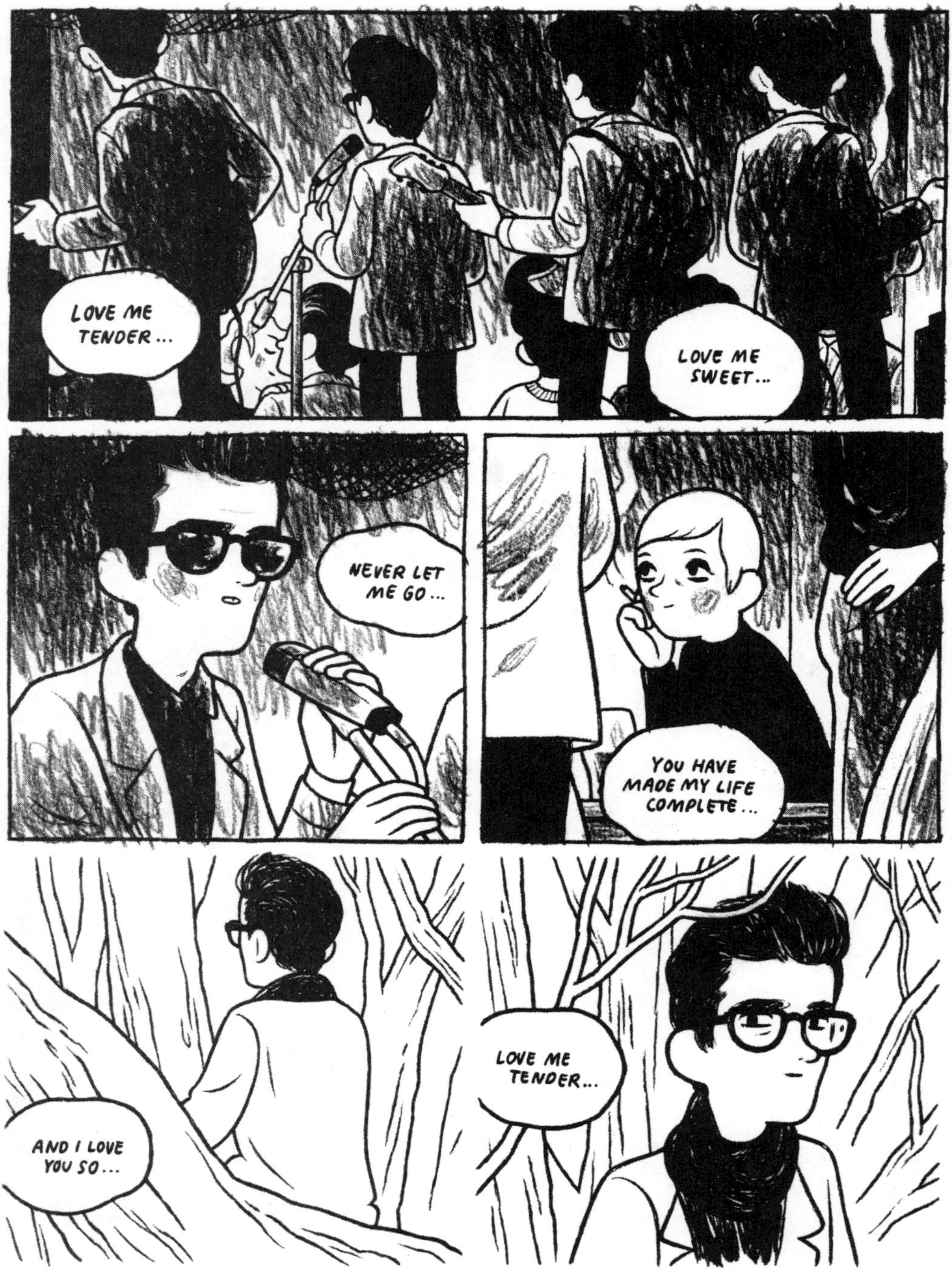
LOVE ME TENDER...
LOVE ME SWEET...
NEVER LET ME GO...
YOU HAVE MADE MY LIFE COMPLETE...
AND I LOVE YOU SO...
LOVE ME TENDER...

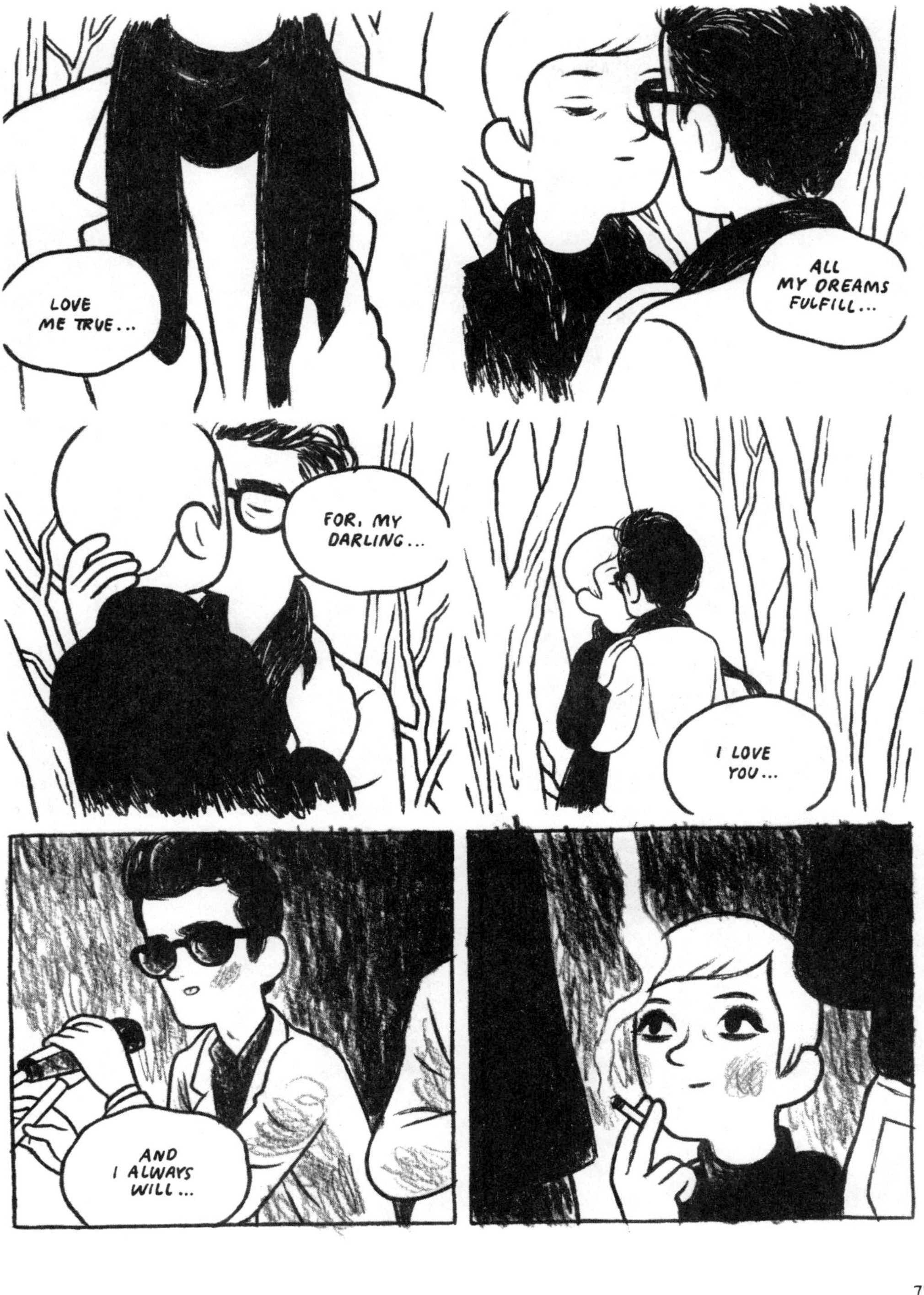
LOVE ME TRUE...
ALL MY DREAMS FULFILL...
FOR, MY DARLING...
I LOVE YOU...
AND I ALWAYS WILL...

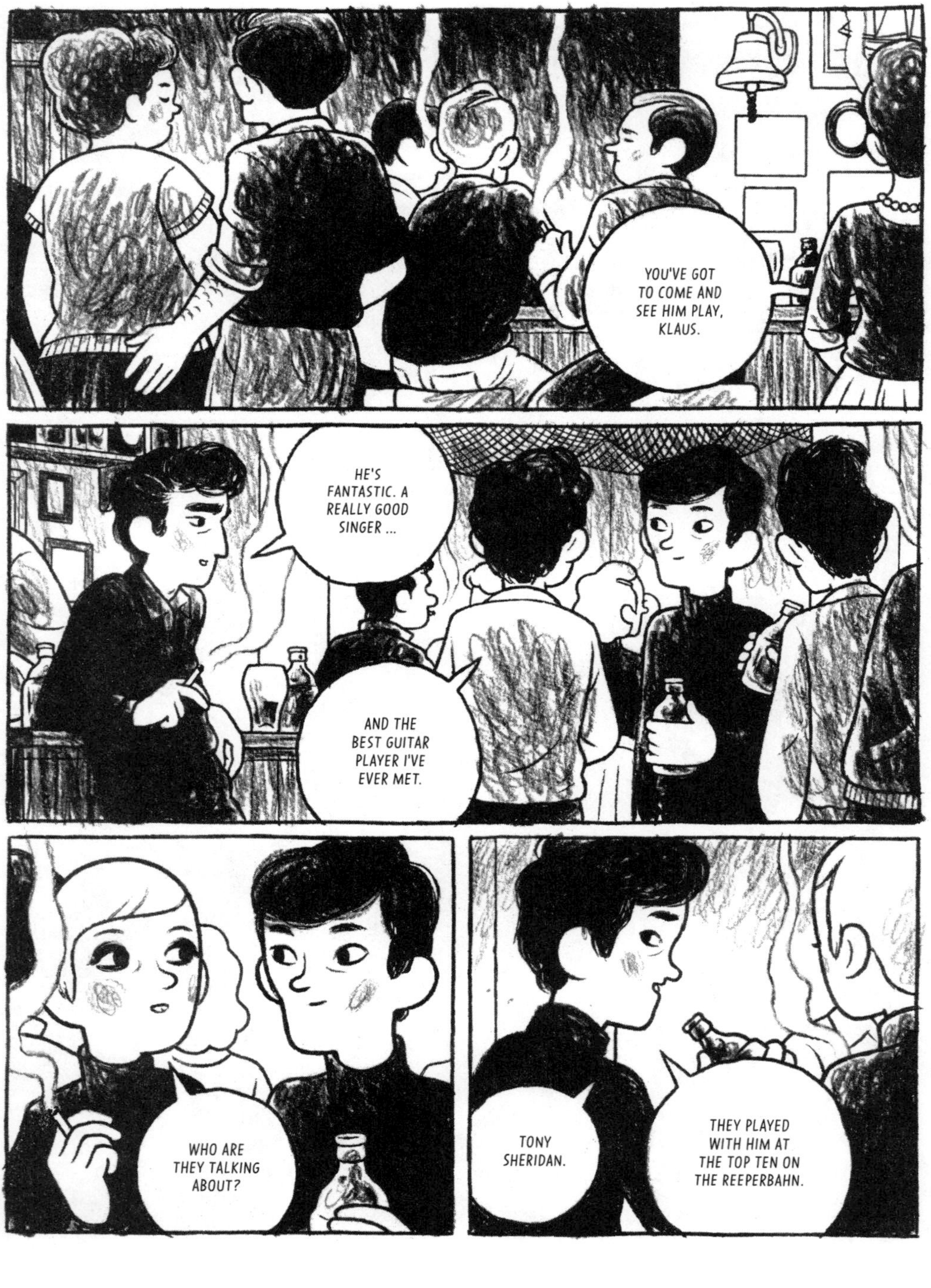
YOU'VE GOT TO COME AND SEE HIM PLAY, KLAUS.
HE'S FANTASTIC. A REALLY GOOD SINGER ...
AND THE BEST GUITAR PLAYER I'VE EVER MET.
WHO ARE THEY TALKING ABOUT?
TONY SHERIDAN.
THEY PLAYED WITH HIM AT THE TOP TEN ON THE REEPERBAHN.

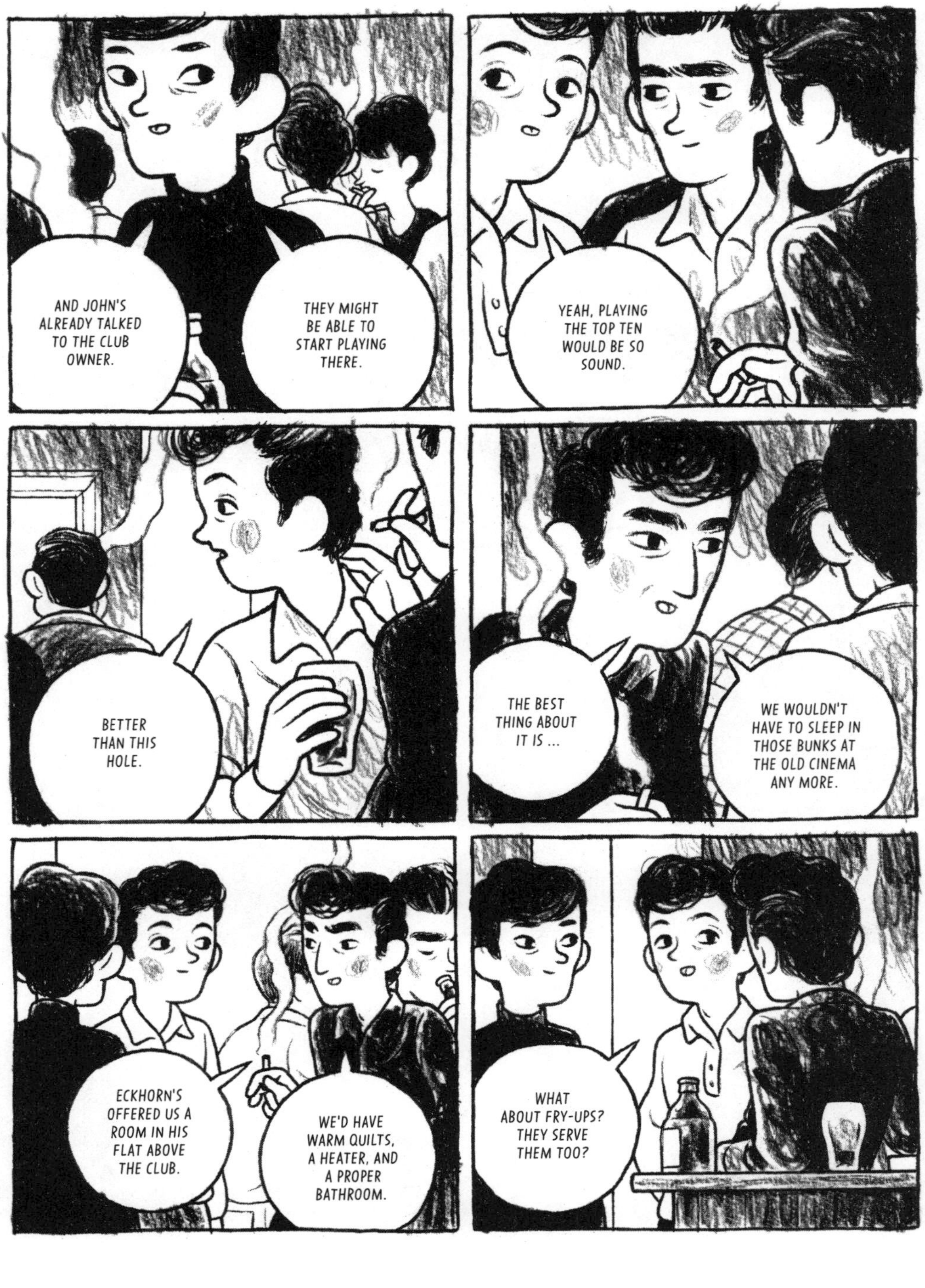
AND JOHN'S ALREADY TALKED TO THE CLUB OWNER.
THEY MIGHT BE ABLE TO START PLAYING THERE.
YEAH, PLAYING THE TOP TEN WOULD BE SO SOUND.
BETTER THAN THIS HOLE.
THE BEST THING ABOUT IT IS ...
WE WOULDN'T HAVE TO SLEEP IN THOSE BUNKS AT THE OLD CINEMA ANY MORE.
ECKHORN'S OFFERED US A ROOM IN HIS FLAT ABOVE THE CLUB.
WE'D HAVE WARM QUILTS, A HEATER, AND A PROPER BATHROOM.
WHAT ABOUT FRY-UPS? THEY SERVE THEM TOO?

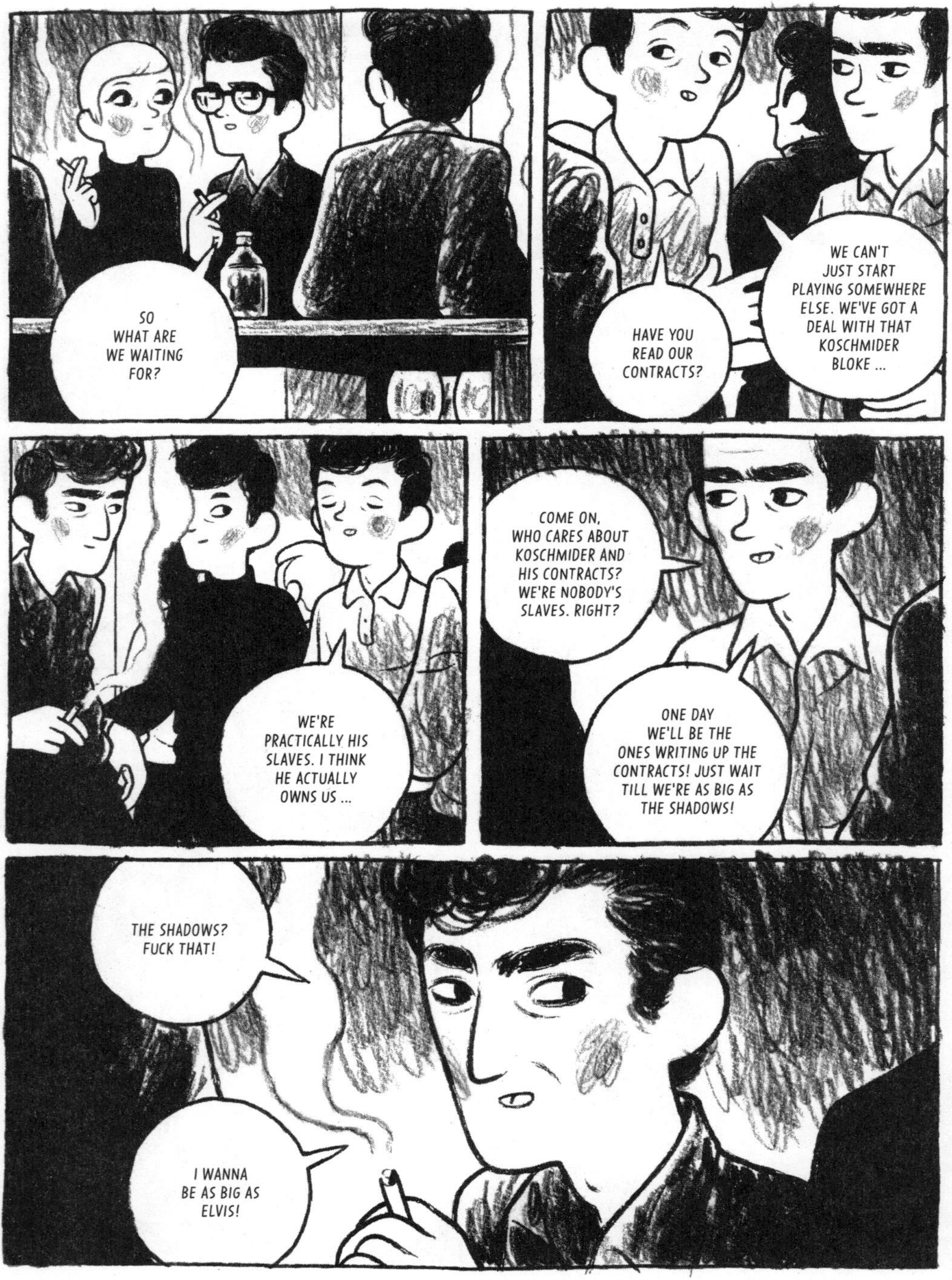
SO WHAT ARE WE WAITING FOR?
HAVE YOU READ OUR CONTRACTS?
WE CAN'T JUST START PLAYING SOMEWHERE ELSE. WE'VE GOT A DEAL WITH THAT KOSCHMIDER BLOKE ...
WE'RE PRACTICALLY HIS SLAVES. I THINK HE ACTUALLY OWNS US ...
COME ON, WHO CARES ABOUT KOSCHMIDER AND HIS CONTRACTS? WE'RE NOBODY'S SLAVES. RIGHT?
ONE DAY WE'LL BE THE ONES WRITING UP THE CONTRACTS! JUST WAIT TILL WE'RE AS BIG AS THE SHADOWS!
THE SHADOWS? FUCK THAT!
I WANNA BE AS BIG AS ELVIS!

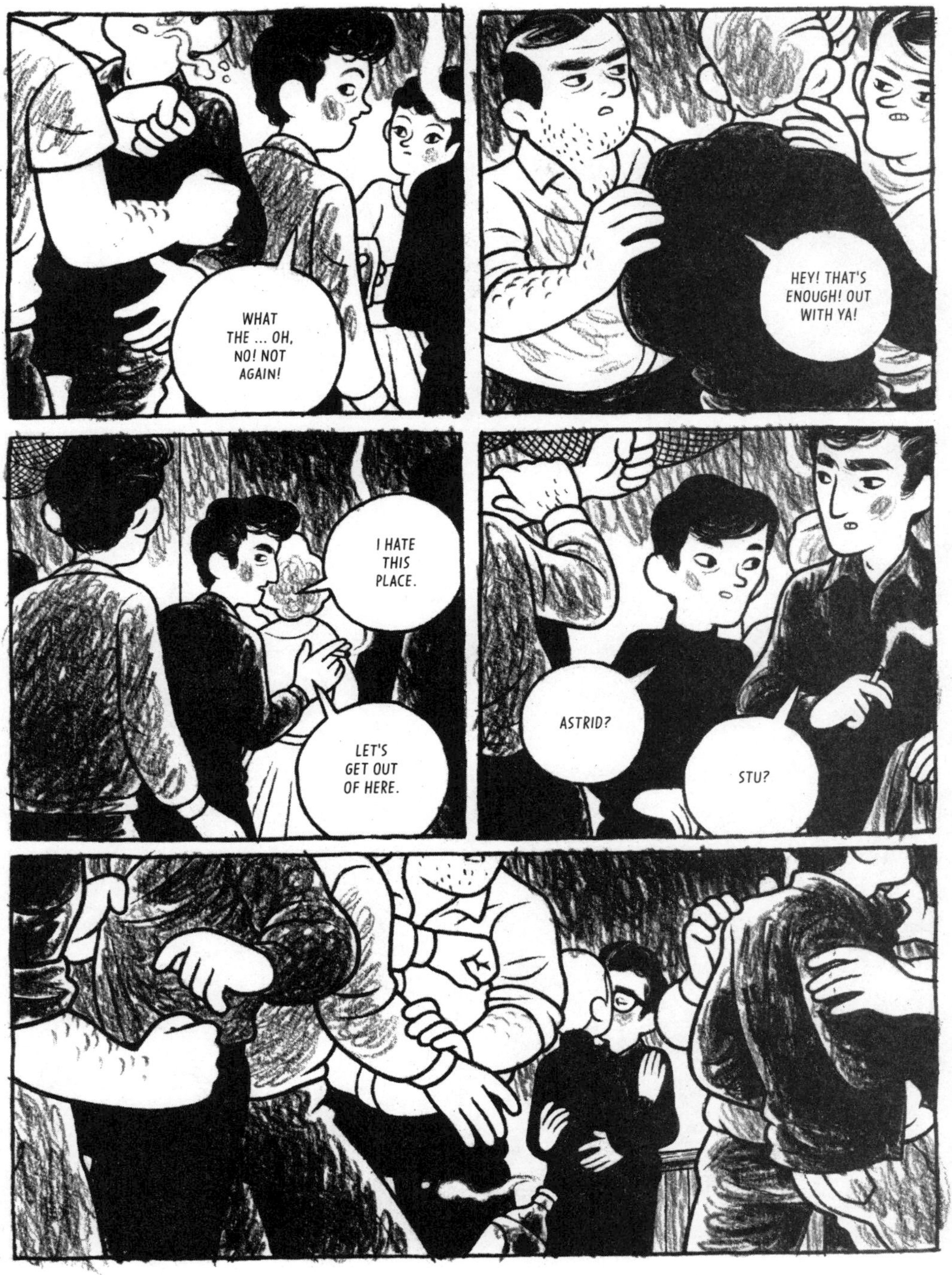
WHAT THE ... OH, NO! NOT AGAIN!
HEY! THAT'S ENOUGH! OUT WITH YA!
I HATE THIS PLACE.
LET'S GET OUT OF HERE.
ASTRID?
STU?

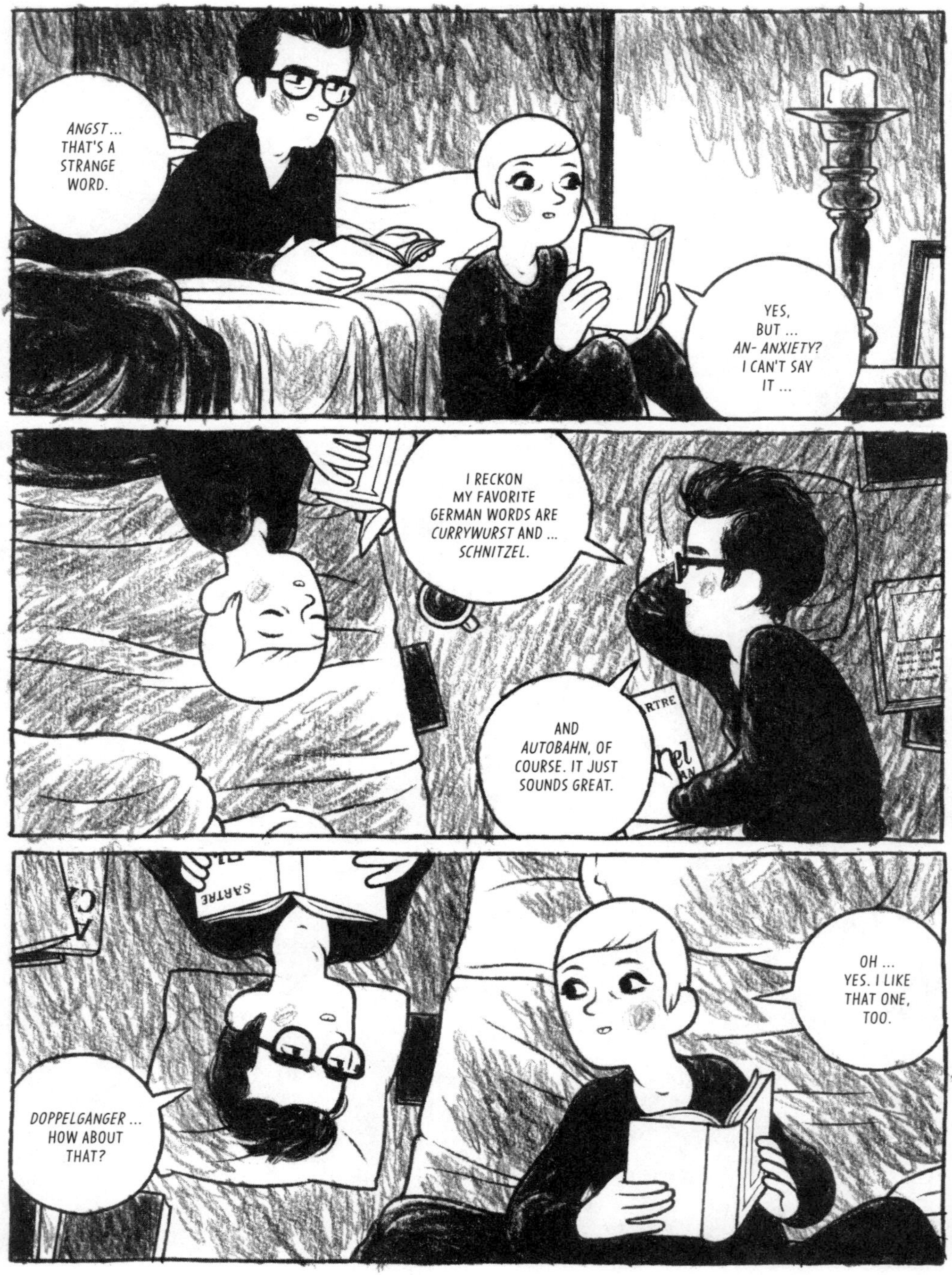
ANGST ... THAT'S A STRANGE WORD.
YES, BUT ... AN- ANXIETY? I CAN'T SAY IT ...
I RECKON MY FAVORITE GERMAN WORDS ARE CURRYWURST AND ... SCHNITZEL.
AND AUTOBAHN, OF COURSE. IT JUST SOUNDS GREAT.
DOPPELGANGER ... HOW ABOUT THAT?
OH ... YES. I LIKE THAT ONE, TOO.

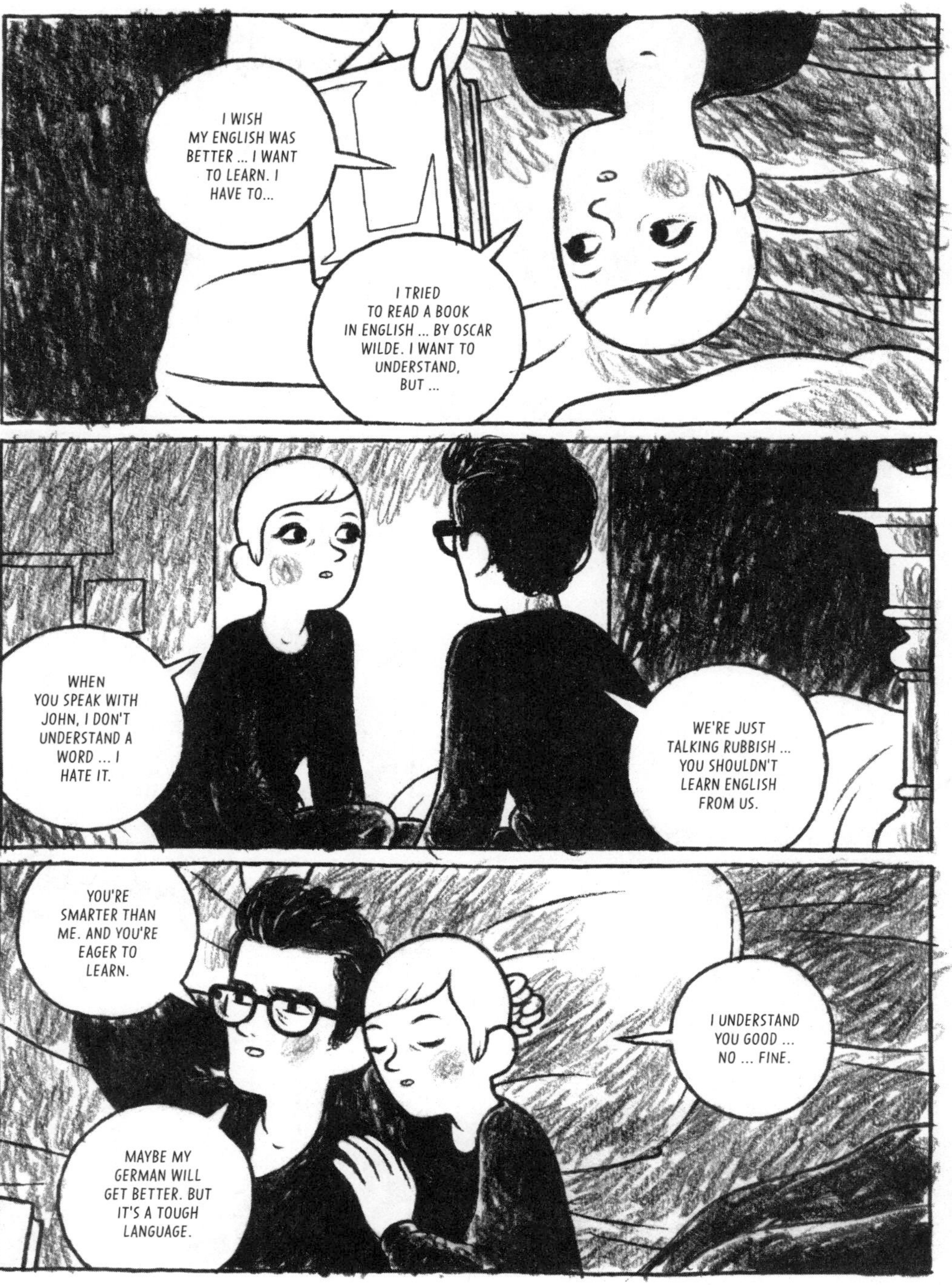
I WISH MY ENGLISH WAS BETTER ... I WANT TO LEARN. I HAVE TO...
I TRIED TO READ A BOOK IN ENGLISH ... BY OSCAR WILDE. I WANT TO UNDERSTAND, BUT ...
WHEN YOU SPEAK WITH JOHN, I DON'T UNDERSTAND A WORD ... I HATE IT.
WE'RE JUST TALKING RUBBISH ... YOU SHOULDN'T LEARN ENGLISH FROM US.
YOU'RE SMARTER THAN ME. AND YOU'RE EAGER TO LEARN.
I UNDERSTAND YOU GOOD ... NO ... FINE.
MAYBE MY GERMAN WILL GET BETTER. BUT IT'S A TOUGH LANGUAGE.

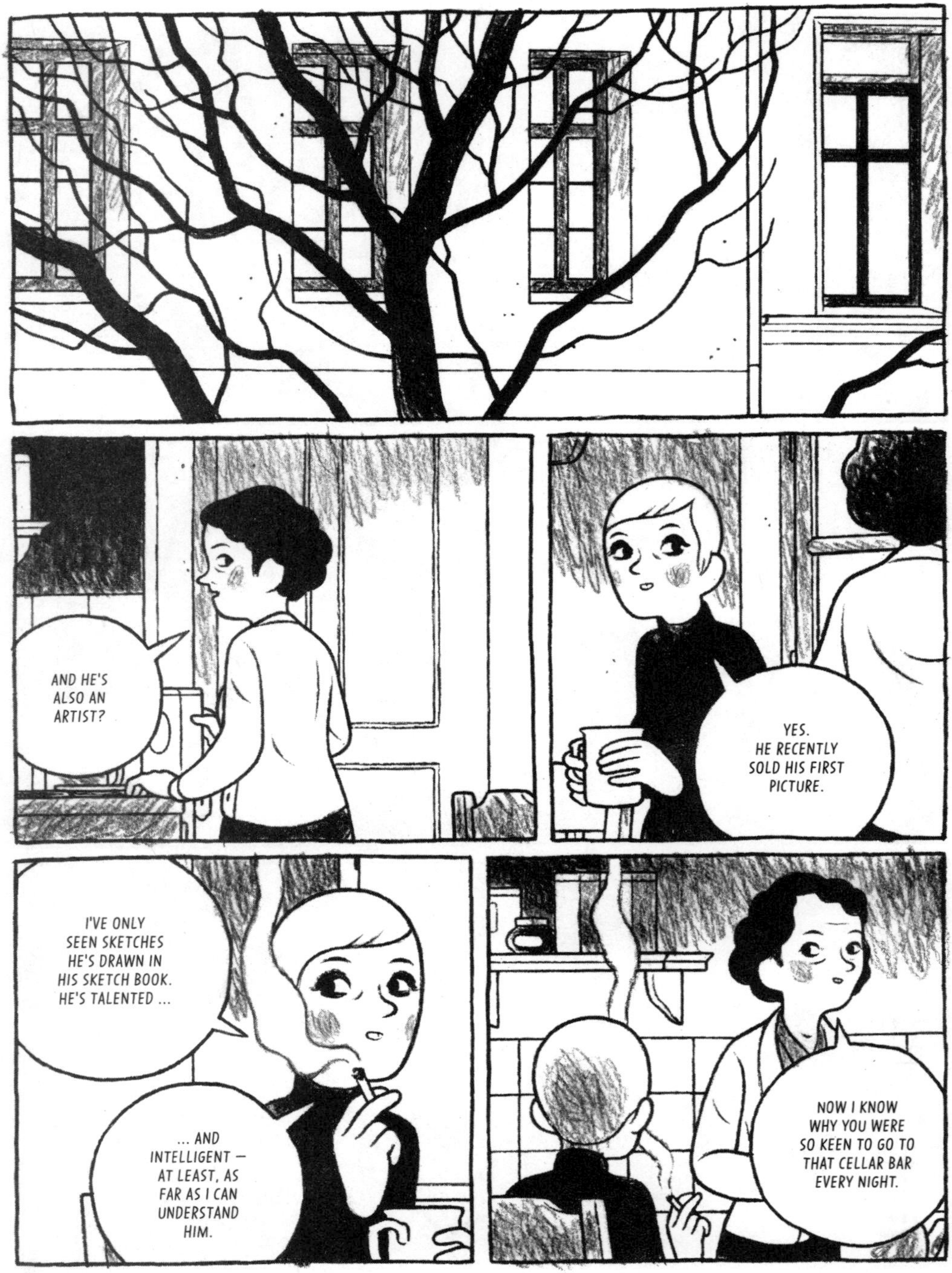
AND HE'S ALSO AN ARTIST?
YES. HE RECENTLY SOLD HIS FIRST PICTURE.
I'VE ONLY SEEN SKETCHES HE'S DRAWN IN HIS SKETCH BOOK. HE'S TALENTED ...
... AND INTELLIGENT — AT LEAST, AS FAR AS I CAN UNDERSTAND HIM.
NOW I KNOW WHY YOU WERE SO KEEN TO GO TO THAT CELLAR BAR EVERY NIGHT.

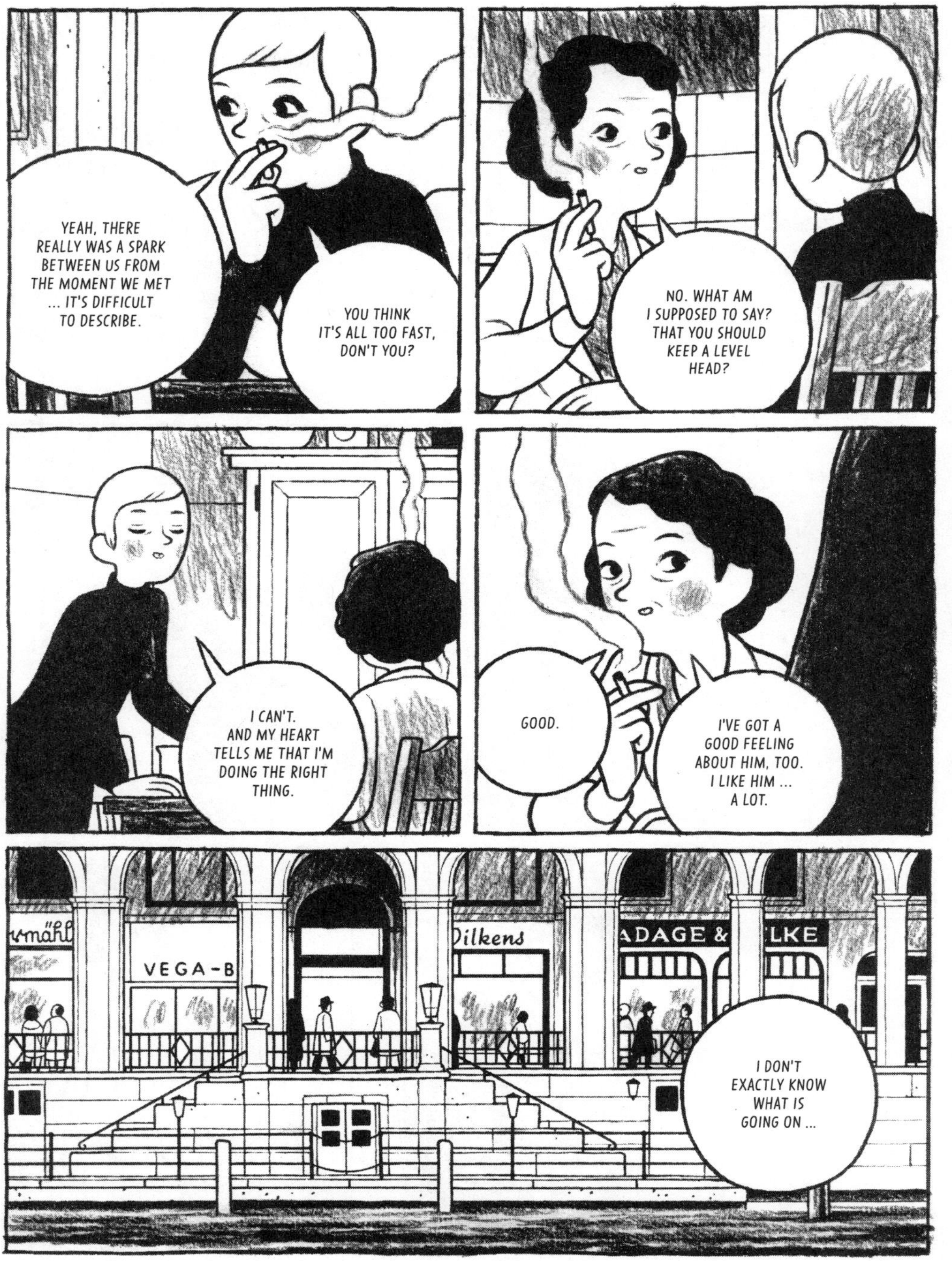
YEAH, THERE REALLY WAS A SPARK BETWEEN US FROM THE MOMENT WE MET ... IT'S DIFFICULT TO DESCRIBE.
YOU THINK IT'S ALL TOO FAST, DON'T YOU?
NO. WHAT AM I SUPPOSED TO SAY? THAT YOU SHOULD KEEP A LEVEL HEAD?
I CAN'T. AND MY HEART TELLS ME THAT I'M DOING THE RIGHT THING.
GOOD.
I'VE GOT A GOOD FEELING ABOUT HIM, TOO. I LIKE HIM ... A LOT.
VEGA-B
Dilkens
ADAGE &
LKE
I DON'T EXACTLY KNOW WHAT IS GOING ON ...

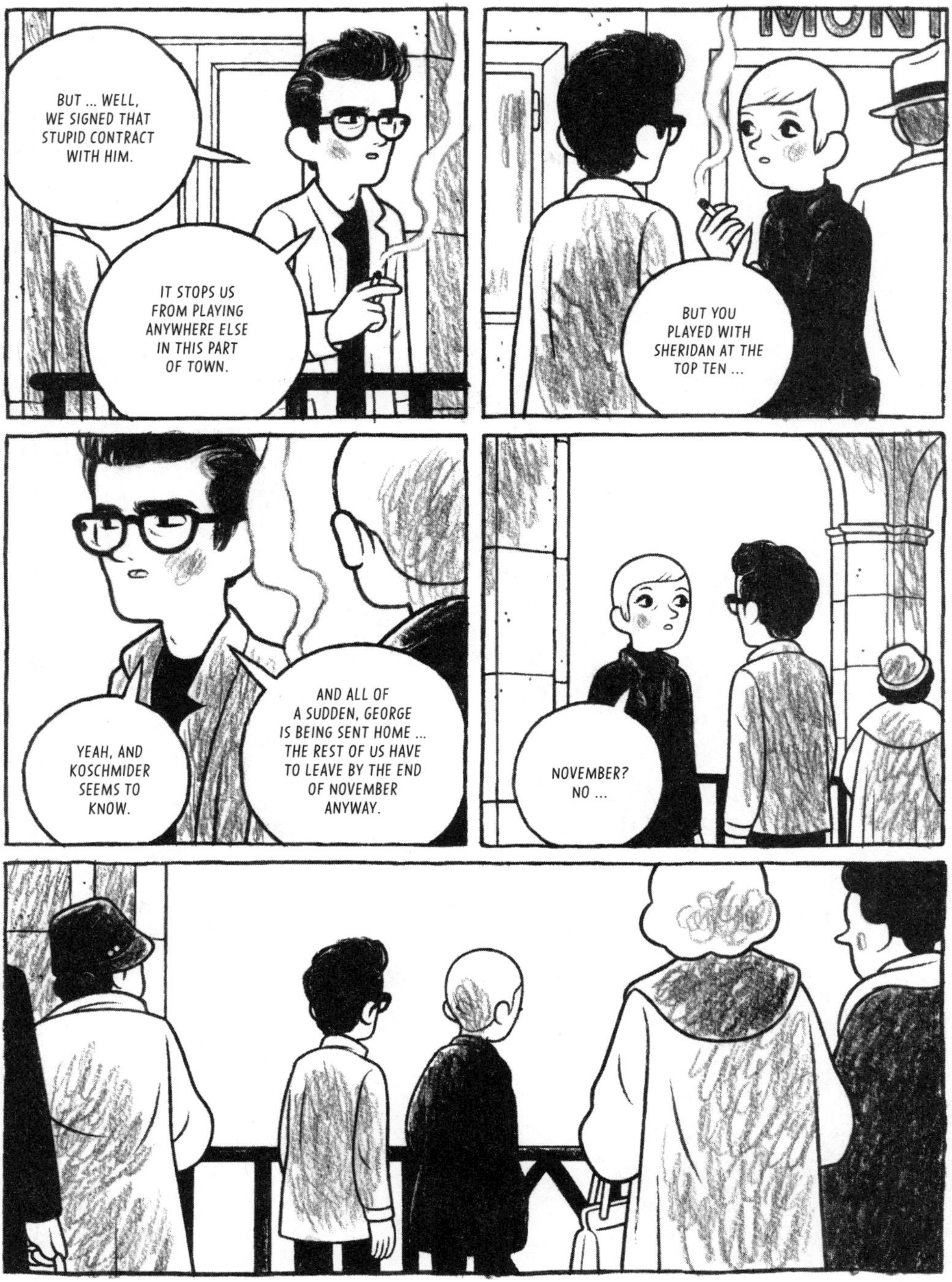
BUT ... WELL, WE SIGNED THAT STUPID CONTRACT WITH HIM.
IT STOPS US FROM PLAYING ANYWHERE ELSE IN THIS PART OF TOWN.
MONT
BUT YOU PLAYED WITH SHERIDAN AT THE TOP TEN ...
YEAH, AND KOSCHMIDER SEEMS TO KNOW.
AND ALL OF A SUDDEN, GEORGE IS BEING SENT HOME ... THE REST OF US HAVE TO LEAVE BY THE END OF NOVEMBER ANYWAY.
NOVEMBER? NO ...

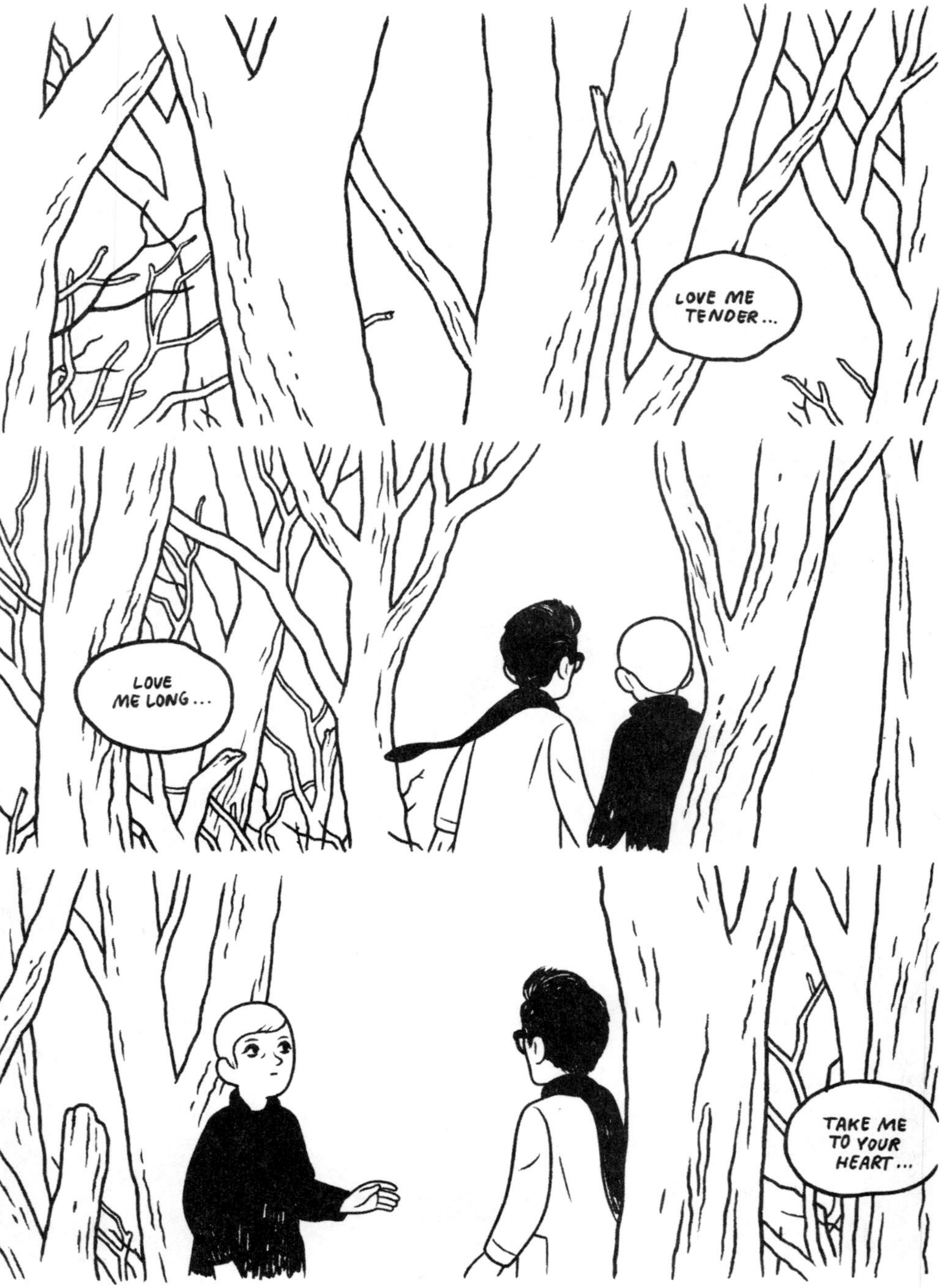
LOVE ME TENDER...
LOVE ME LONG...
TAKE ME TO YOUR HEART...

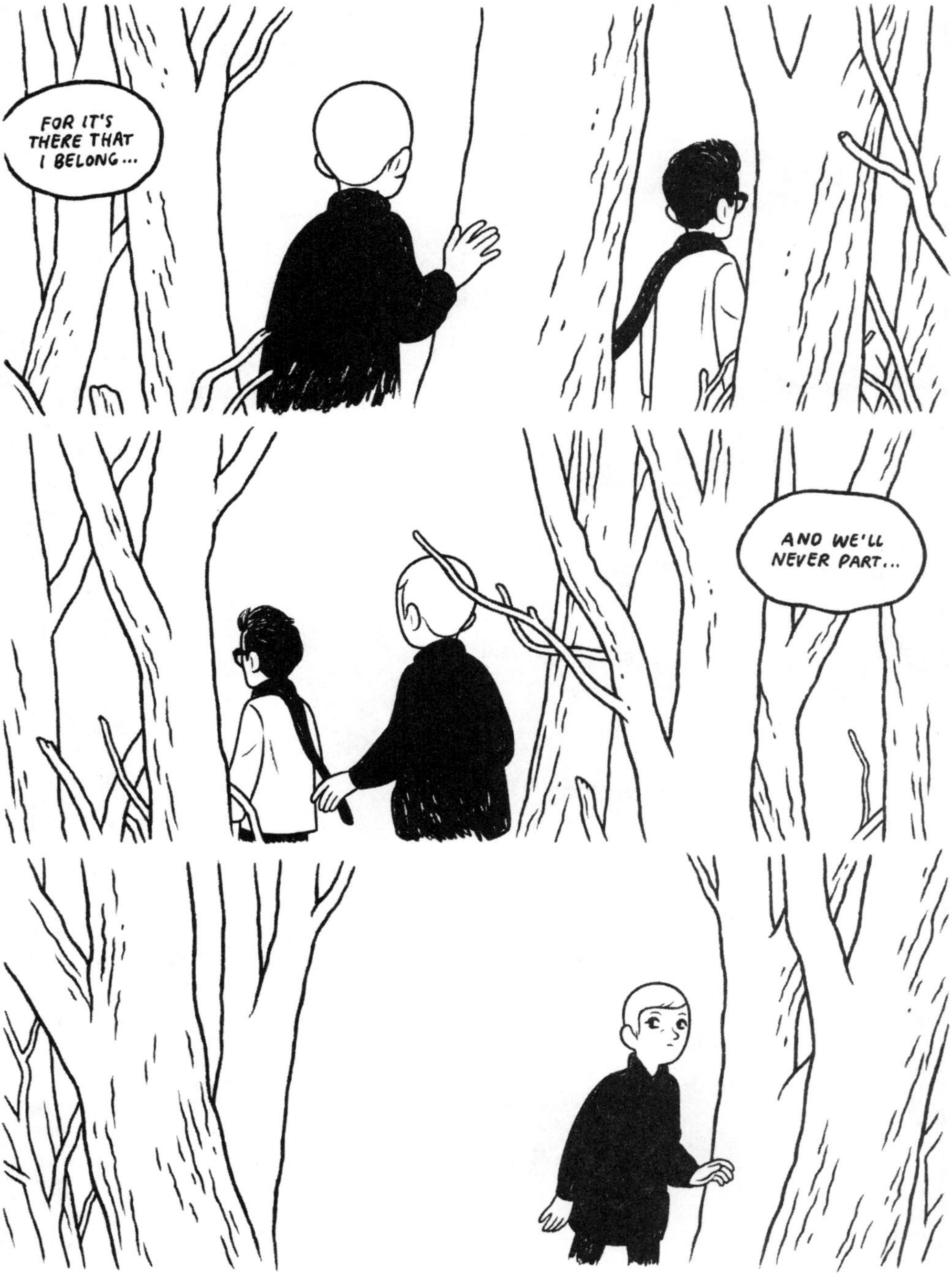
FOR IT'S THERE THAT I BELONG...
AND WE'LL NEVER PART...

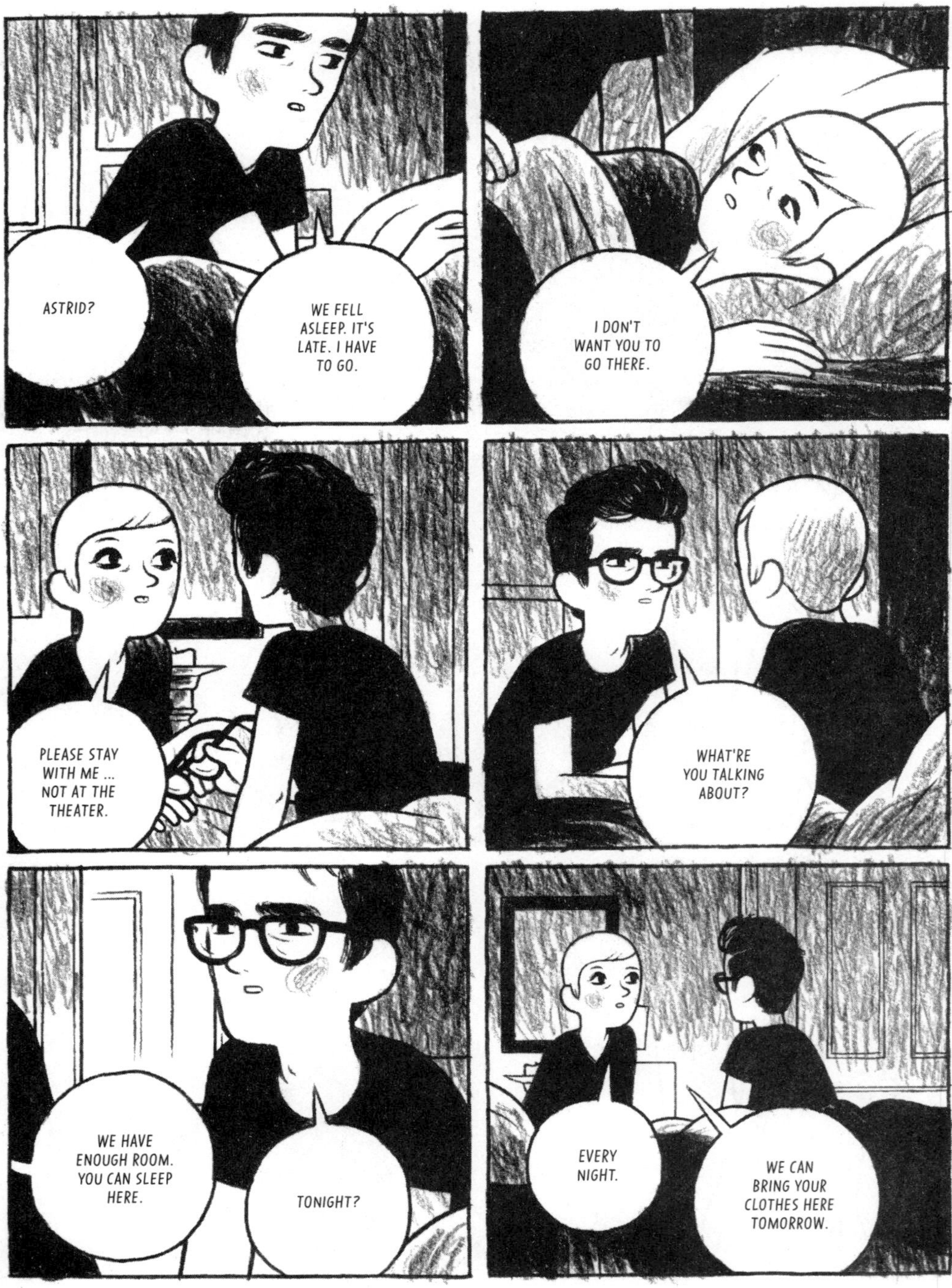
ASTRID?
WE FELL ASLEEP. IT'S LATE. I HAVE TO GO.
I DON'T WANT YOU TO GO THERE.
PLEASE STAY WITH ME ... NOT AT THE THEATER.
WHAT'RE YOU TALKING ABOUT?
WE HAVE ENOUGH ROOM. YOU CAN SLEEP HERE.
TONIGHT?
EVERY NIGHT.
WE CAN BRING YOUR CLOTHES HERE TOMORROW.

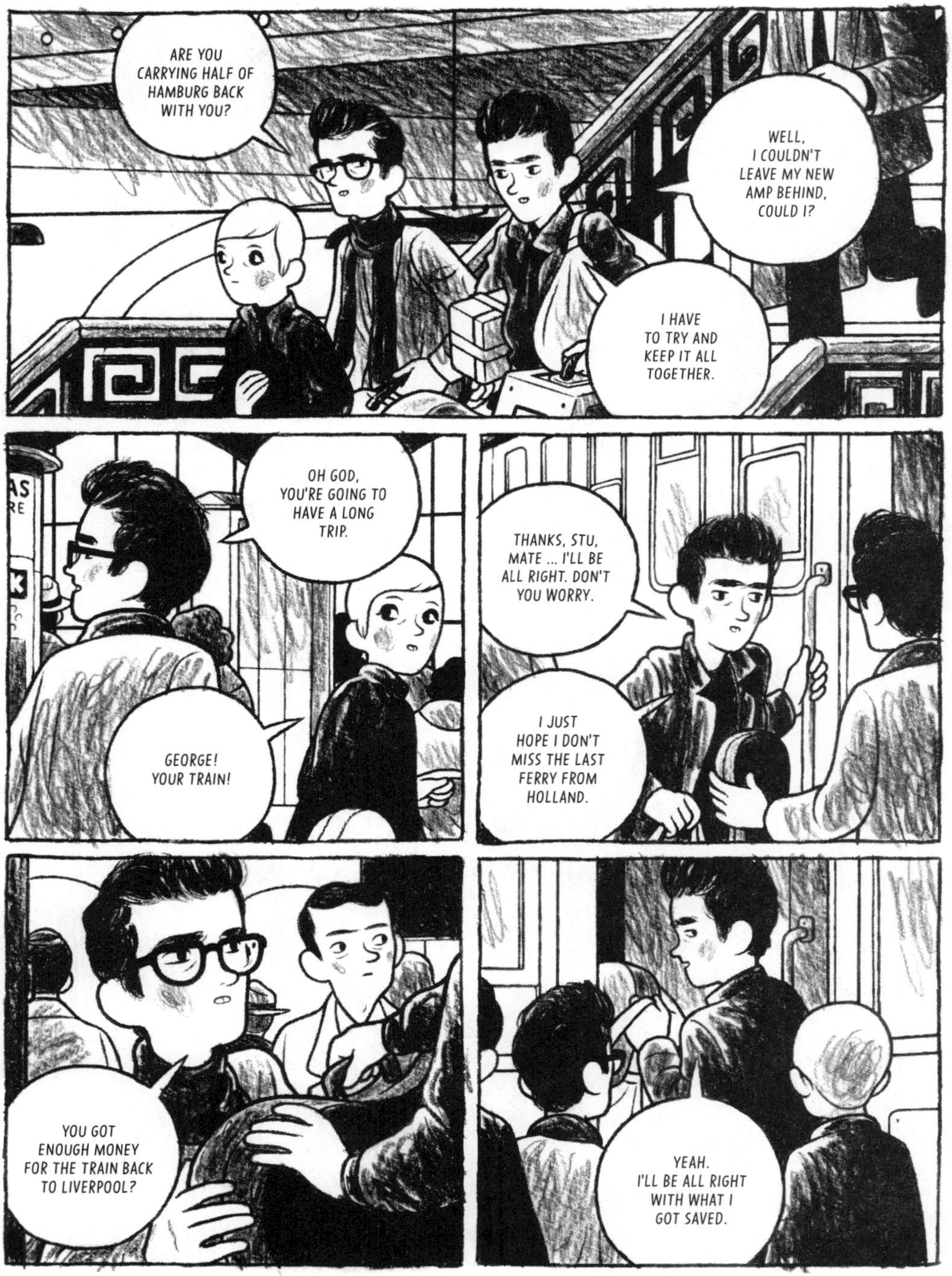
ARE YOU CARRYING HALF OF HAMBURG BACK WITH YOU?
WELL, I COULDN'T LEAVE MY NEW AMP BEHIND, COULD I?
I HAVE TO TRY AND KEEP IT ALL TOGETHER.
OH GOD, YOU'RE GOING TO HAVE A LONG TRIP.
GEORGE! YOUR TRAIN!
THANKS, STU, MATE ... I'LL BE ALL RIGHT. DON'T YOU WORRY.
I JUST HOPE I DON'T MISS THE LAST FERRY FROM HOLLAND.
YOU GOT ENOUGH MONEY FOR THE TRAIN BACK TO LIVERPOOL?
YEAH. I'LL BE ALL RIGHT WITH WHAT I GOT SAVED.

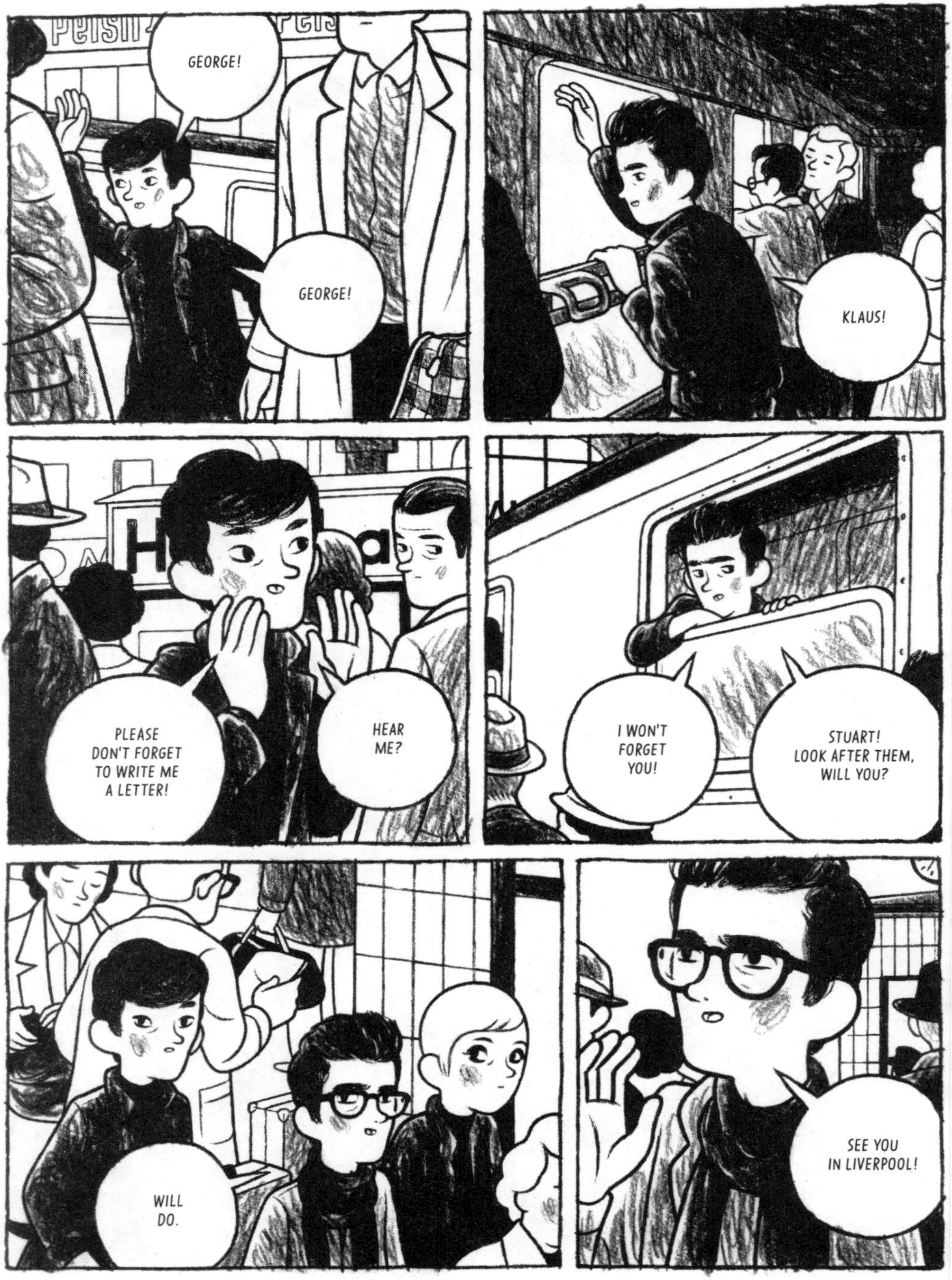
GEORGE!
GEORGE!
KLAUS!
PLEASE DON'T FORGET TO WRITE ME A LETTER!
HEAR ME?
I WON'T FORGET YOU!
STUART! LOOK AFTER THEM, WILL YOU?
WILL DO.
SEE YOU IN LIVERPOOL!

Bahnsteig 4
YEAH, SEE YOU SOON!
BON VOYAGE!
POOR KID ... SAFE TRIP, MATE.

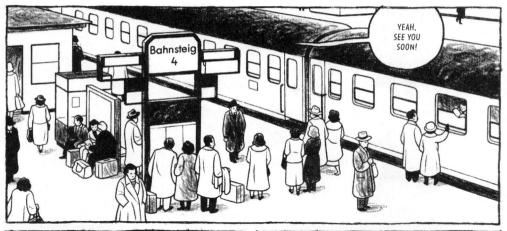

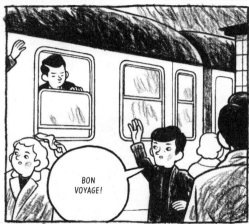

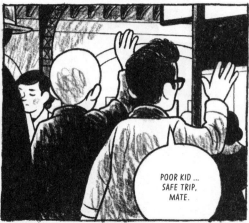

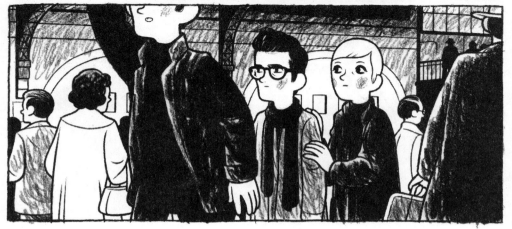

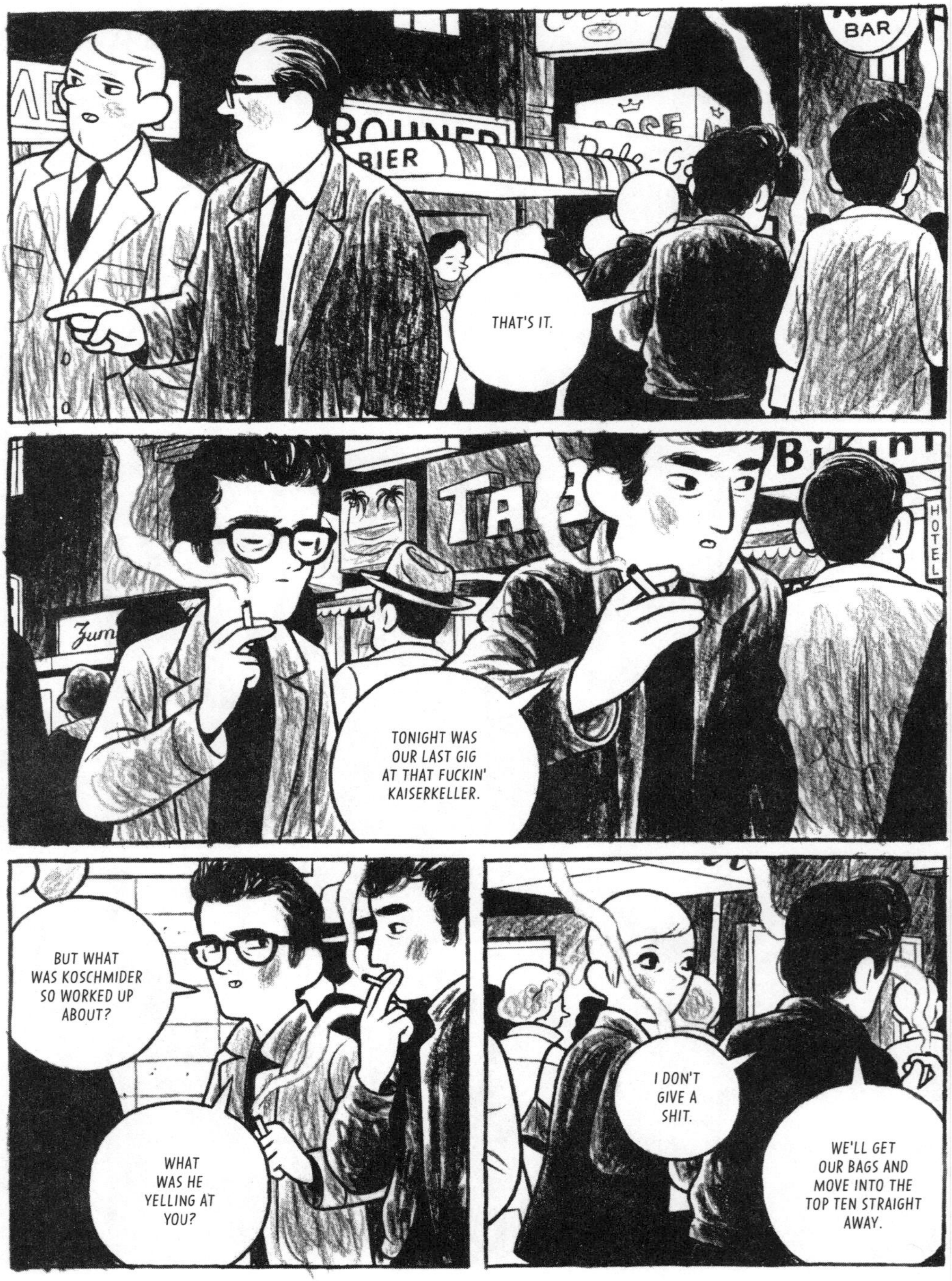
BAR
BIER
HOTEL
THAT'S IT.
TONIGHT WAS OUR LAST GIG AT THAT FUCKIN' KAISERKELLER.
BUT WHAT WAS KOSCHMIDER SO WORKED UP ABOUT?
WHAT WAS HE YELLING AT YOU?
I DON'T GIVE A SHIT.
WE'LL GET OUR BAGS AND MOVE INTO THE TOP TEN STRAIGHT AWAY.

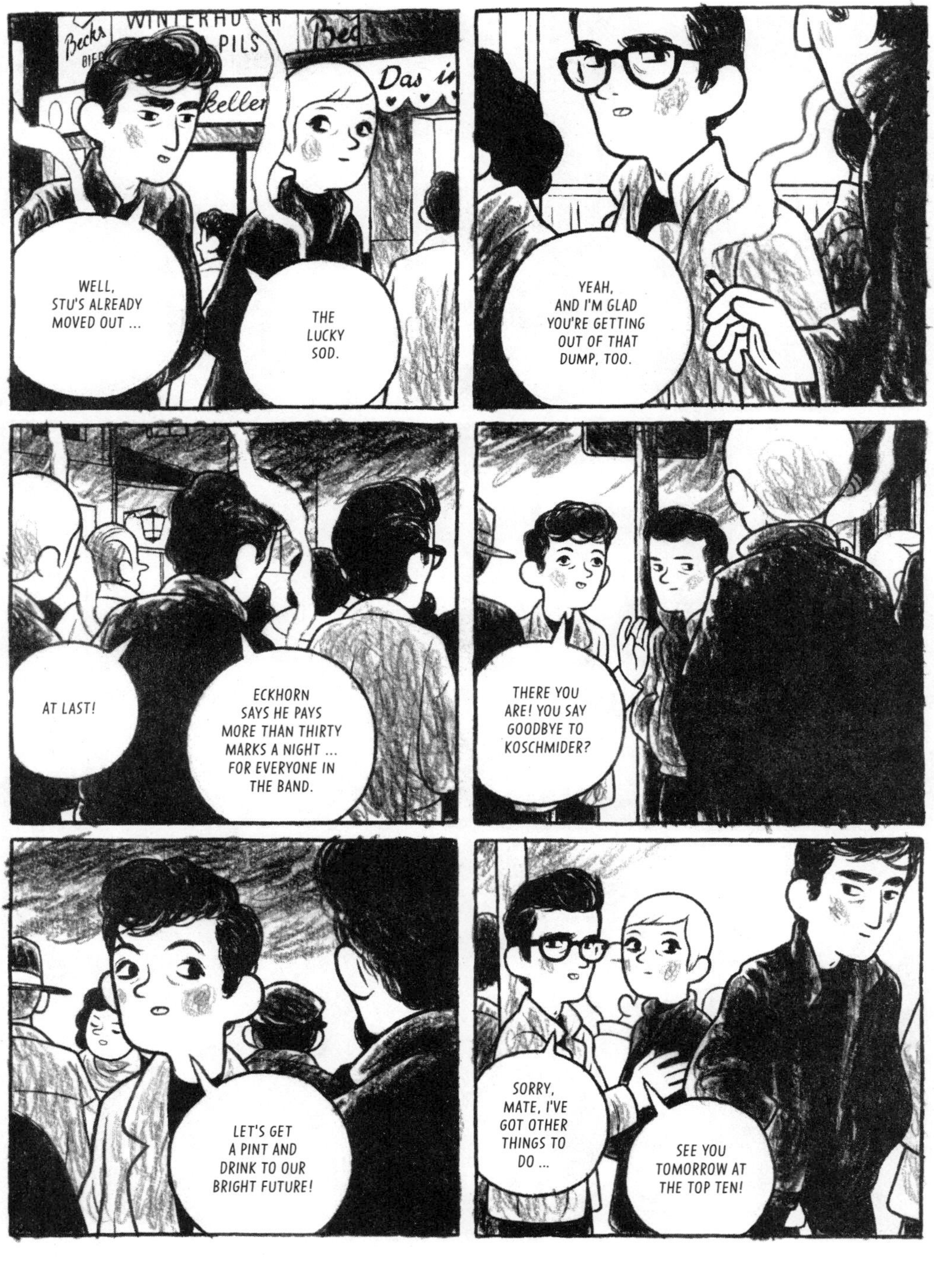
WINTERHUDER PILS
Das in
WELL, STU'S ALREADY MOVED OUT ...
THE LUCKY SOD.
YEAH, AND I'M GLAD YOU'RE GETTING OUT OF THAT DUMP, TOO.
AT LAST!
ECKHORN SAYS HE PAYS MORE THAN THIRTY MARKS A NIGHT ... FOR EVERYONE IN THE BAND.
THERE YOU ARE! YOU SAY GOODBYE TO KOSCHMIDER?
LET'S GET A PINT AND DRINK TO OUR BRIGHT FUTURE!
SORRY, MATE, I'VE GOT OTHER THINGS TO DO ...
SEE YOU TOMORROW AT THE TOP TEN!

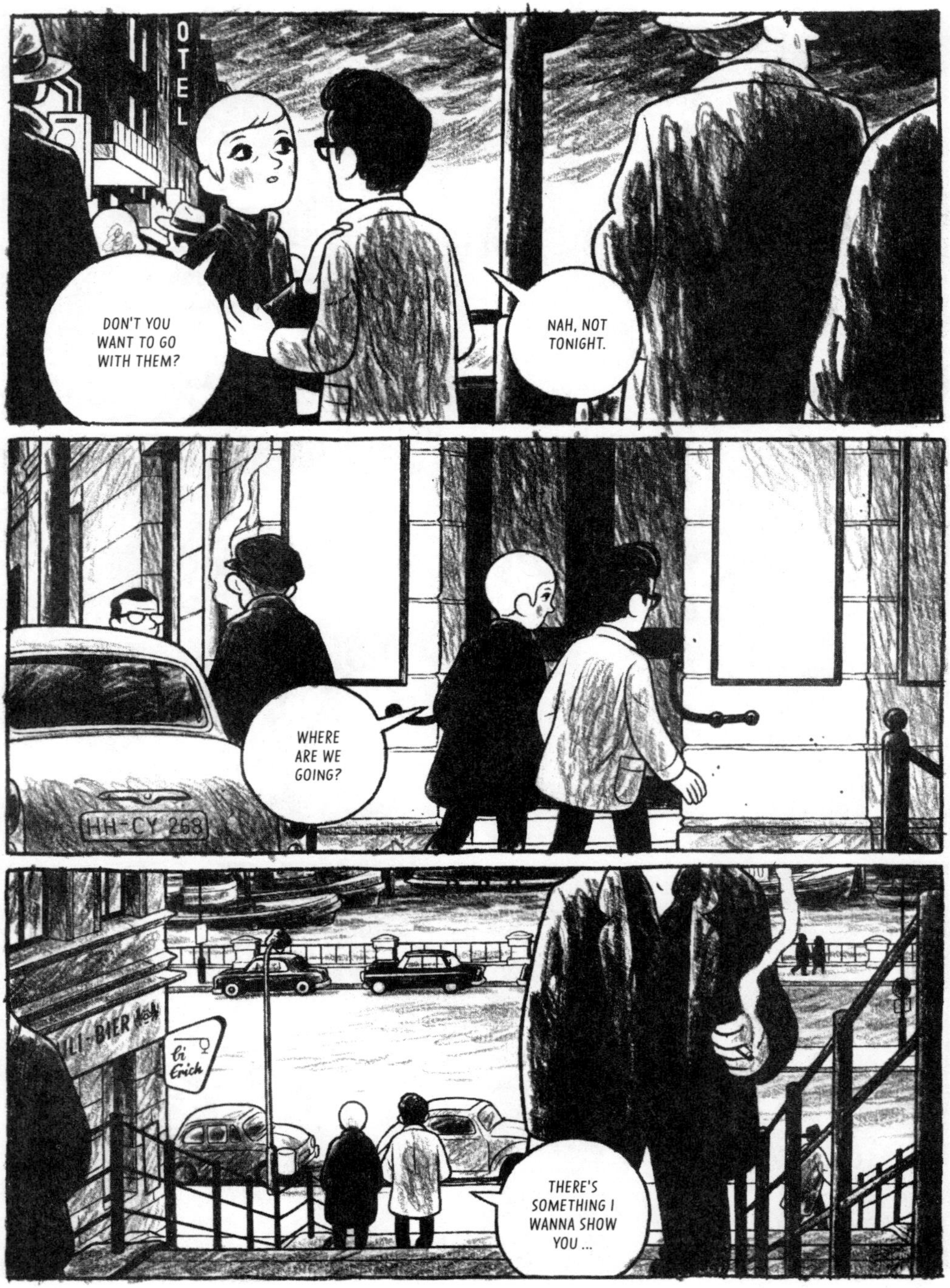
OTEL
DON'T YOU WANT TO GO WITH THEM?
NAH, NOT TONIGHT.
HH-CY 268
WHERE ARE WE GOING?
BIER
bi Erich
THERE'S SOMETHING I WANNA SHOW YOU ...

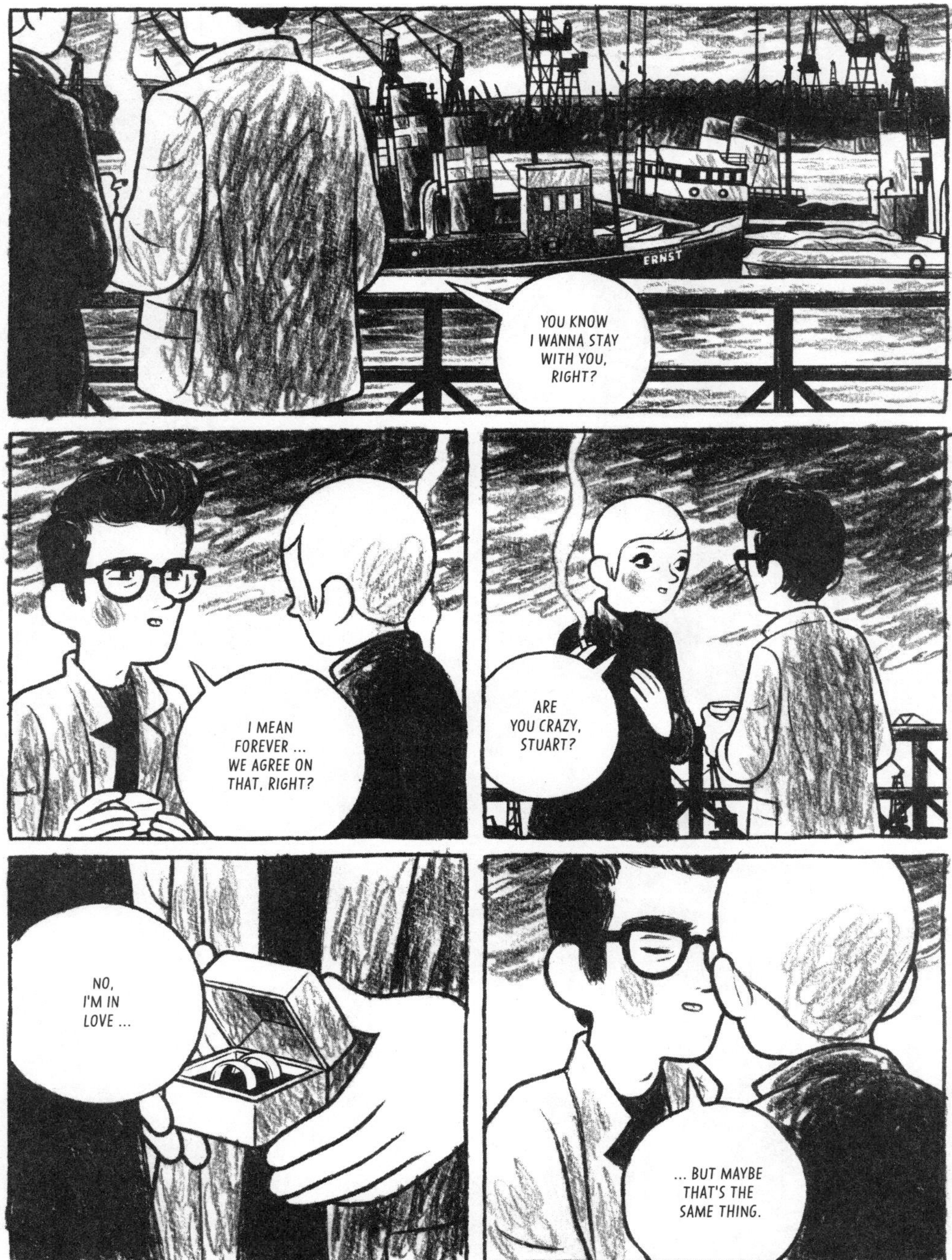
ERNST
YOU KNOW I WANNA STAY WITH YOU, RIGHT?
I MEAN FOREVER ... WE AGREE ON THAT, RIGHT?
ARE YOU CRAZY, STUART?
NO, I'M IN LOVE ...
... BUT MAYBE THAT'S THE SAME THING.

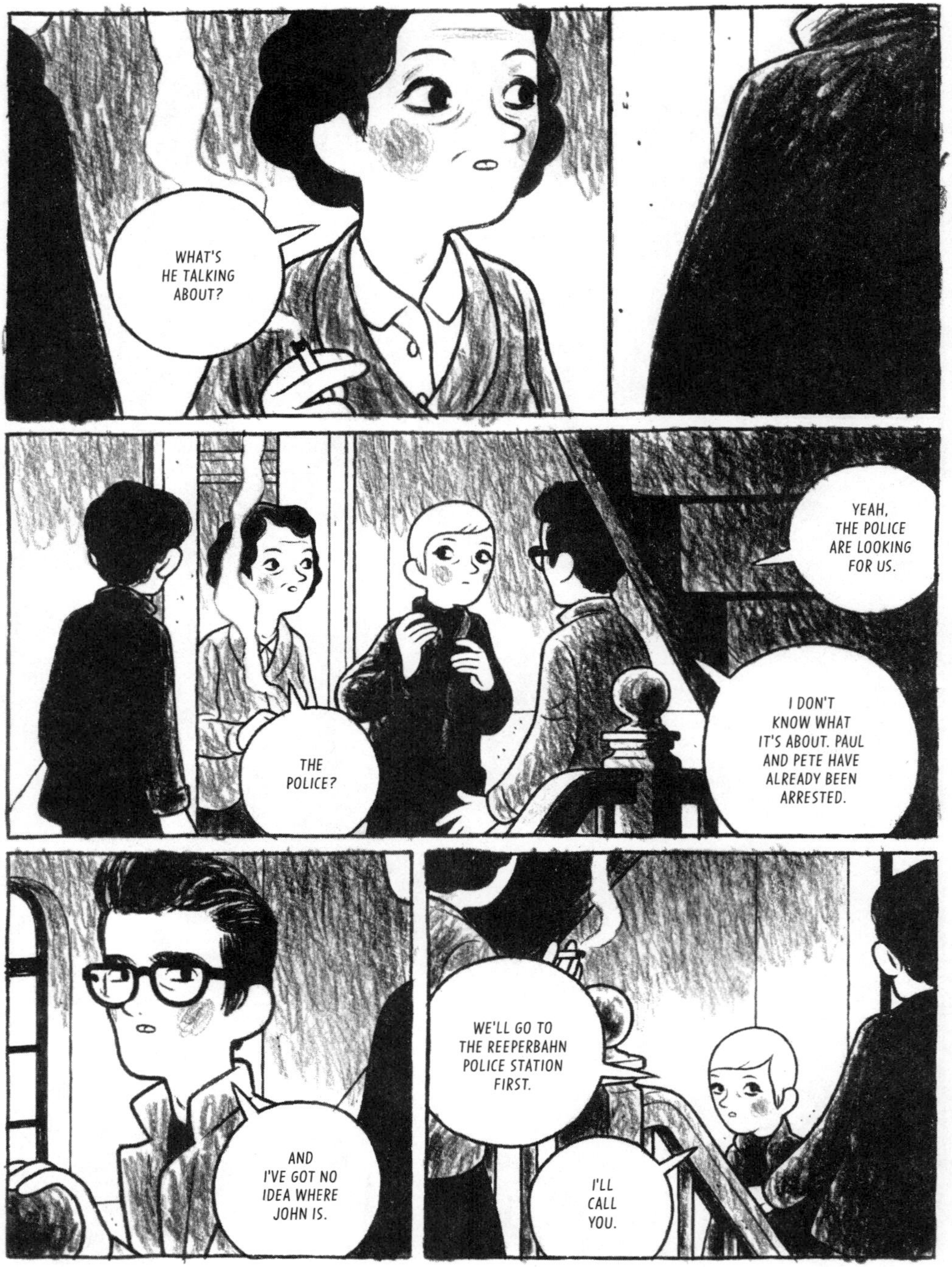
WHAT'S HE TALKING ABOUT?
YEAH, THE POLICE ARE LOOKING FOR US.
THE POLICE?
I DON'T KNOW WHAT IT'S ABOUT. PAUL AND PETE HAVE ALREADY BEEN ARRESTED.
AND I'VE GOT NO IDEA WHERE JOHN IS.
WE'LL GO TO THE REEPERBAHN POLICE STATION FIRST.
I'LL CALL YOU.

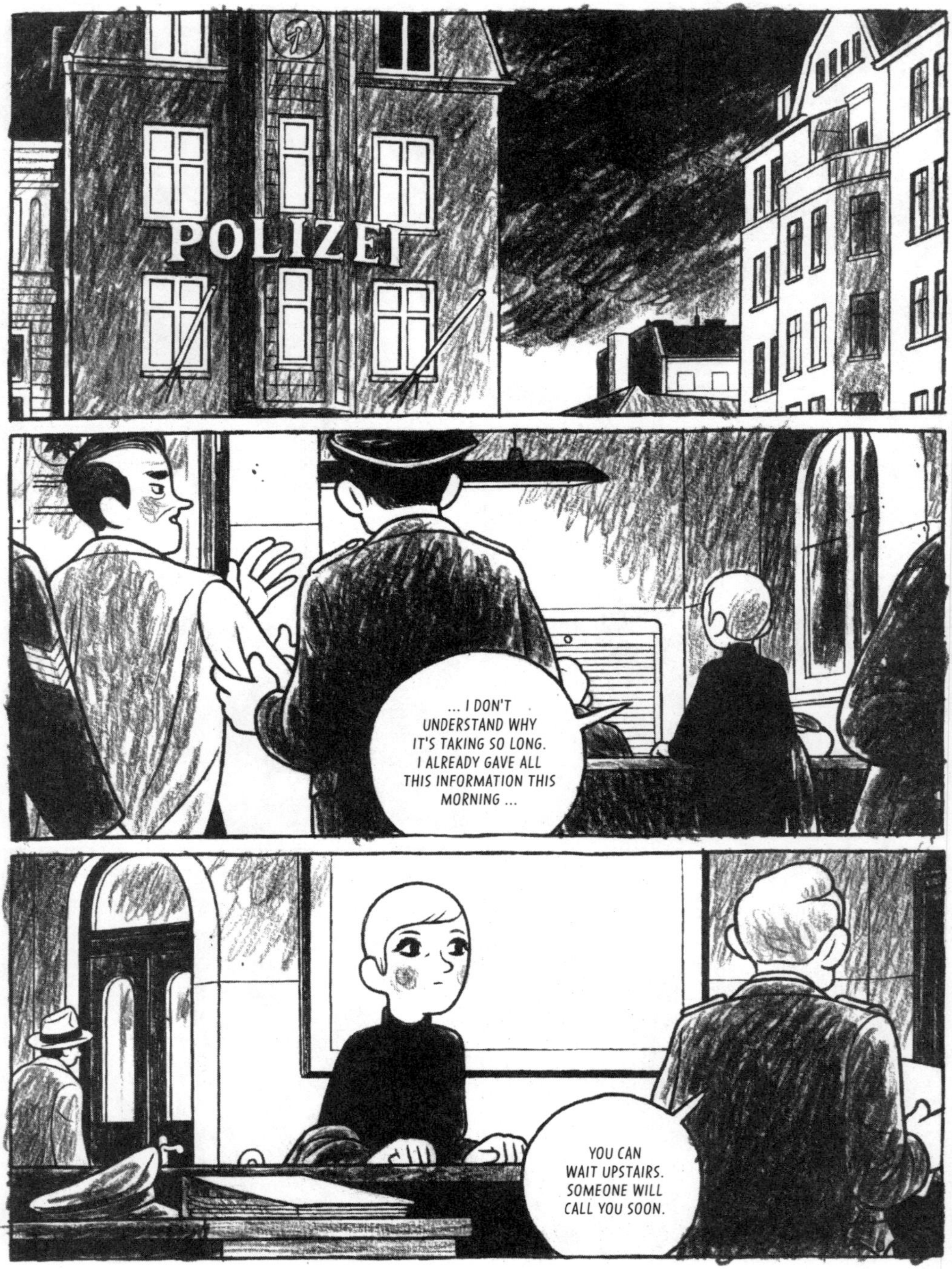
POLIZEI
... I DON'T UNDERSTAND WHY IT'S TAKING SO LONG. I ALREADY GAVE ALL THIS INFORMATION THIS MORNING ...
YOU CAN WAIT UPSTAIRS. SOMEONE WILL CALL YOU SOON.

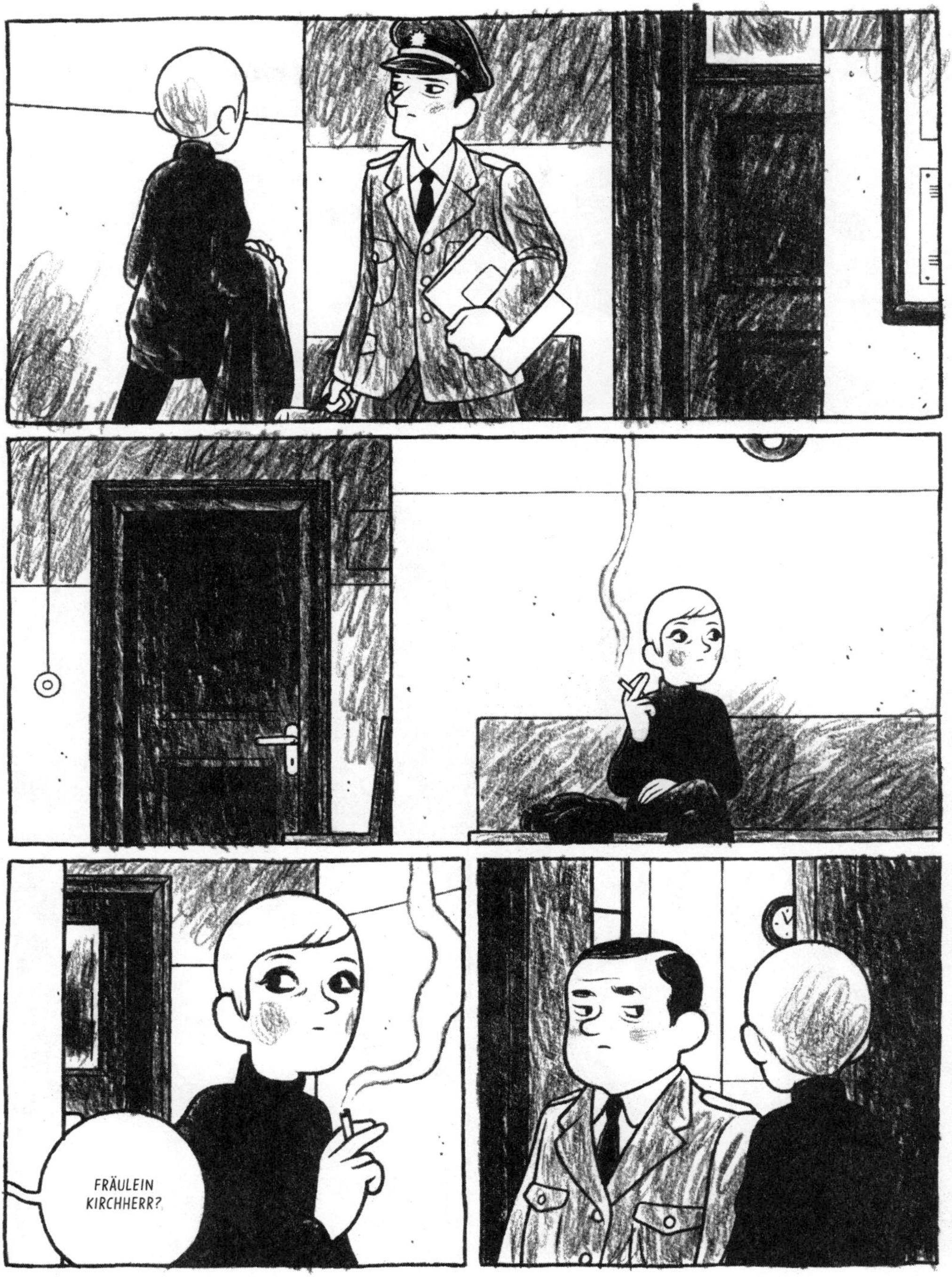
FRÄULEIN KIRCHHERR?

GOOD EVENING.

GOOD EVENING.

WE'RE INVESTIGATING ACCUSATIONS OF ... ARSON AT ... PAUL-ROOSENSTRASSE 33.

BUT YOU'RE ... HERR SUTCLIFFE DOESN'T EVEN LIVE THERE ANYMORE.

HE LIVES WITH ME. WE'RE ENGAGED AND ...

YES, HE SAID THAT AND GAVE THIS ADDRESS ...

IS IT YOUR ADDRESS?

YES, THAT'S ...

YOUR ID CARD PLEASE ...

THANK YOU. WE STILL NEED TO CHECK THE GENTLEMEN'S RESIDENCE PERMITS.

AND, OF COURSE, THEIR WORK PERMITS.

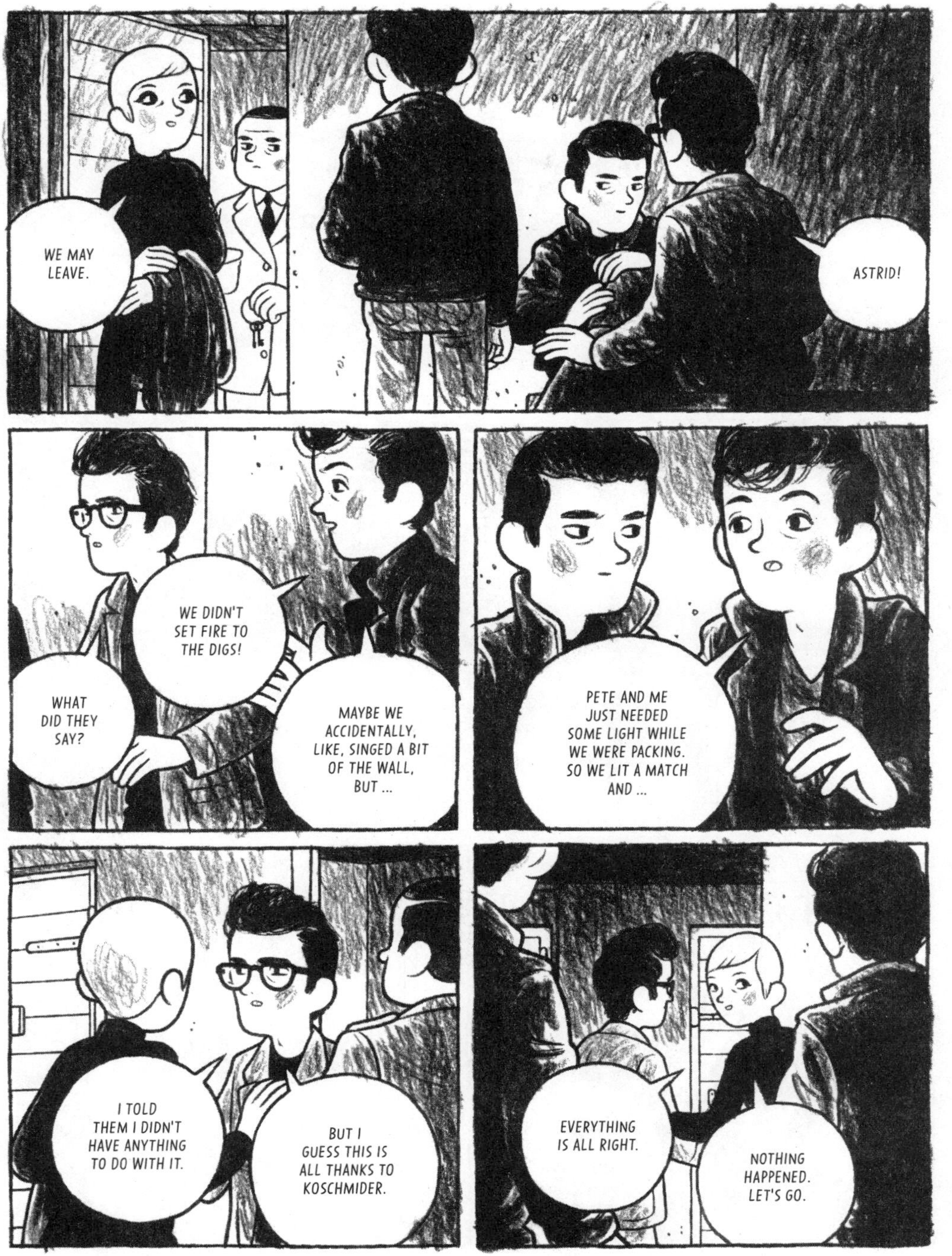
WE MAY LEAVE.
ASTRID!
WE DIDN'T SET FIRE TO THE DIGS!
WHAT DID THEY SAY?
MAYBE WE ACCIDENTALLY, LIKE, SINGED A BIT OF THE WALL, BUT ...
PETE AND ME JUST NEEDED SOME LIGHT WHILE WE WERE PACKING. SO WE LIT A MATCH AND ...
I TOLD THEM I DIDN'T HAVE ANYTHING TO DO WITH IT.
BUT I GUESS THIS IS ALL THANKS TO KOSCHMIDER.
EVERYTHING IS ALL RIGHT.
NOTHING HAPPENED. LET'S GO.

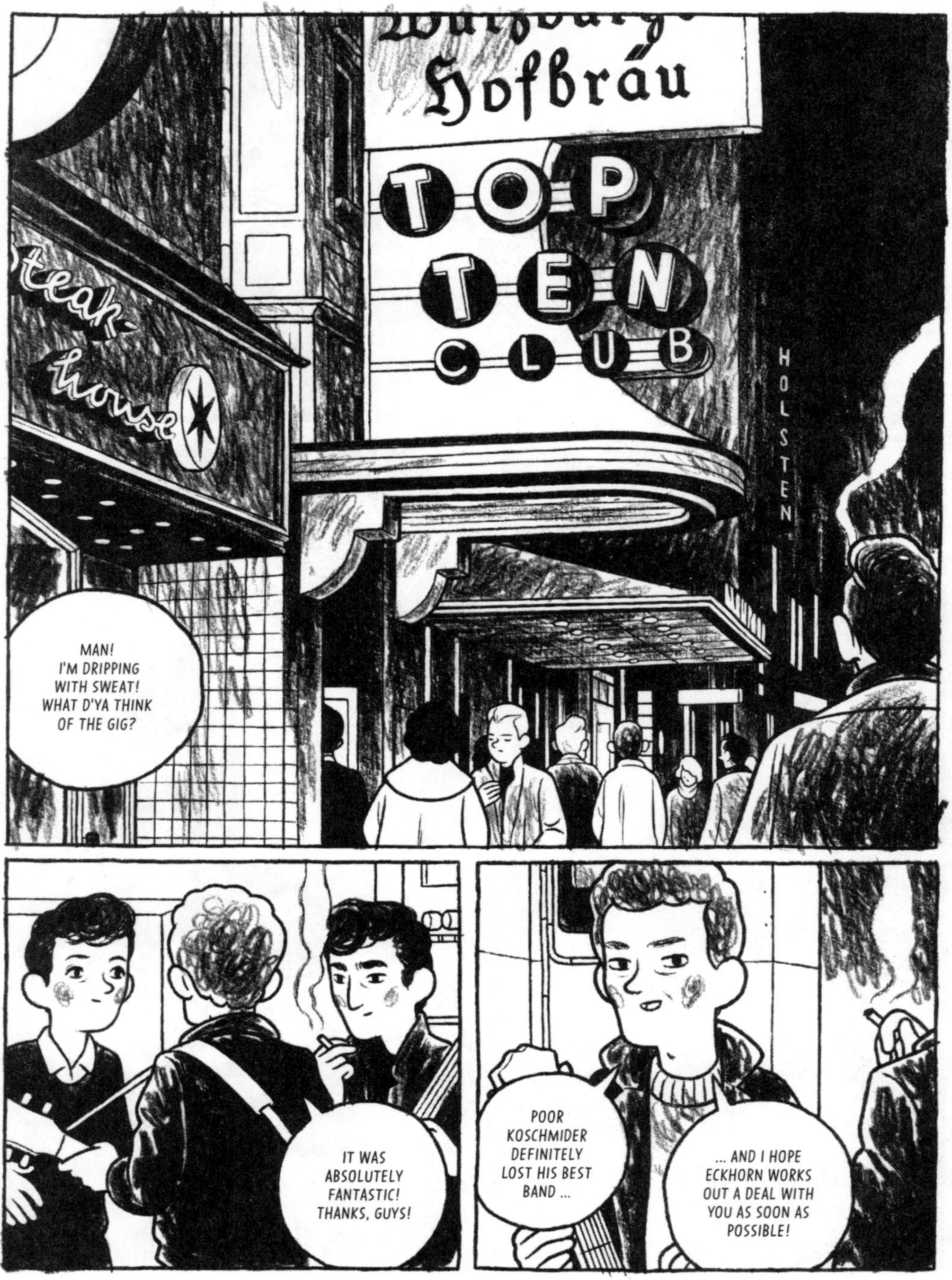
Hofbräu
TOP TEN CLUB
Steak-house
HOLSTEN
MAN! I'M DRIPPING WITH SWEAT! WHAT D'YA THINK OF THE GIG?
IT WAS ABSOLUTELY FANTASTIC! THANKS, GUYS!
POOR KOSCHMIDER DEFINITELY LOST HIS BEST BAND ...
... AND I HOPE ECKHORN WORKS OUT A DEAL WITH YOU AS SOON AS POSSIBLE!

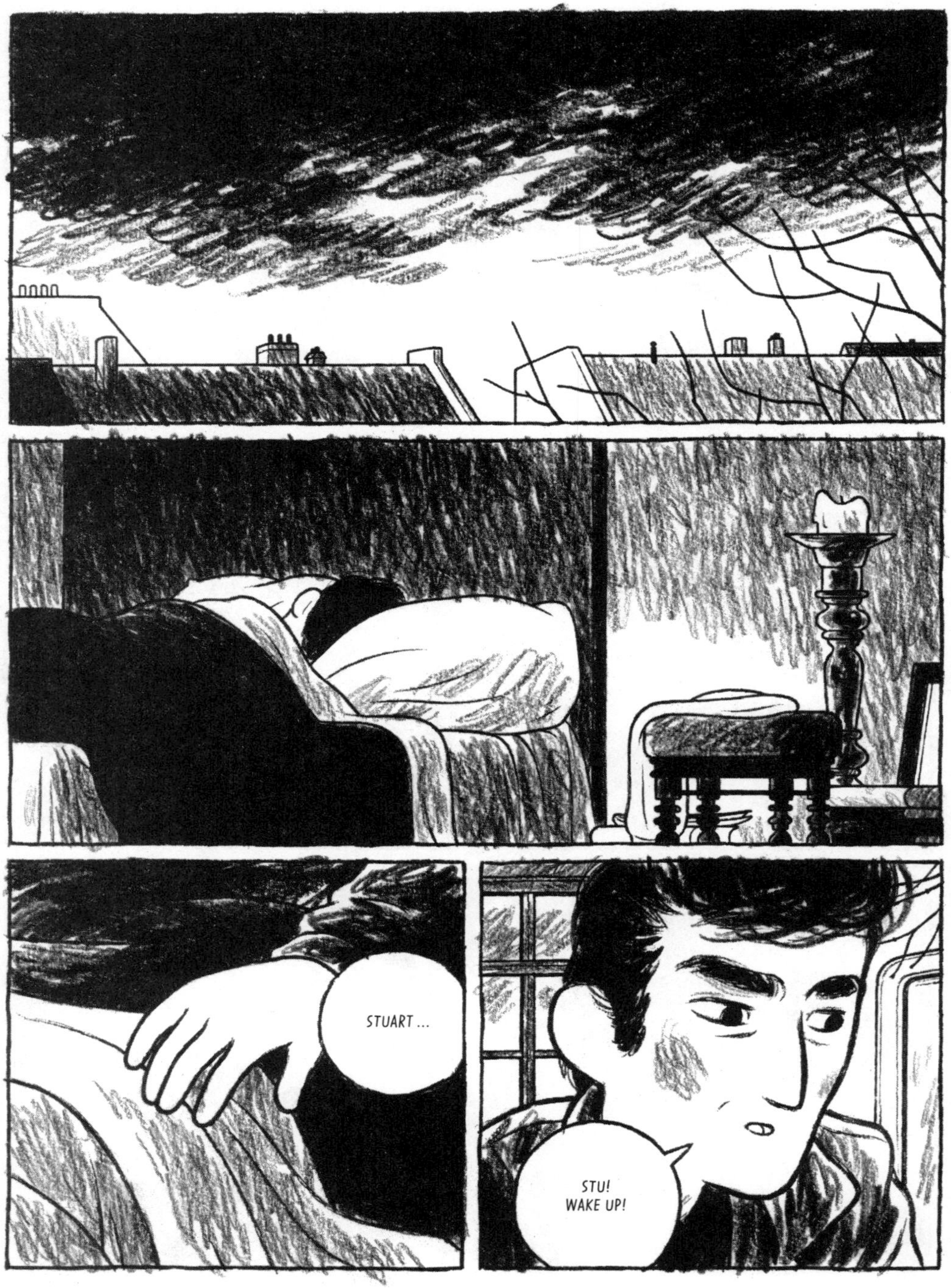
STUART ...
STU! WAKE UP!

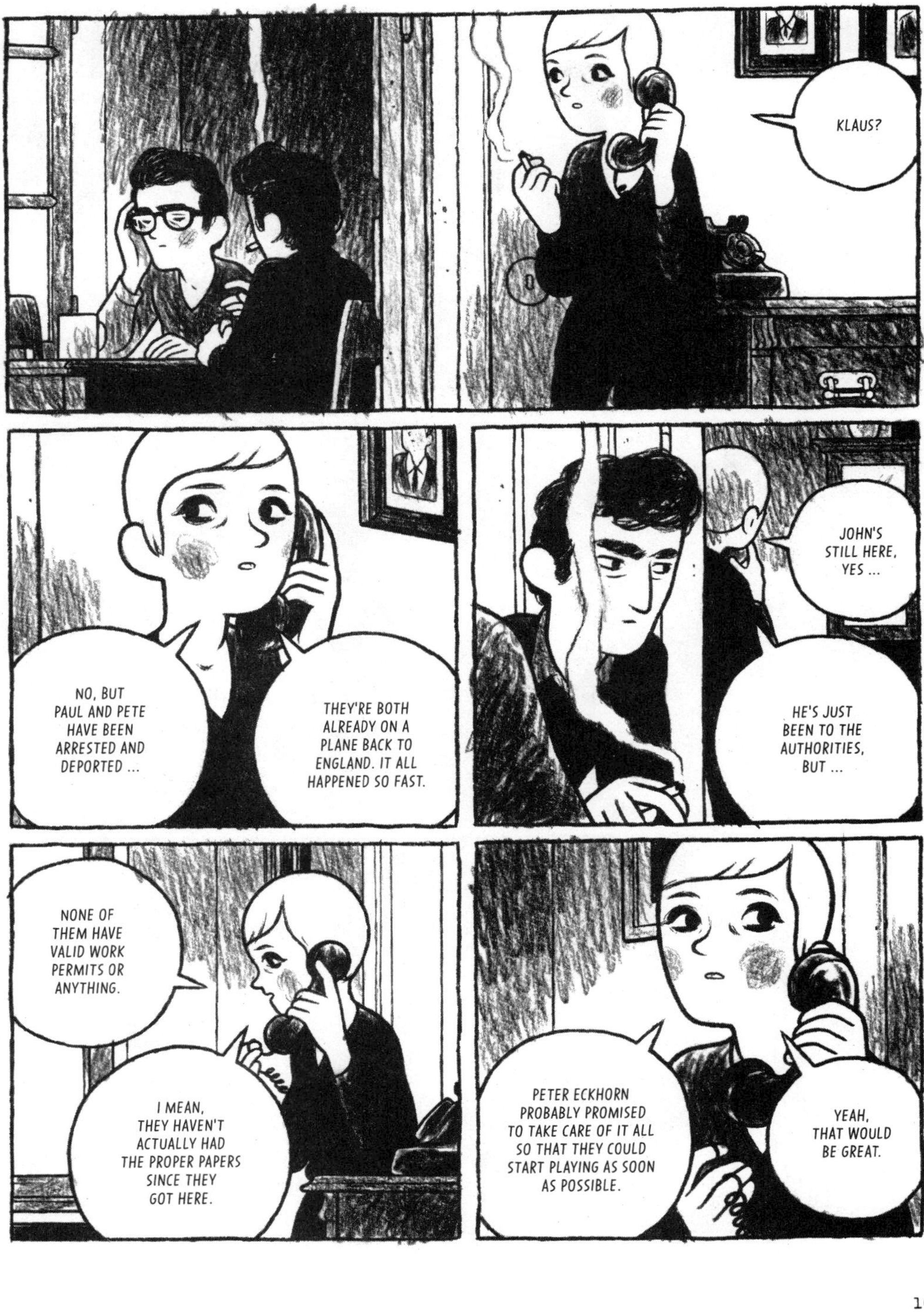
KLAUS?
NO, BUT PAUL AND PETE HAVE BEEN ARRESTED AND DEPORTED ...
THEY'RE BOTH ALREADY ON A PLANE BACK TO ENGLAND. IT ALL HAPPENED SO FAST.
JOHN'S STILL HERE, YES ...
HE'S JUST BEEN TO THE AUTHORITIES, BUT ...
NONE OF THEM HAVE VALID WORK PERMITS OR ANYTHING.
I MEAN, THEY HAVEN'T ACTUALLY HAD THE PROPER PAPERS SINCE THEY GOT HERE.
PETER ECKHORN PROBABLY PROMISED TO TAKE CARE OF IT ALL SO THAT THEY COULD START PLAYING AS SOON AS POSSIBLE.
YEAH, THAT WOULD BE GREAT.

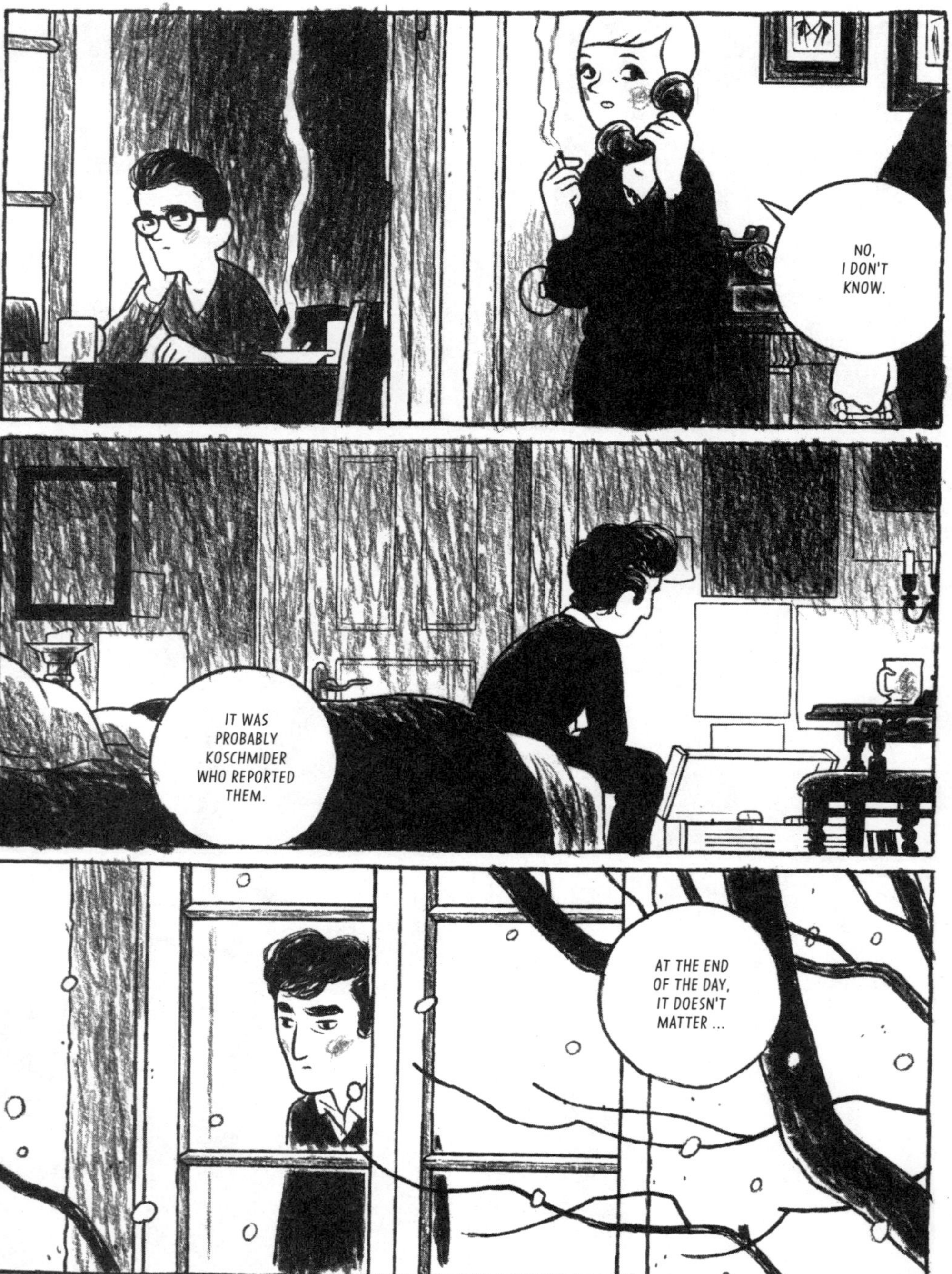
NO, I DON'T KNOW.
IT WAS PROBABLY KOSCHMIDER WHO REPORTED THEM.
AT THE END OF THE DAY, IT DOESN'T MATTER ...

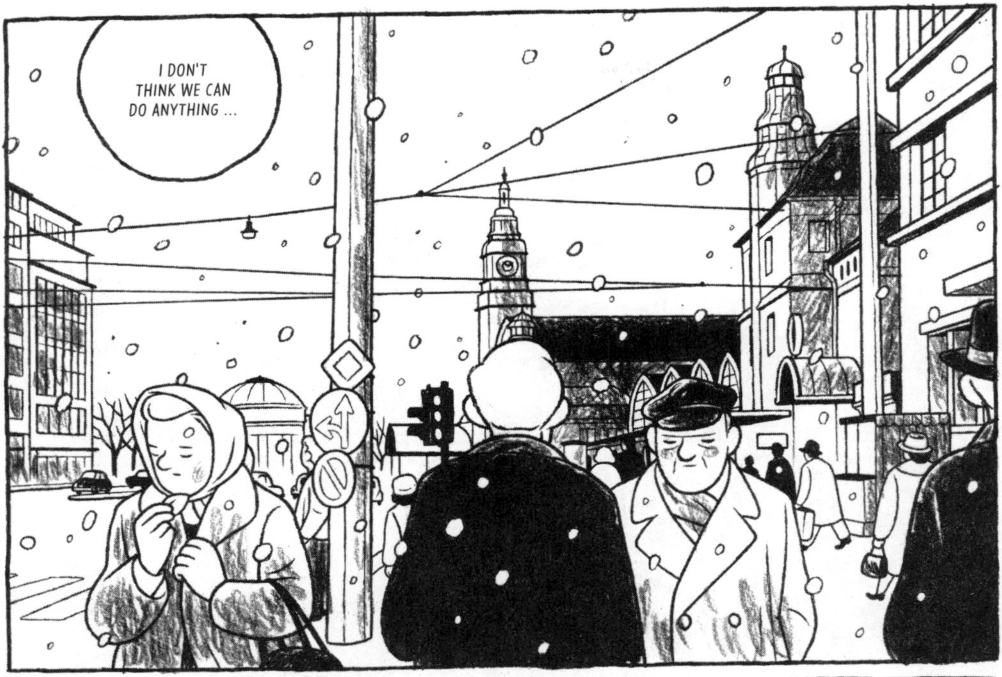
I DON'T THINK WE CAN DO ANYTHING ...

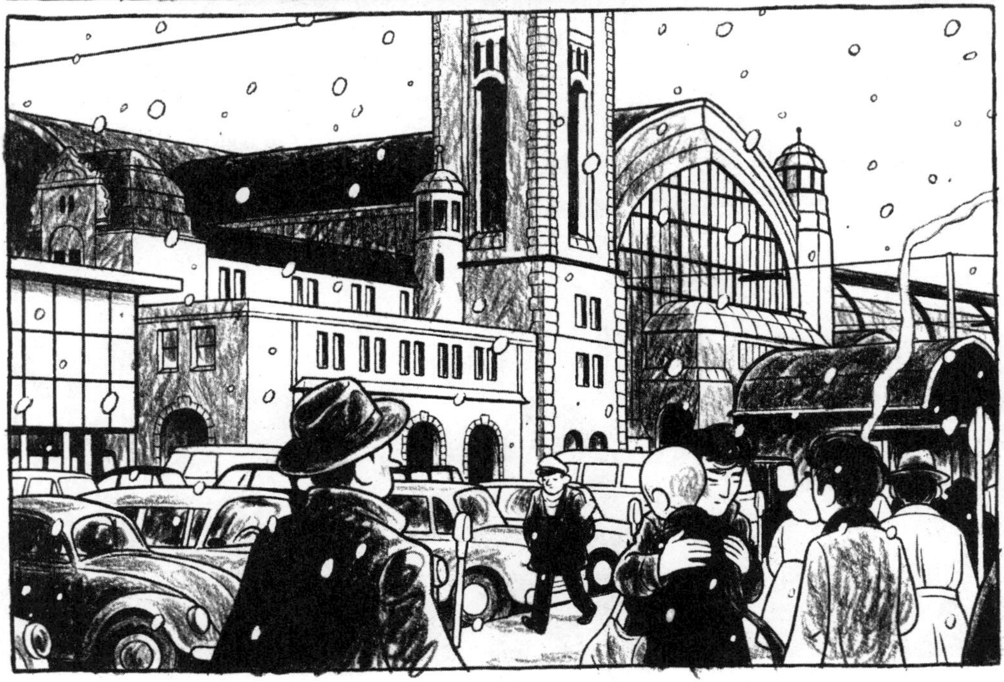

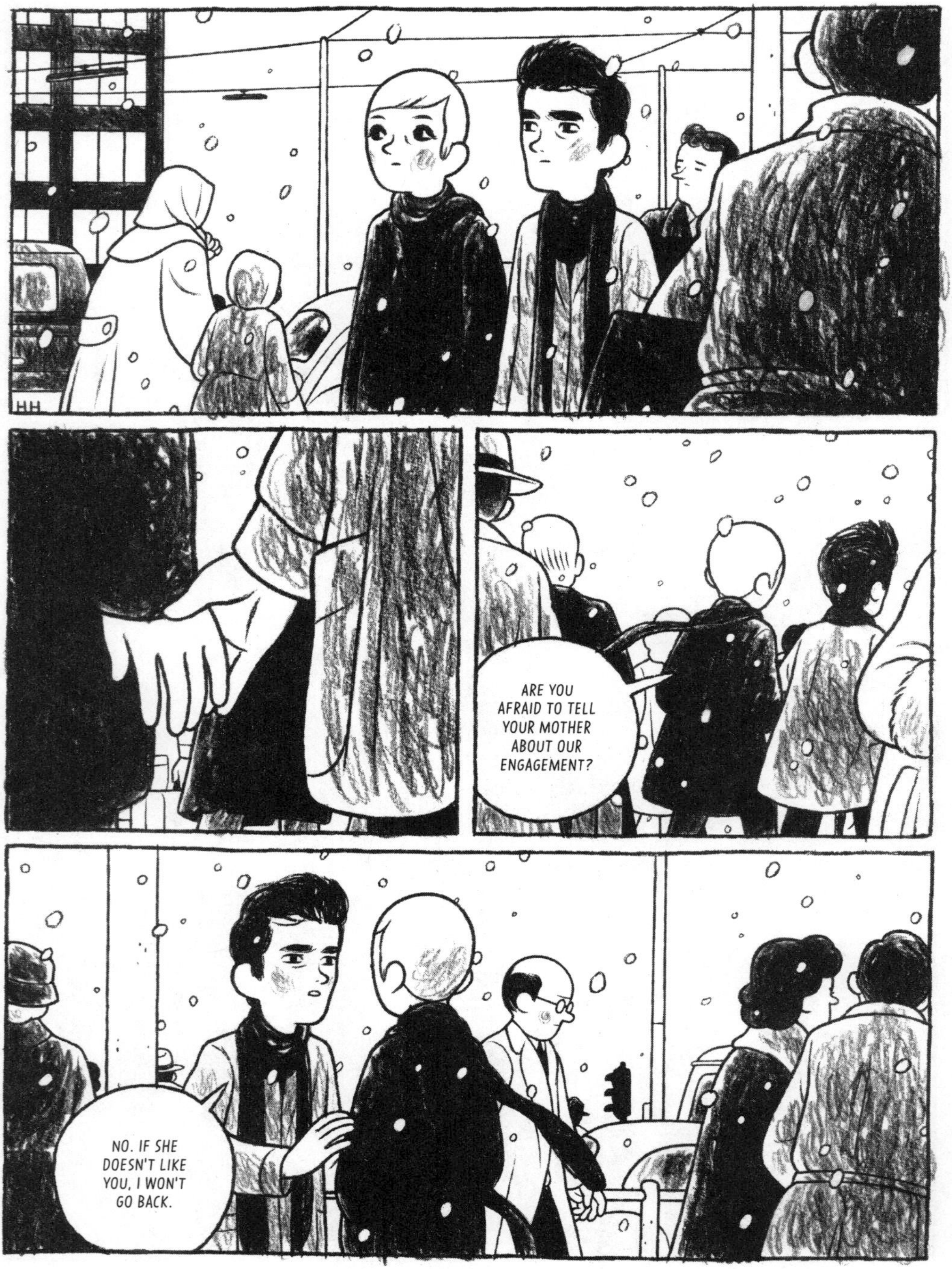
ARE YOU AFRAID TO TELL YOUR MOTHER ABOUT OUR ENGAGEMENT?
NO. IF SHE DOESN'T LIKE YOU, I WON'T GO BACK.

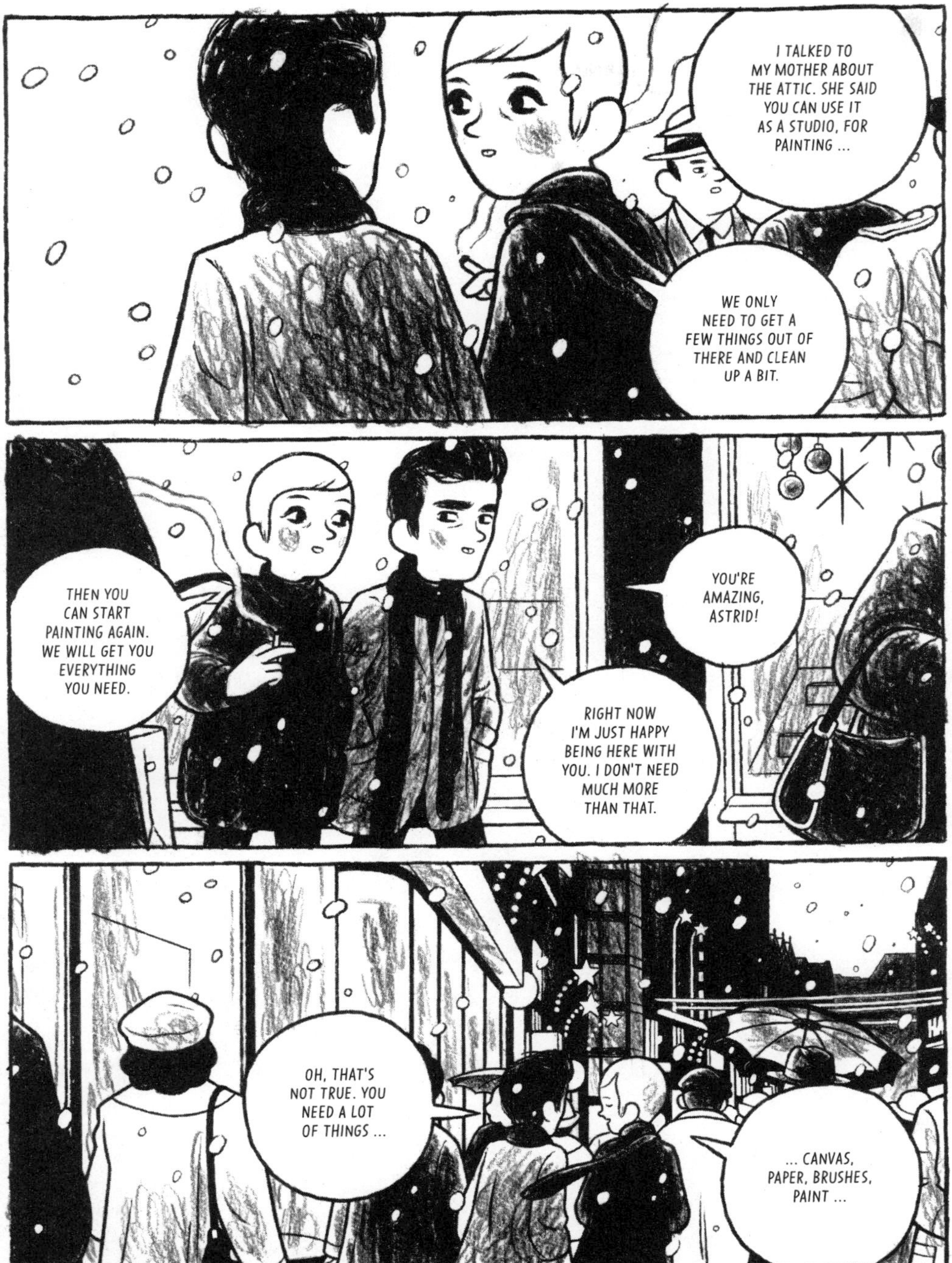
I TALKED TO MY MOTHER ABOUT THE ATTIC. SHE SAID YOU CAN USE IT AS A STUDIO, FOR PAINTING ...
WE ONLY NEED TO GET A FEW THINGS OUT OF THERE AND CLEAN UP A BIT.
THEN YOU CAN START PAINTING AGAIN. WE WILL GET YOU EVERYTHING YOU NEED.
YOU'RE AMAZING, ASTRID!
RIGHT NOW I'M JUST HAPPY BEING HERE WITH YOU. I DON'T NEED MUCH MORE THAN THAT.
OH, THAT'S NOT TRUE. YOU NEED A LOT OF THINGS ...
... CANVAS, PAPER, BRUSHES, PAINT ...

»Paolozzi«

March 1961

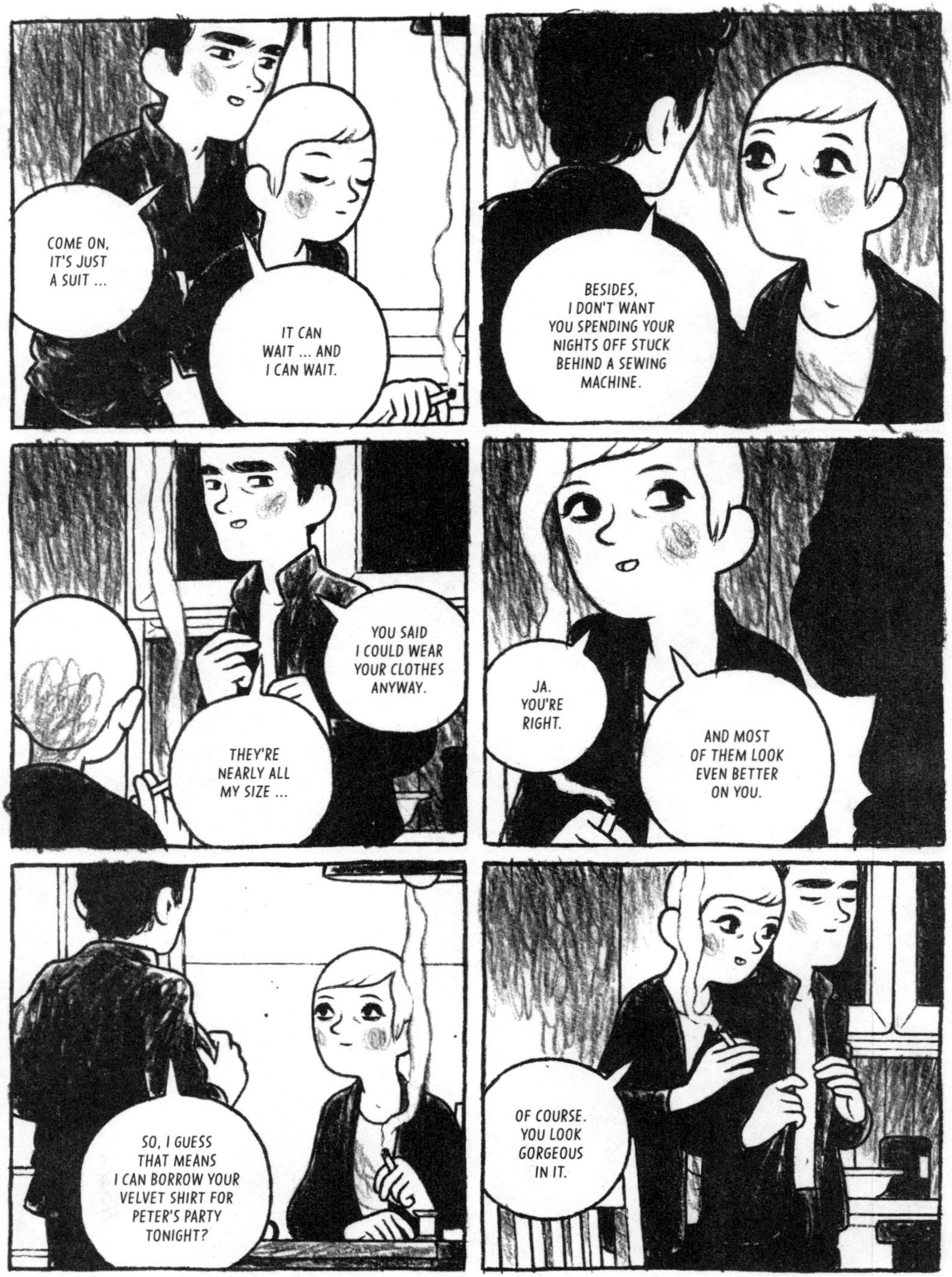
COME ON, IT'S JUST A SUIT ...
IT CAN WAIT ... AND I CAN WAIT.
BESIDES, I DON'T WANT YOU SPENDING YOUR NIGHTS OFF STUCK BEHIND A SEWING MACHINE.
YOU SAID I COULD WEAR YOUR CLOTHES ANYWAY.
THEY'RE NEARLY ALL MY SIZE ...
JA. YOU'RE RIGHT.
AND MOST OF THEM LOOK EVEN BETTER ON YOU.
SO, I GUESS THAT MEANS I CAN BORROW YOUR VELVET SHIRT FOR PETER'S PARTY TONIGHT?
OF COURSE. YOU LOOK GORGEOUS IN IT.

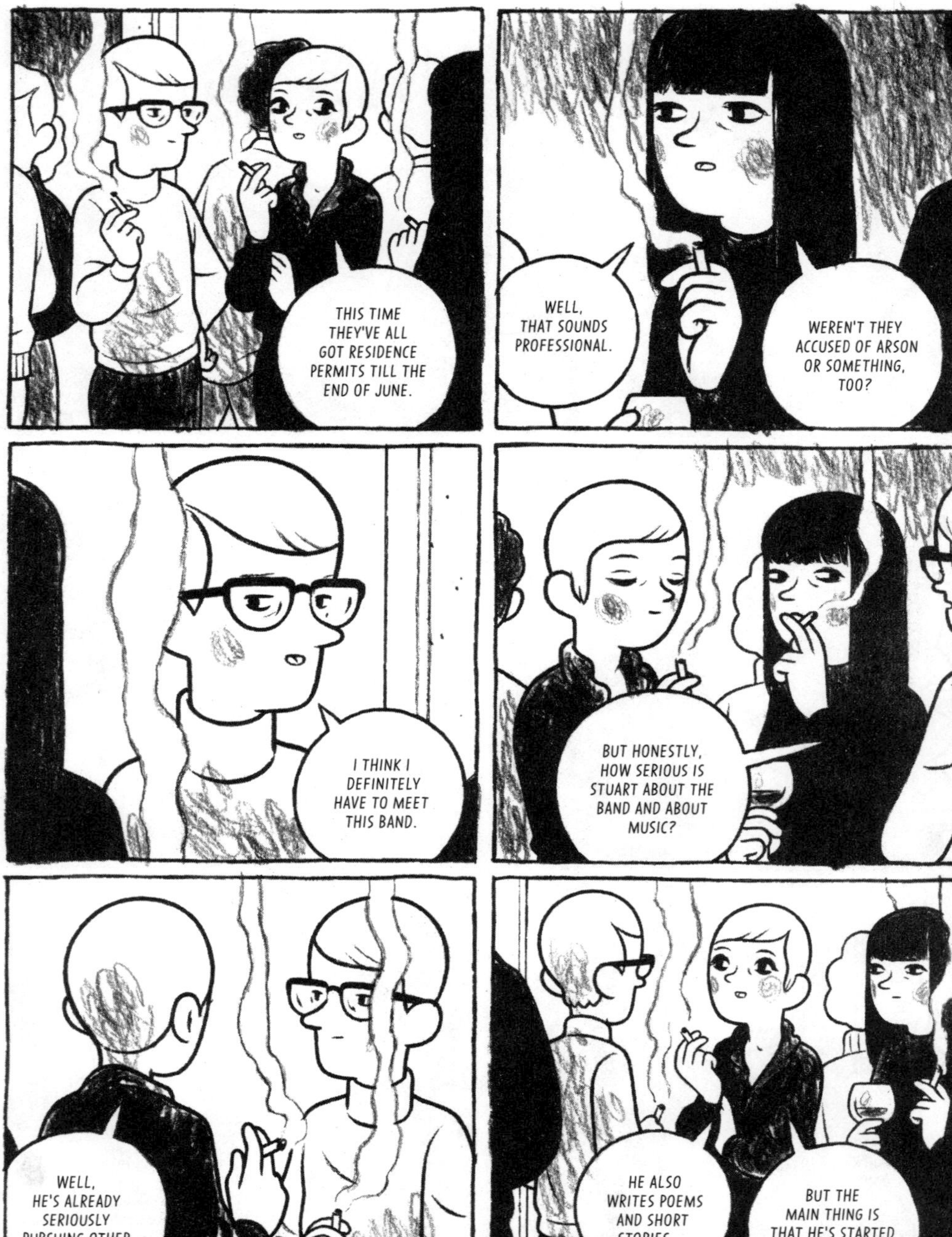
THIS TIME THEY'VE ALL GOT RESIDENCE PERMITS TILL THE END OF JUNE.
WELL, THAT SOUNDS PROFESSIONAL.
WEREN'T THEY ACCUSED OF ARSON OR SOMETHING, TOO?
I THINK I DEFINITELY HAVE TO MEET THIS BAND.
BUT HONESTLY, HOW SERIOUS IS STUART ABOUT THE BAND AND ABOUT MUSIC?
WELL, HE'S ALREADY SERIOUSLY PURSUING OTHER THINGS.
HE ALSO WRITES POEMS AND SHORT STORIES ...
BUT THE MAIN THING IS THAT HE'S STARTED PAINTING AGAIN.

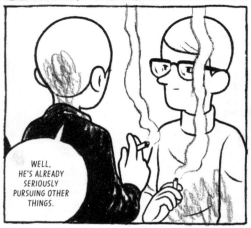

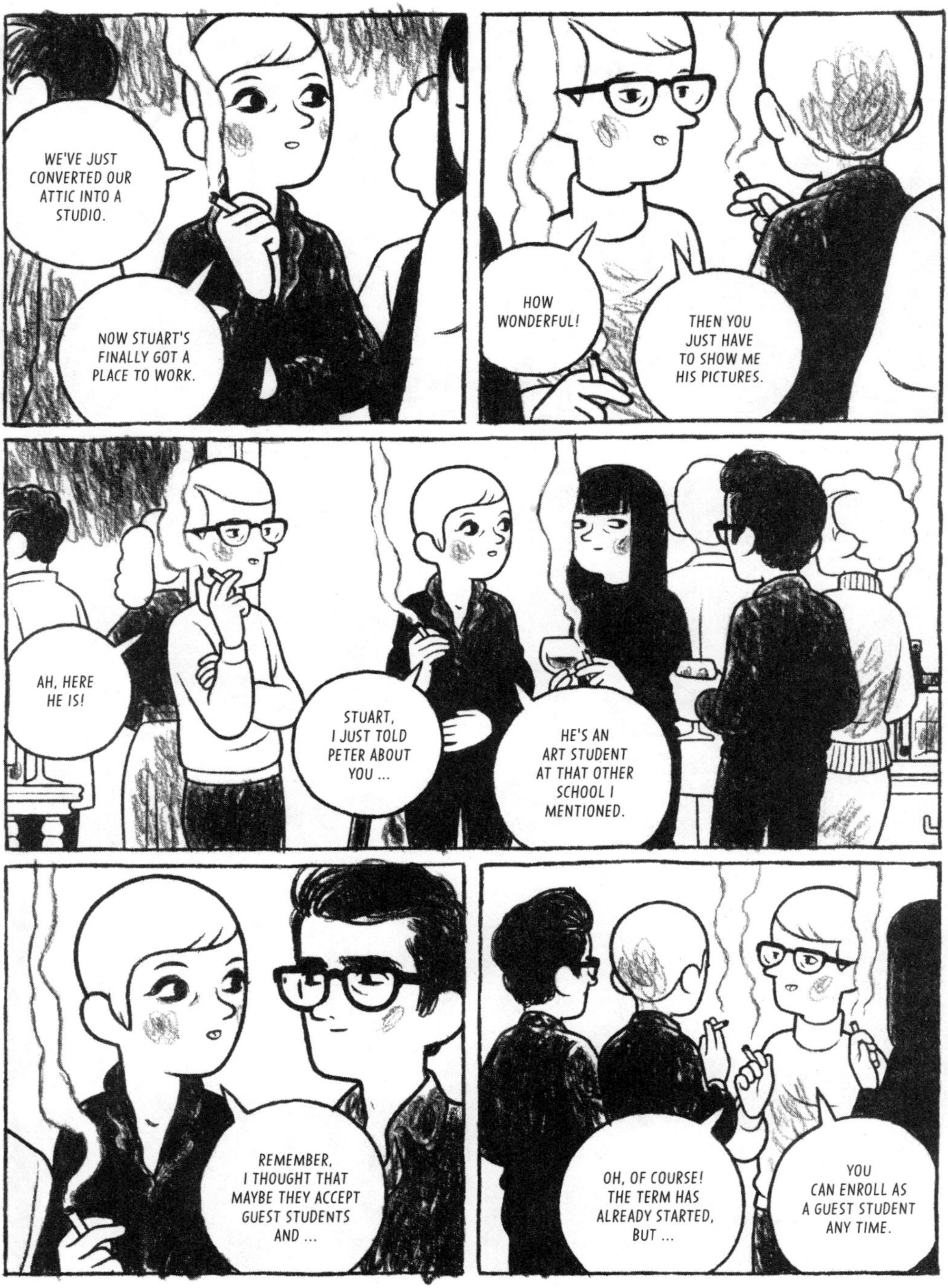
WE'VE JUST CONVERTED OUR ATTIC INTO A STUDIO.
NOW STUART'S FINALLY GOT A PLACE TO WORK.
HOW WONDERFUL!
THEN YOU JUST HAVE TO SHOW ME HIS PICTURES.
AH, HERE HE IS!
STUART, I JUST TOLD PETER ABOUT YOU ...
HE'S AN ART STUDENT AT THAT OTHER SCHOOL I MENTIONED.
REMEMBER, I THOUGHT THAT MAYBE THEY ACCEPT GUEST STUDENTS AND ...
OH, OF COURSE! THE TERM HAS ALREADY STARTED, BUT ...
YOU CAN ENROLL AS A GUEST STUDENT ANY TIME.

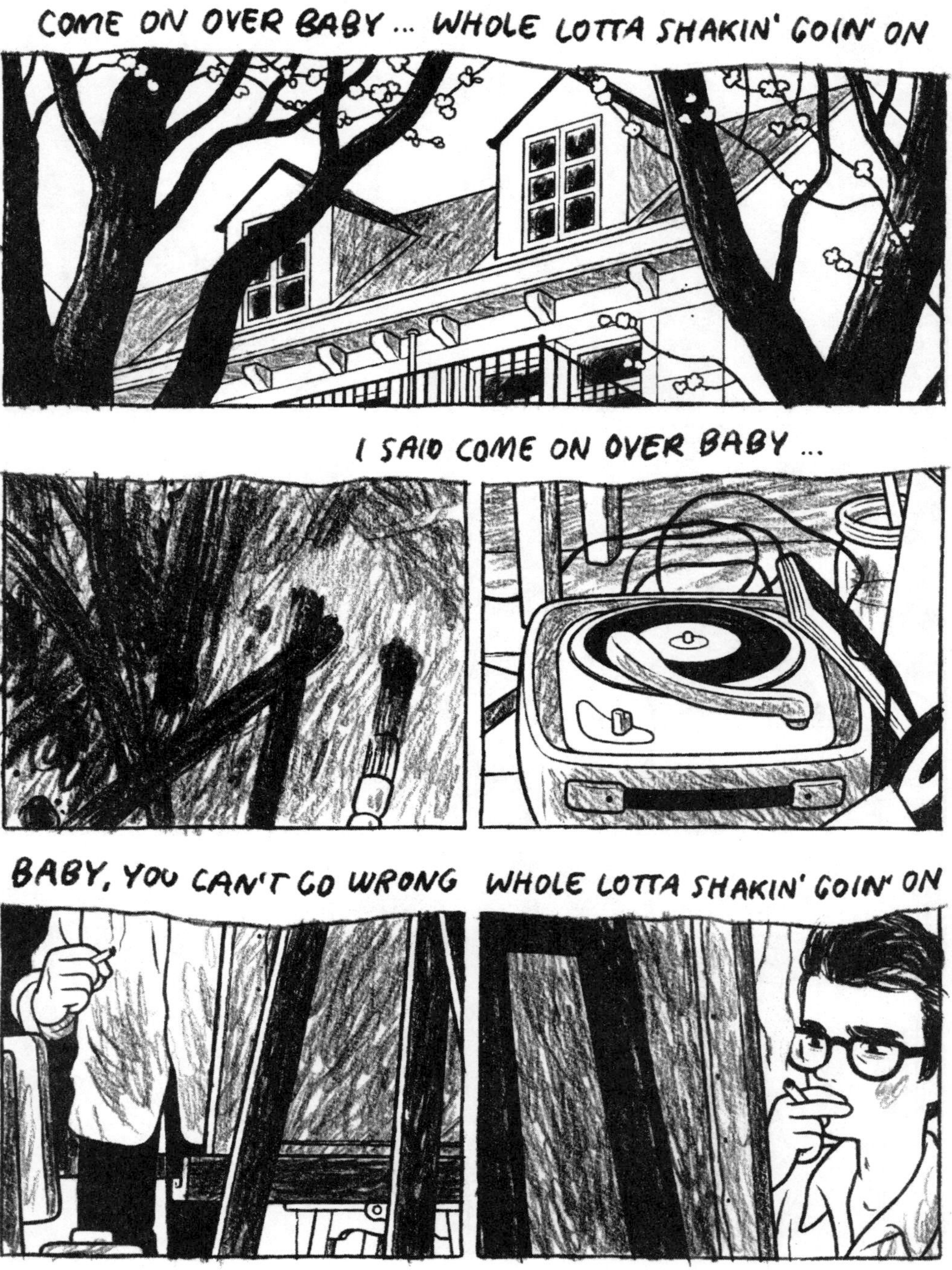
COME ON OVER BABY ... WHOLE LOTTA SHAKIN' GOIN' ON
I SAID COME ON OVER BABY ...
BABY, YOU CAN'T GO WRONG
WHOLE LOTTA SHAKIN' GOIN' ON

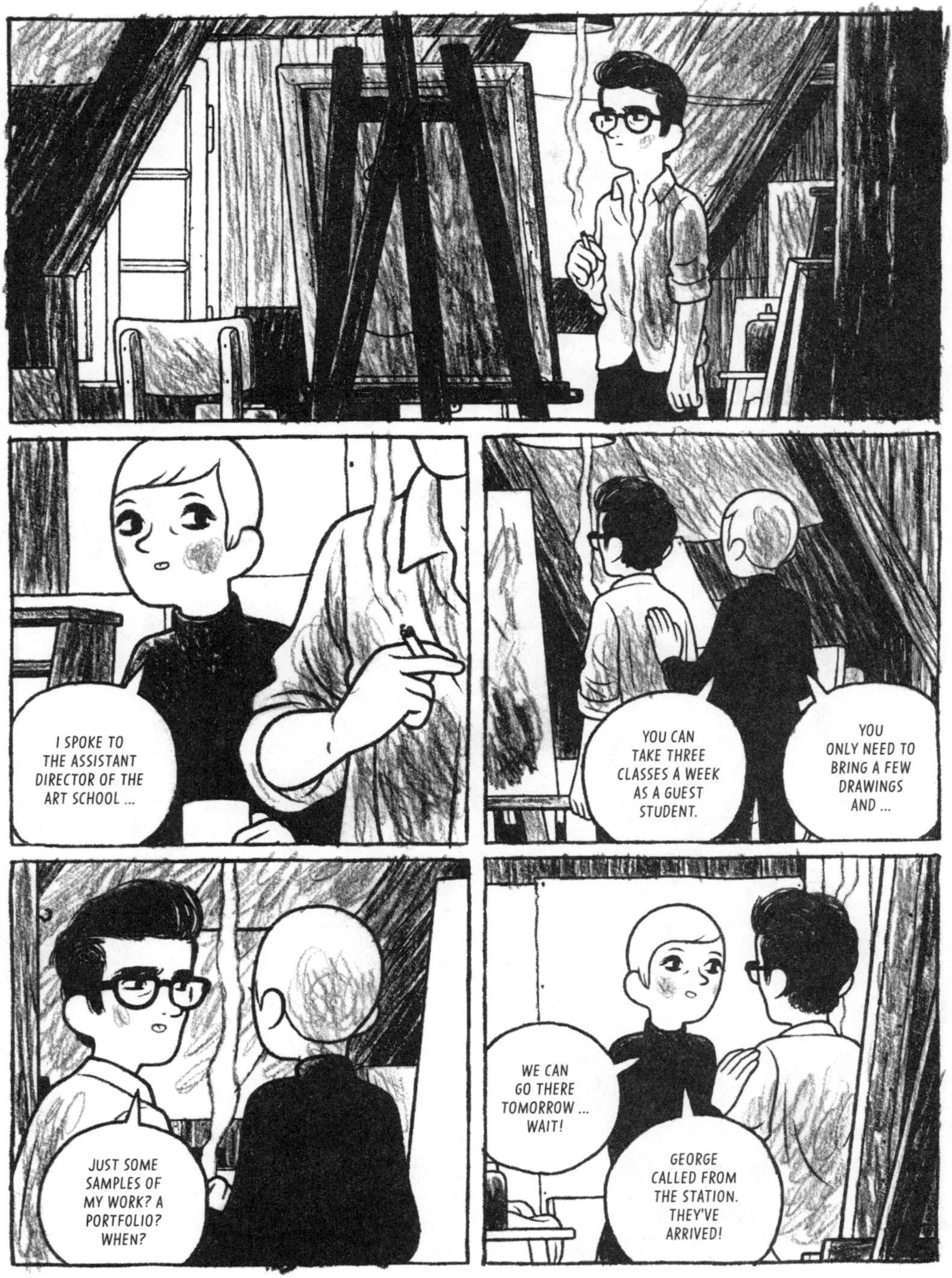
I SPOKE TO THE ASSISTANT DIRECTOR OF THE ART SCHOOL ...
YOU CAN TAKE THREE CLASSES A WEEK AS A GUEST STUDENT.
YOU ONLY NEED TO BRING A FEW DRAWINGS AND ...
JUST SOME SAMPLES OF MY WORK? A PORTFOLIO? WHEN?
WE CAN GO THERE TOMORROW ... WAIT!
GEORGE CALLED FROM THE STATION. THEY'VE ARRIVED!

ASTRID!
JOHN! GEORGE!
WELCOME BACK TO HAMBURG!
OH, WIE GEHT ES IHN, MRS. KIRCHHERR?*
DANKE, GUT!
YOU'RE BOTH LOOKING GOOD. STILL MADLY IN LOVE?

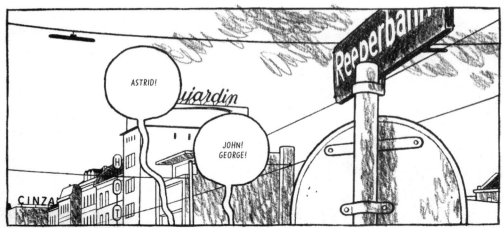

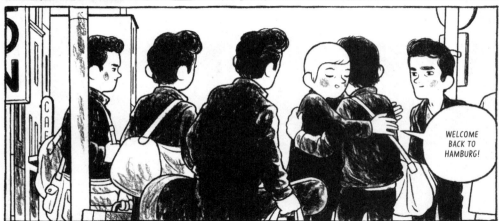

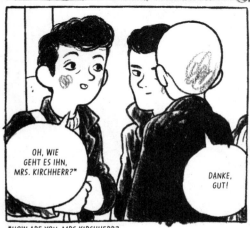

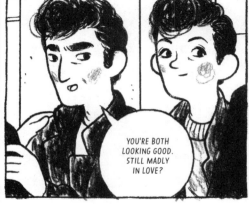

*HOW ARE YOU, MRS KIRCHHERR?

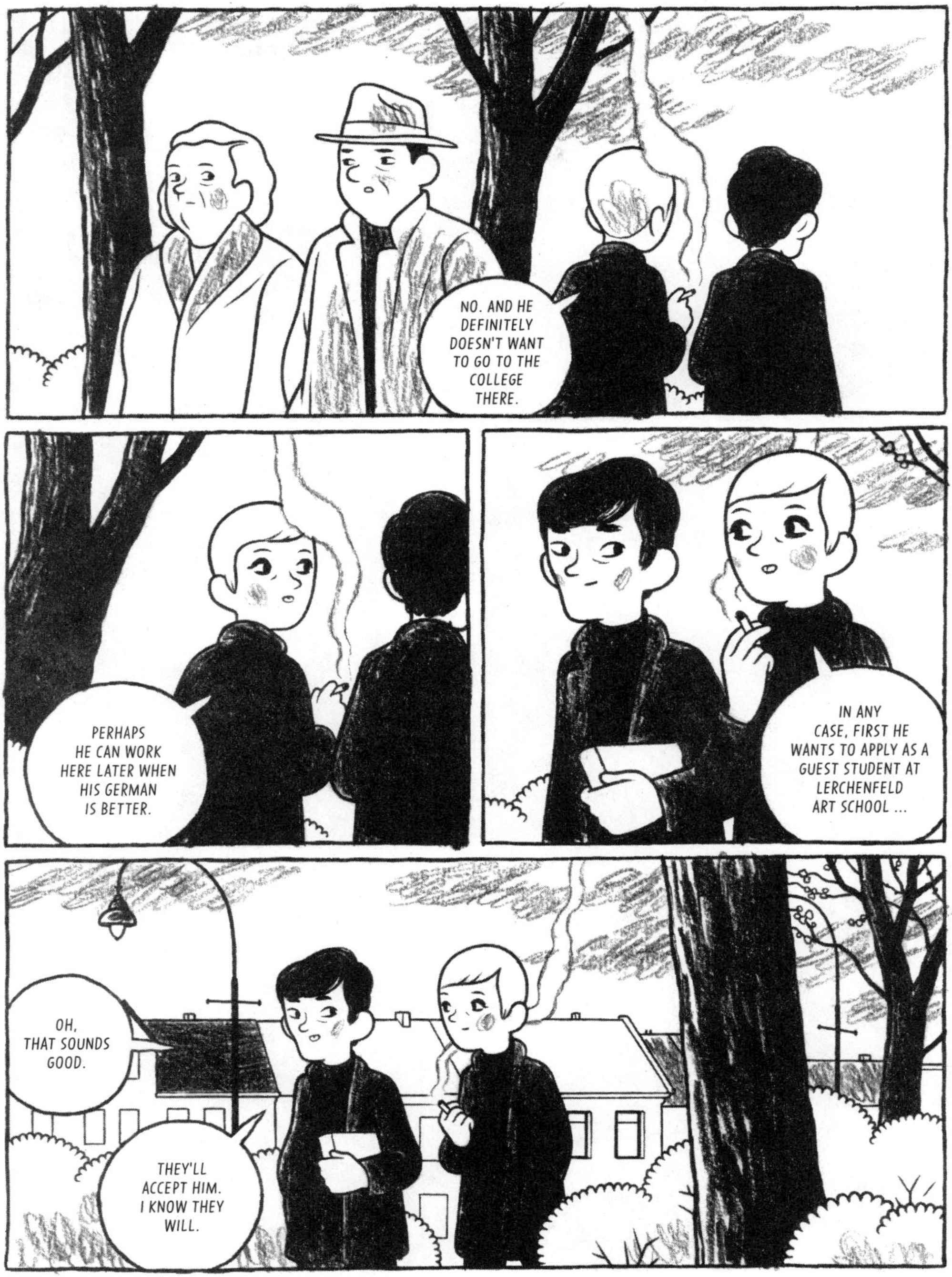
NO. AND HE DEFINITELY DOESN'T WANT TO GO TO THE COLLEGE THERE.
PERHAPS HE CAN WORK HERE LATER WHEN HIS GERMAN IS BETTER.
IN ANY CASE, FIRST HE WANTS TO APPLY AS A GUEST STUDENT AT LERCHENFELD ART SCHOOL ...
OH, THAT SOUNDS GOOD.
THEY'LL ACCEPT HIM. I KNOW THEY WILL.

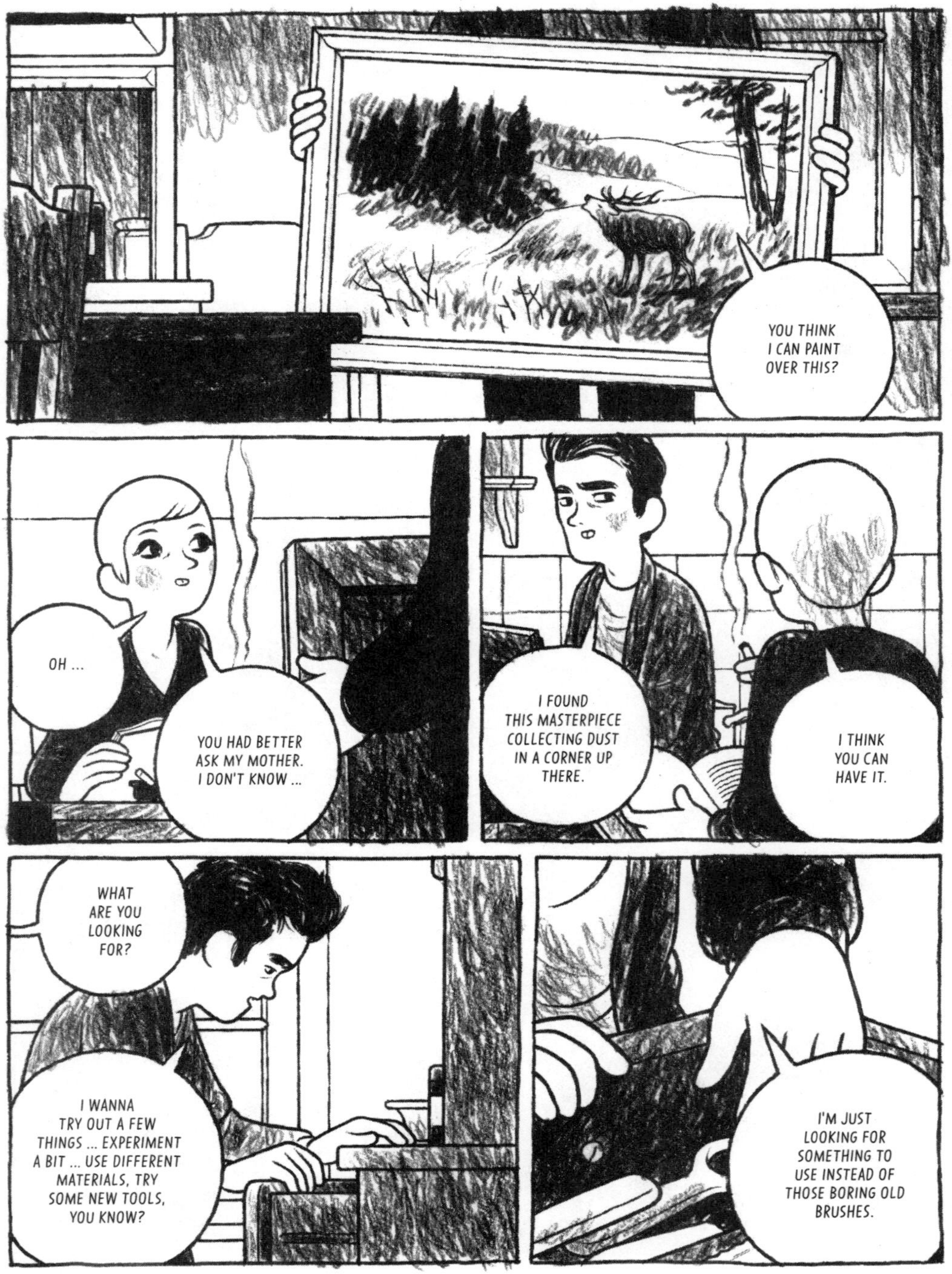

YOU THINK I CAN PAINT OVER THIS?
OH ...
YOU HAD BETTER ASK MY MOTHER. I DON'T KNOW ...
I FOUND THIS MASTERPIECE COLLECTING DUST IN A CORNER UP THERE.
I THINK YOU CAN HAVE IT.
WHAT ARE YOU LOOKING FOR?
I WANNA TRY OUT A FEW THINGS ... EXPERIMENT A BIT ... USE DIFFERENT MATERIALS, TRY SOME NEW TOOLS, YOU KNOW?
I'M JUST LOOKING FOR SOMETHING TO USE INSTEAD OF THOSE BORING OLD BRUSHES.

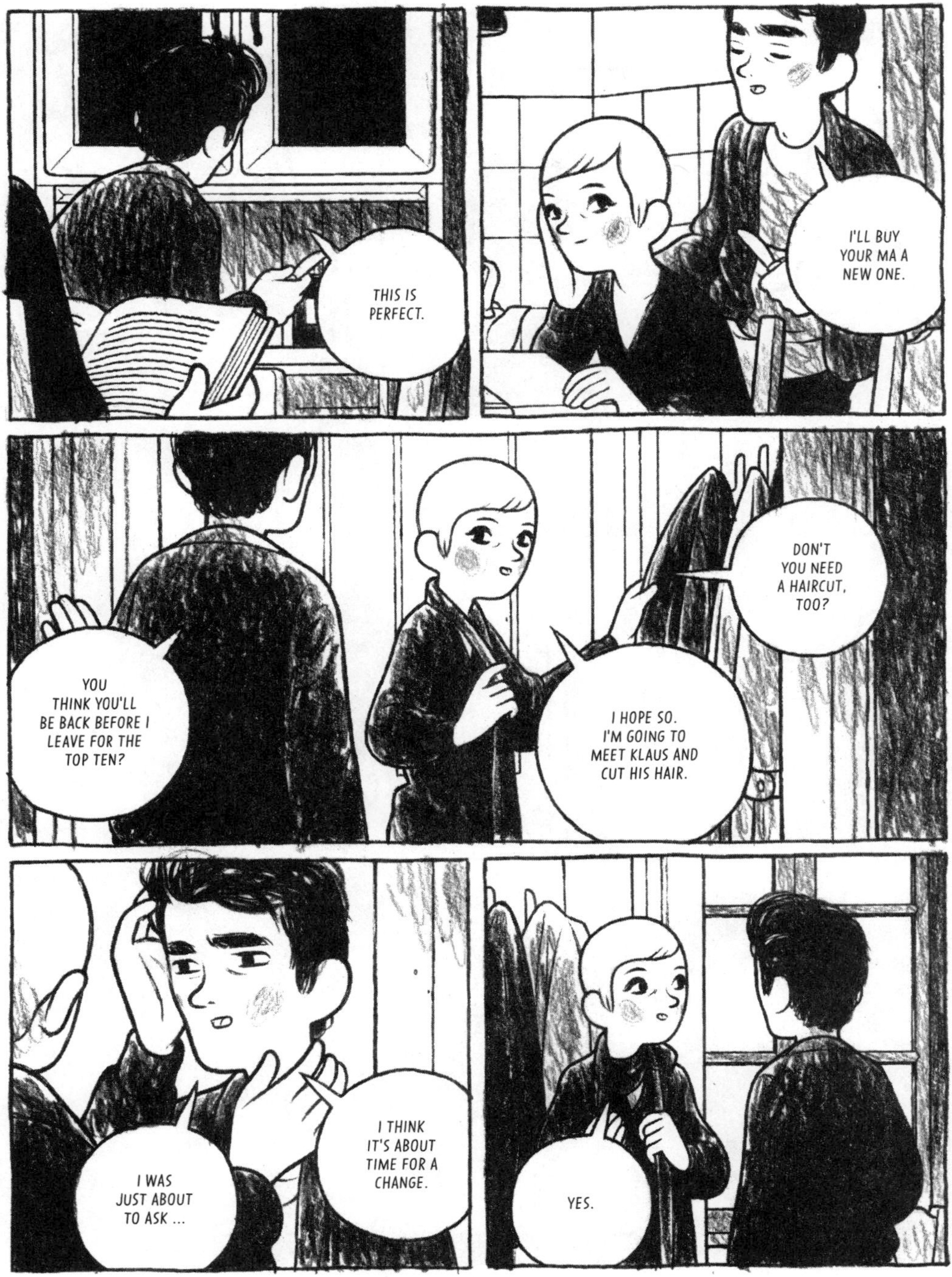
THIS IS PERFECT.
I'LL BUY YOUR MA A NEW ONE.
DON'T YOU NEED A HAIRCUT, TOO?
I HOPE SO. I'M GOING TO MEET KLAUS AND CUT HIS HAIR.
YOU THINK YOU'LL BE BACK BEFORE I LEAVE FOR THE TOP TEN?
I THINK IT'S ABOUT TIME FOR A CHANGE.
I WAS JUST ABOUT TO ASK ...
YES.

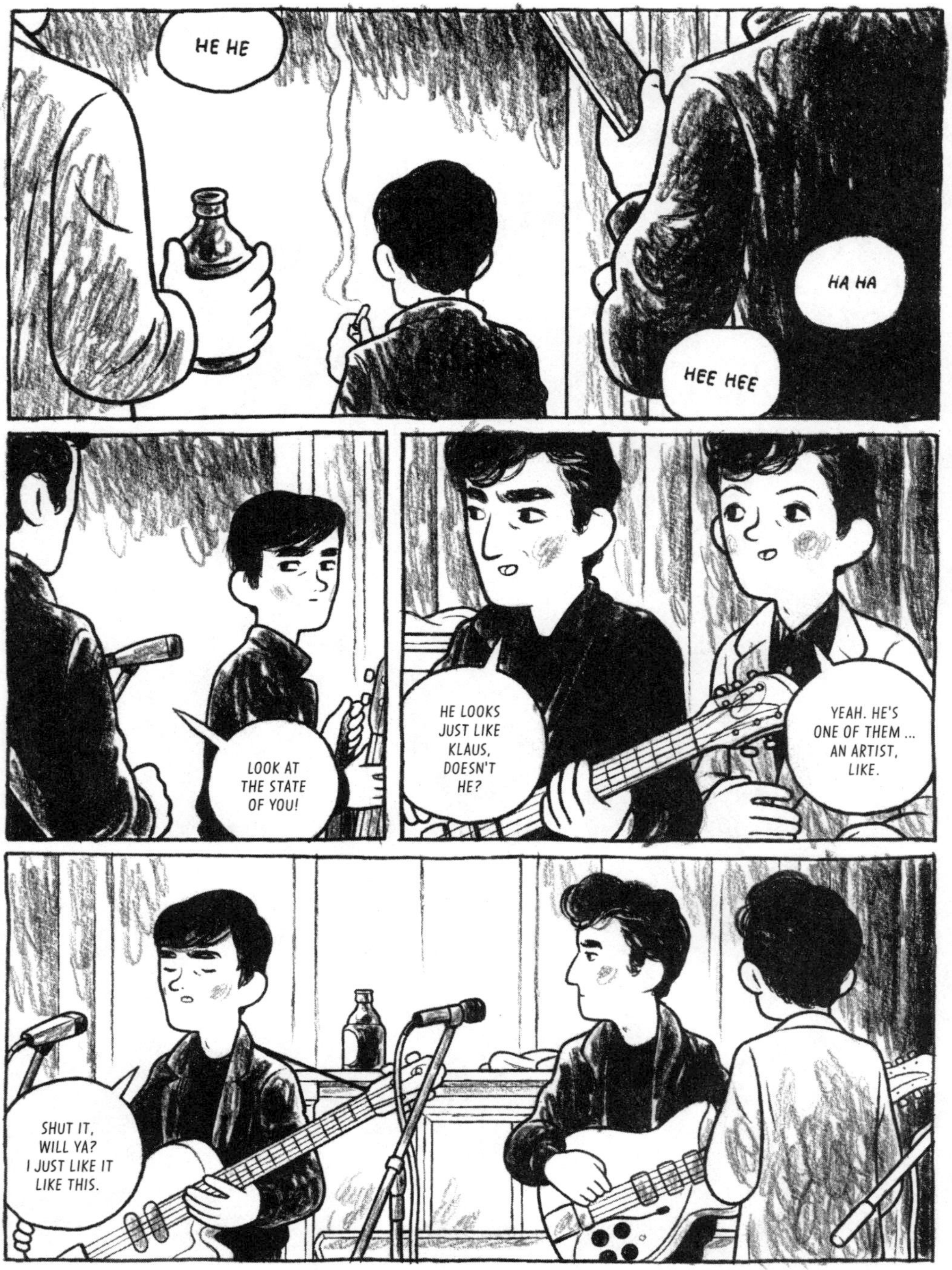
HE HE
HA HA
HEE HEE
LOOK AT THE STATE OF YOU!
HE LOOKS JUST LIKE KLAUS, DOESN'T HE?
YEAH. HE'S ONE OF THEM ... AN ARTIST, LIKE.
SHUT IT, WILL YA? I JUST LIKE IT LIKE THIS.

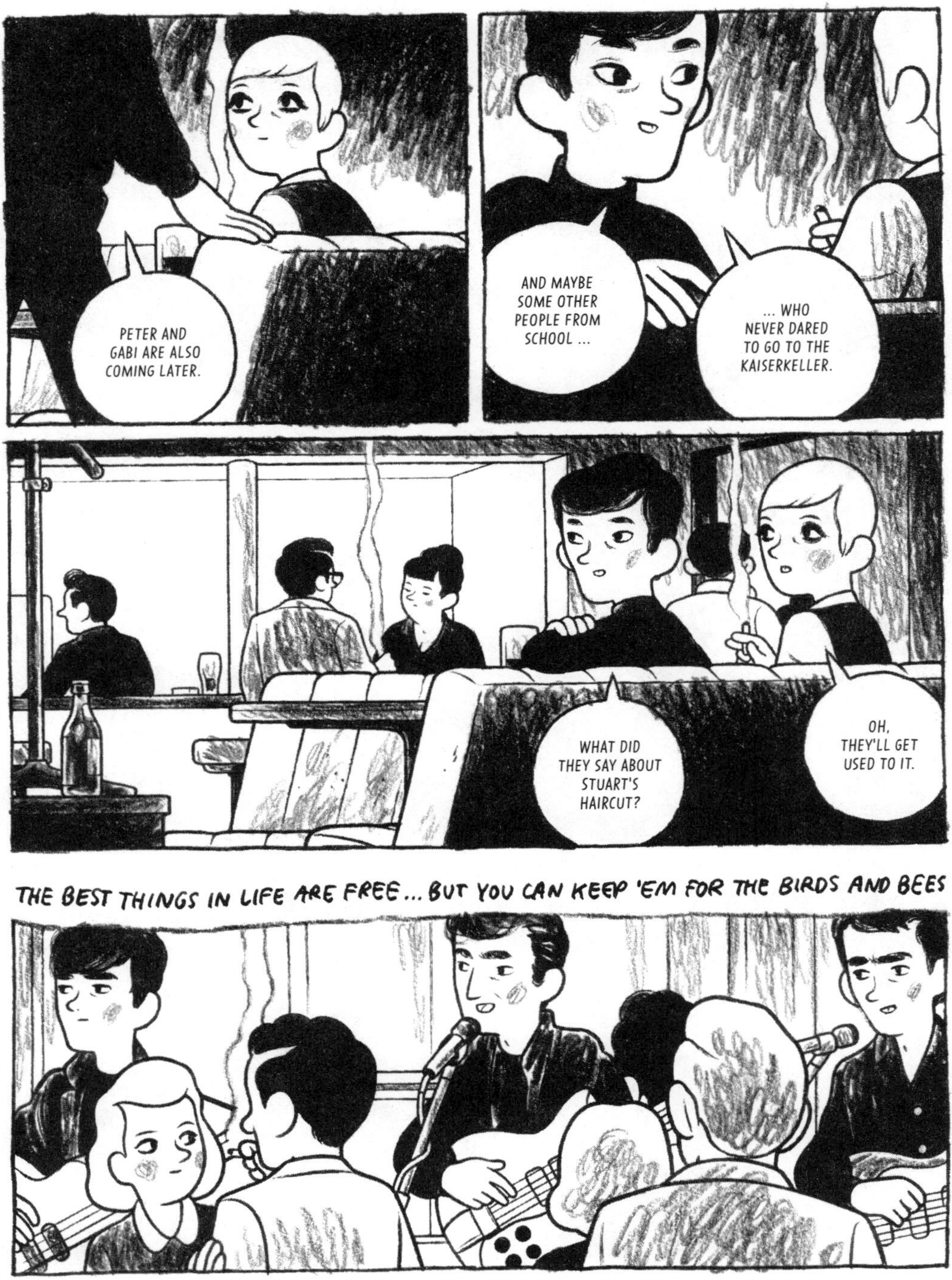
PETER AND GABI ARE ALSO COMING LATER.
AND MAYBE SOME OTHER PEOPLE FROM SCHOOL ...
... WHO NEVER DARED TO GO TO THE KAISERKELLER.
WHAT DID THEY SAY ABOUT STUART'S HAIRCUT?
OH, THEY'LL GET USED TO IT.
THE BEST THINGS IN LIFE ARE FREE... BUT YOU CAN KEEP 'EM FOR THE BIRDS AND BEES

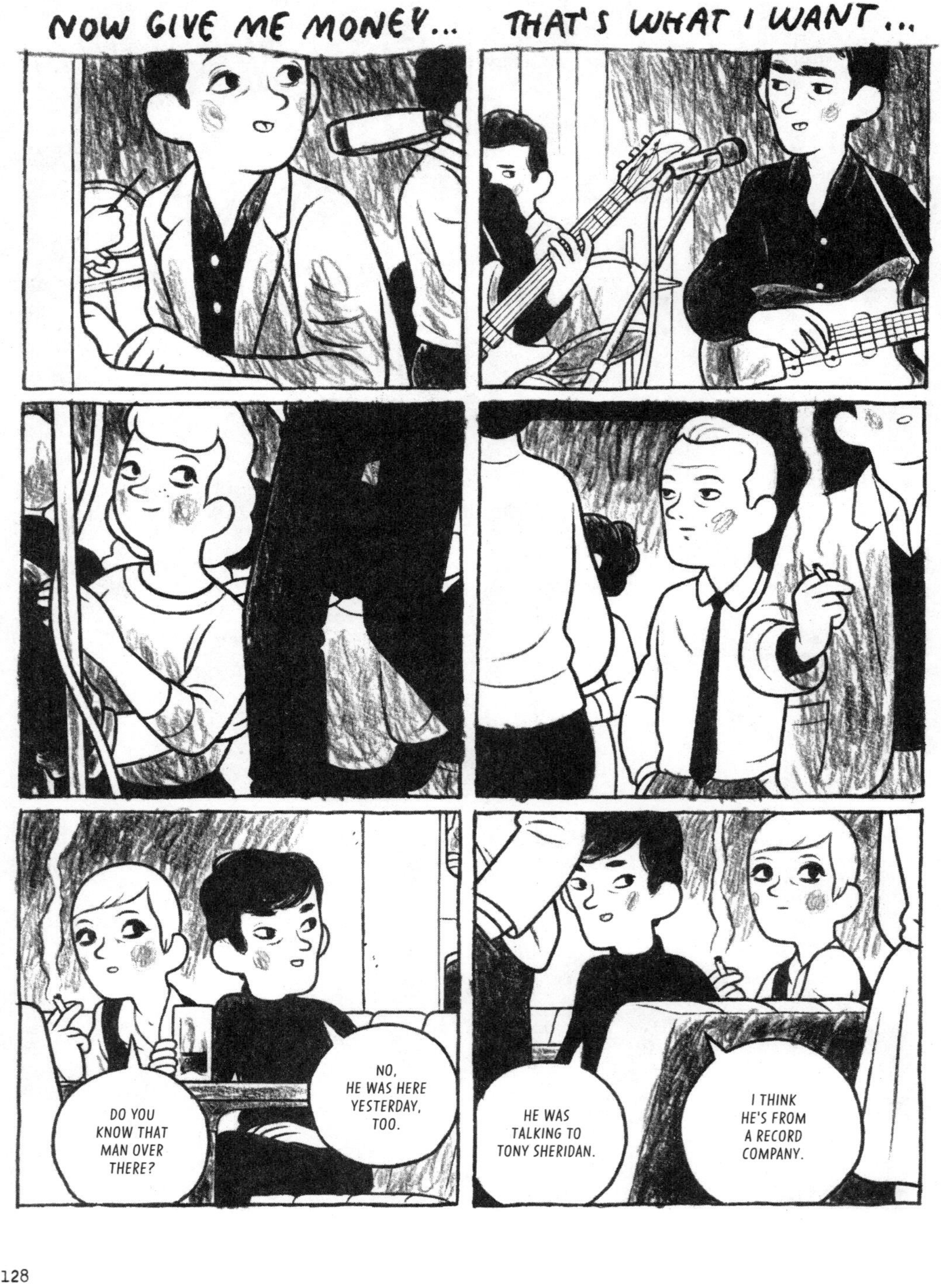
NOW GIVE ME MONEY... THAT'S WHAT I WANT...
DO YOU KNOW THAT MAN OVER THERE?
NO, HE WAS HERE YESTERDAY, TOO.
HE WAS TALKING TO TONY SHERIDAN.
I THINK HE'S FROM A RECORD COMPANY.

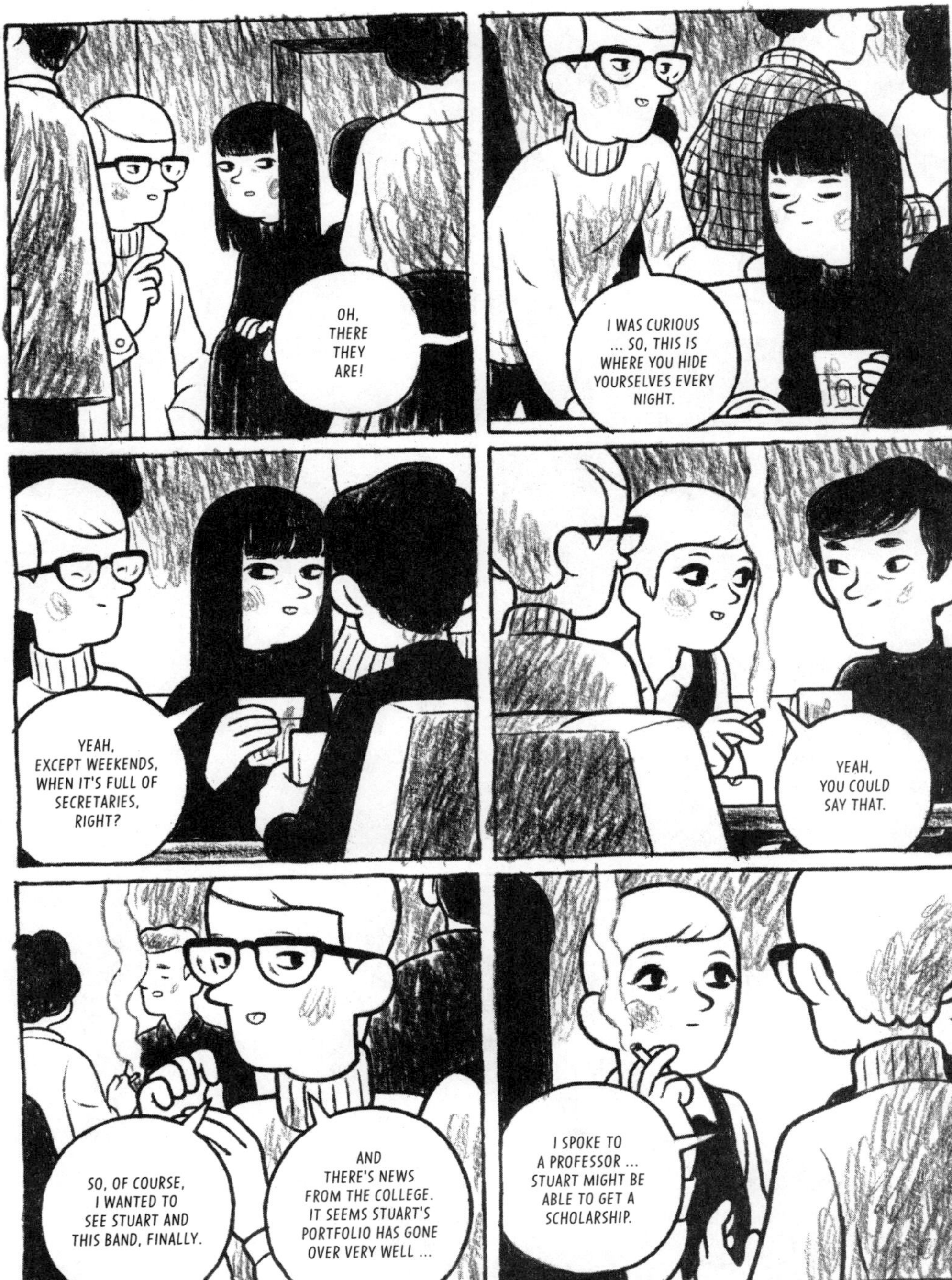
OH, THERE THEY ARE!
I WAS CURIOUS ... SO, THIS IS WHERE YOU HIDE YOURSELVES EVERY NIGHT.
YEAH, EXCEPT WEEKENDS, WHEN IT'S FULL OF SECRETARIES, RIGHT?
YEAH, YOU COULD SAY THAT.
SO, OF COURSE, I WANTED TO SEE STUART AND THIS BAND, FINALLY.
AND THERE'S NEWS FROM THE COLLEGE. IT SEEMS STUART'S PORTFOLIO HAS GONE OVER VERY WELL ...
I SPOKE TO A PROFESSOR ... STUART MIGHT BE ABLE TO GET A SCHOLARSHIP.

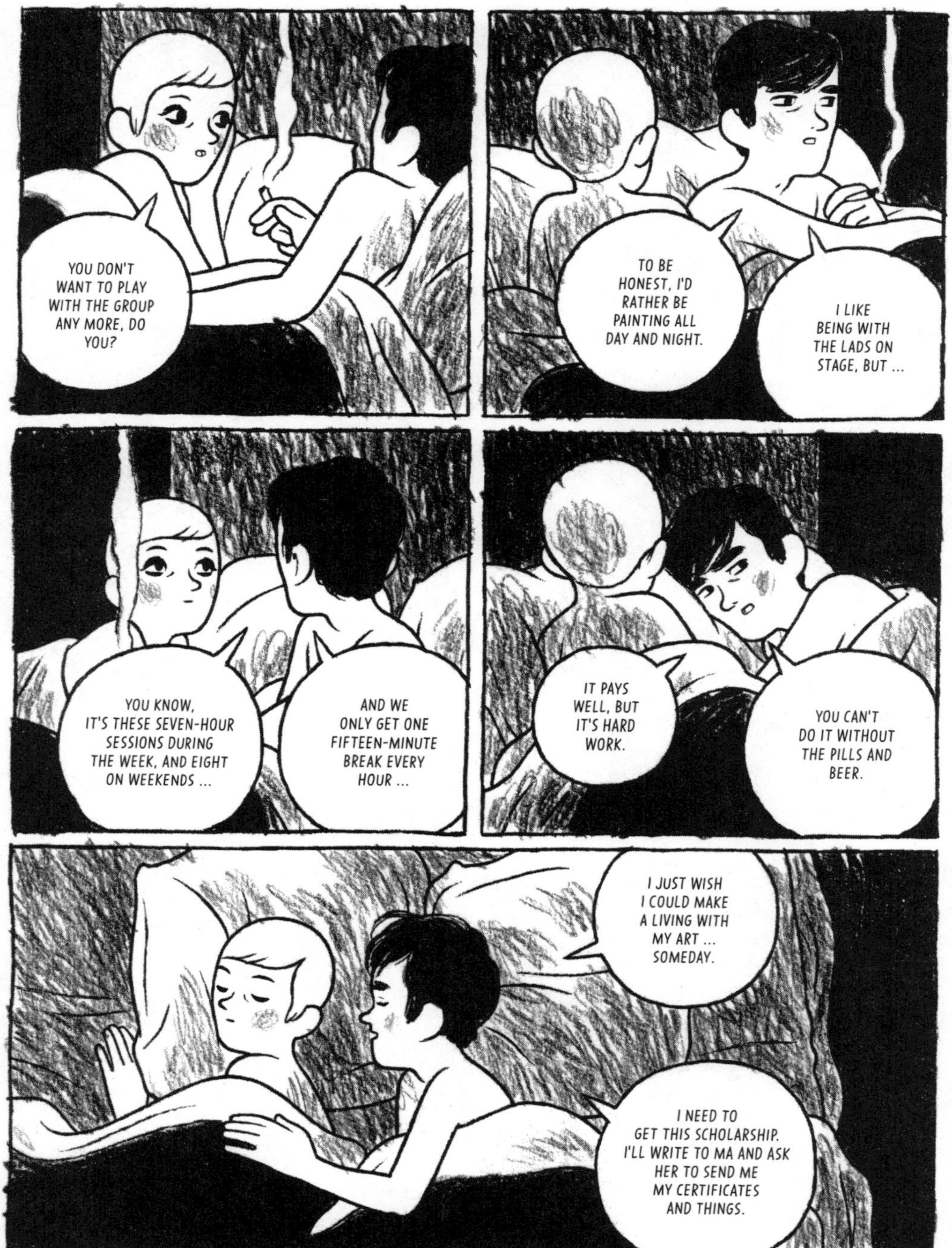
YOU DON'T WANT TO PLAY WITH THE GROUP ANY MORE, DO YOU?
TO BE HONEST, I'D RATHER BE PAINTING ALL DAY AND NIGHT.
I LIKE BEING WITH THE LADS ON STAGE, BUT ...
YOU KNOW, IT'S THESE SEVEN-HOUR SESSIONS DURING THE WEEK, AND EIGHT ON WEEKENDS ...
AND WE ONLY GET ONE FIFTEEN-MINUTE BREAK EVERY HOUR ...
IT PAYS WELL, BUT IT'S HARD WORK.
YOU CAN'T DO IT WITHOUT THE PILLS AND BEER.
I JUST WISH I COULD MAKE A LIVING WITH MY ART ... SOMEDAY.
I NEED TO GET THIS SCHOLARSHIP. I'LL WRITE TO MA AND ASK HER TO SEND ME MY CERTIFICATES AND THINGS.

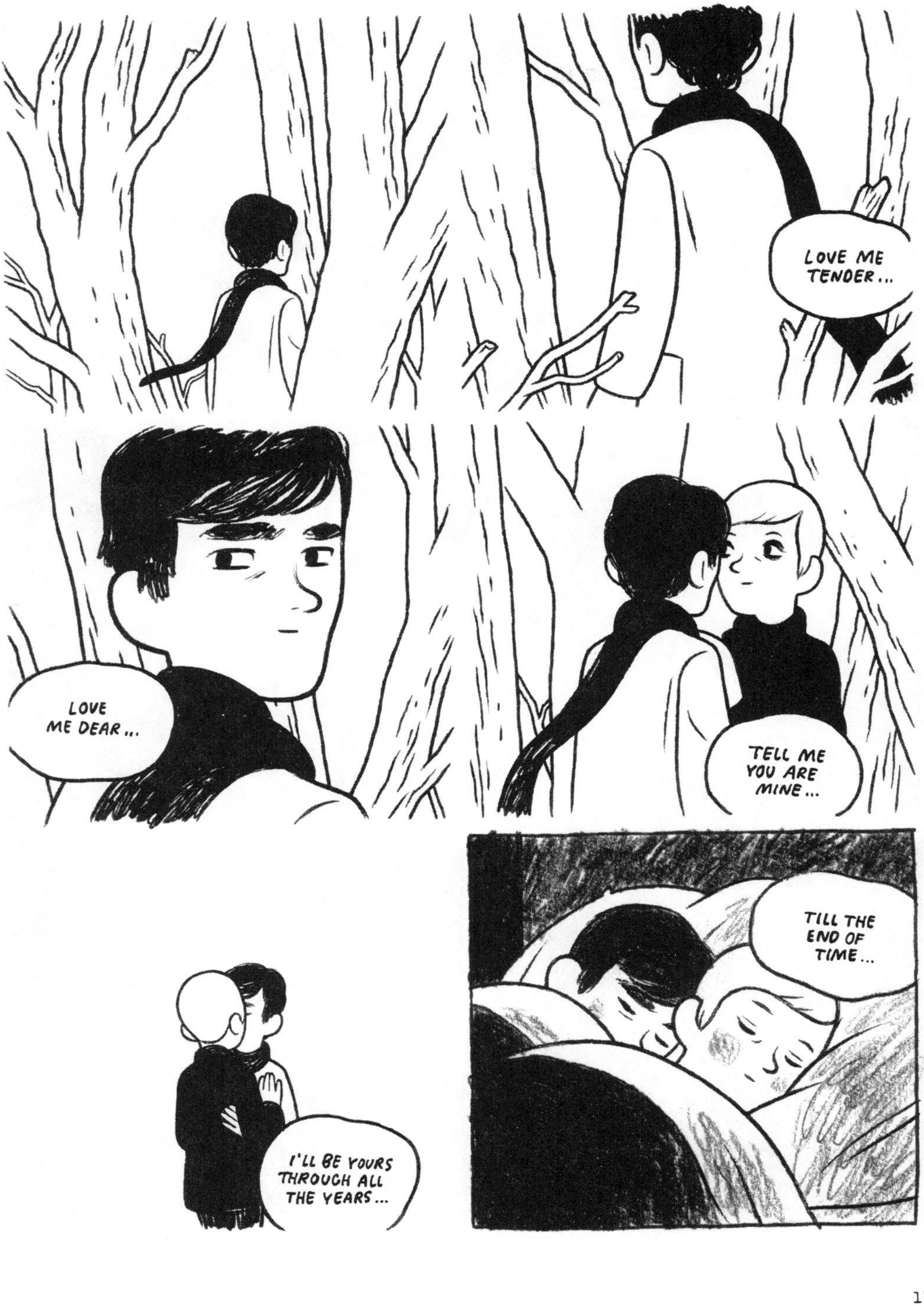
LOVE ME TENDER...
LOVE ME DEAR...
TELL ME YOU ARE MINE...
I'LL BE YOURS THROUGH ALL THE YEARS...
TILL THE END OF TIME...

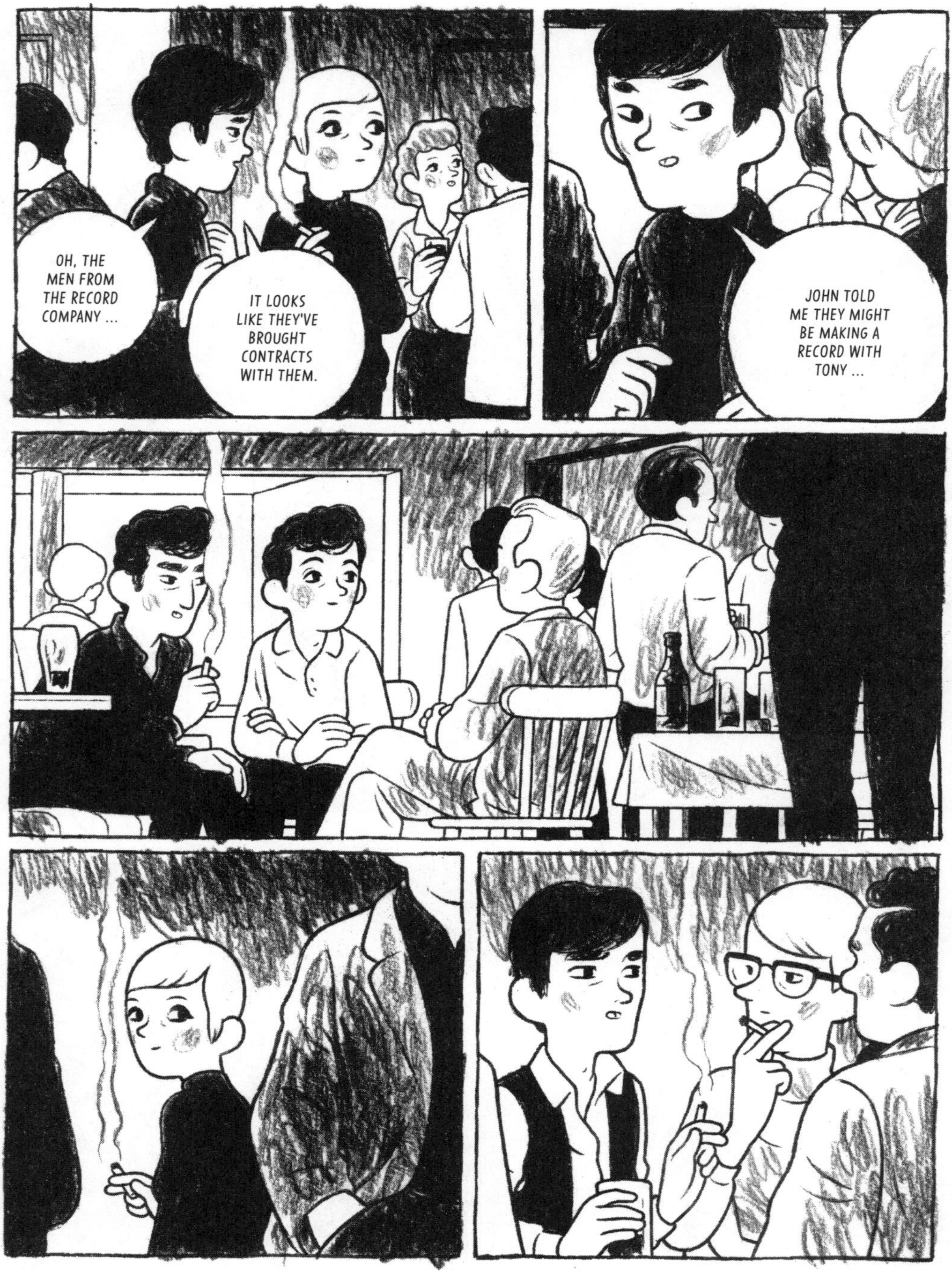
OH, THE MEN FROM THE RECORD COMPANY ...
IT LOOKS LIKE THEY'VE BROUGHT CONTRACTS WITH THEM.
JOHN TOLD ME THEY MIGHT BE MAKING A RECORD WITH TONY ...

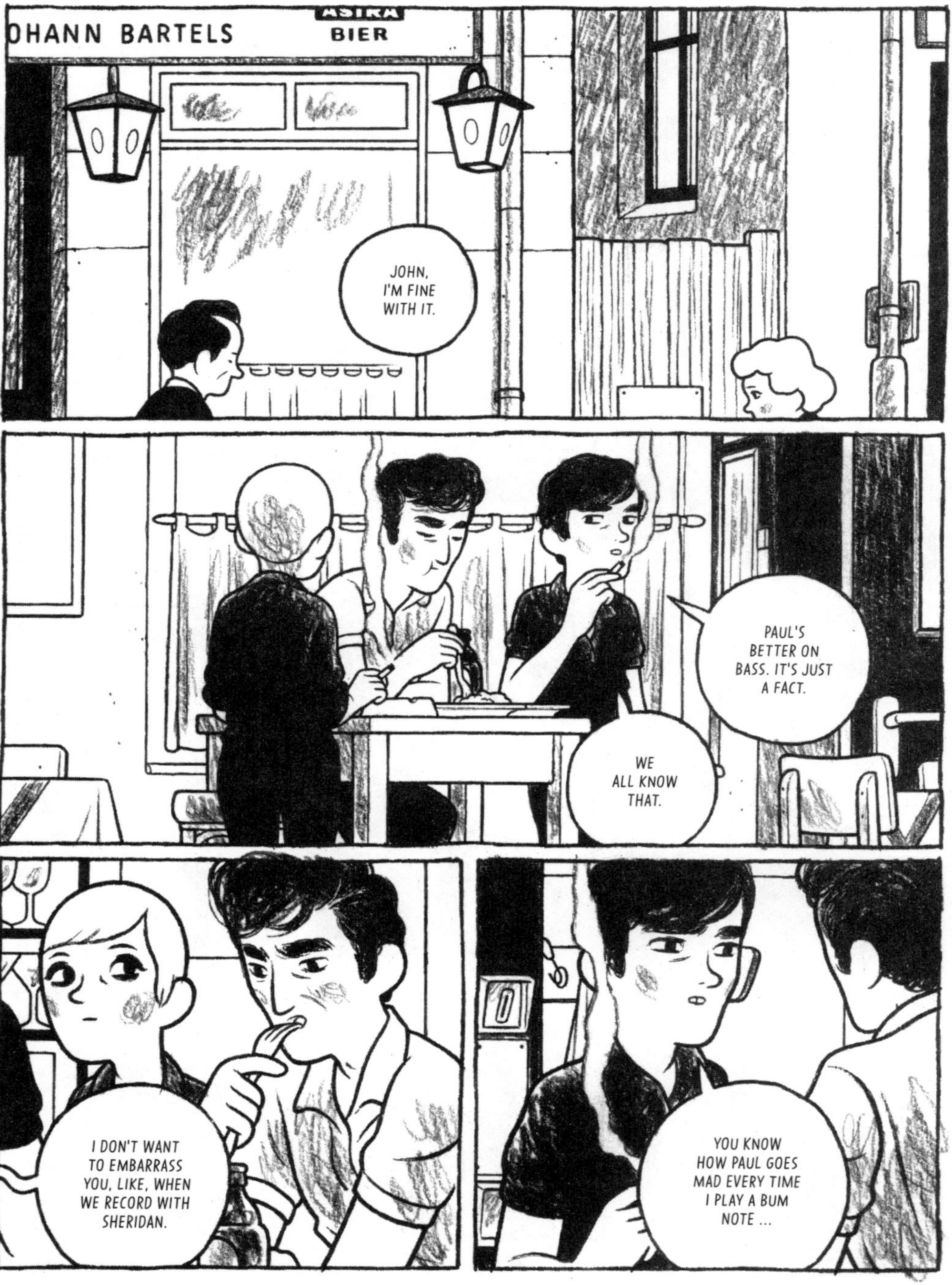
OHANN BARTELS
ASTRA
BIER
JOHN, I'M FINE WITH IT.
PAUL'S BETTER ON BASS. IT'S JUST A FACT.
WE ALL KNOW THAT.
I DON'T WANT TO EMBARRASS YOU, LIKE, WHEN WE RECORD WITH SHERIDAN.
YOU KNOW HOW PAUL GOES MAD EVERY TIME I PLAY A BUM NOTE ...

135

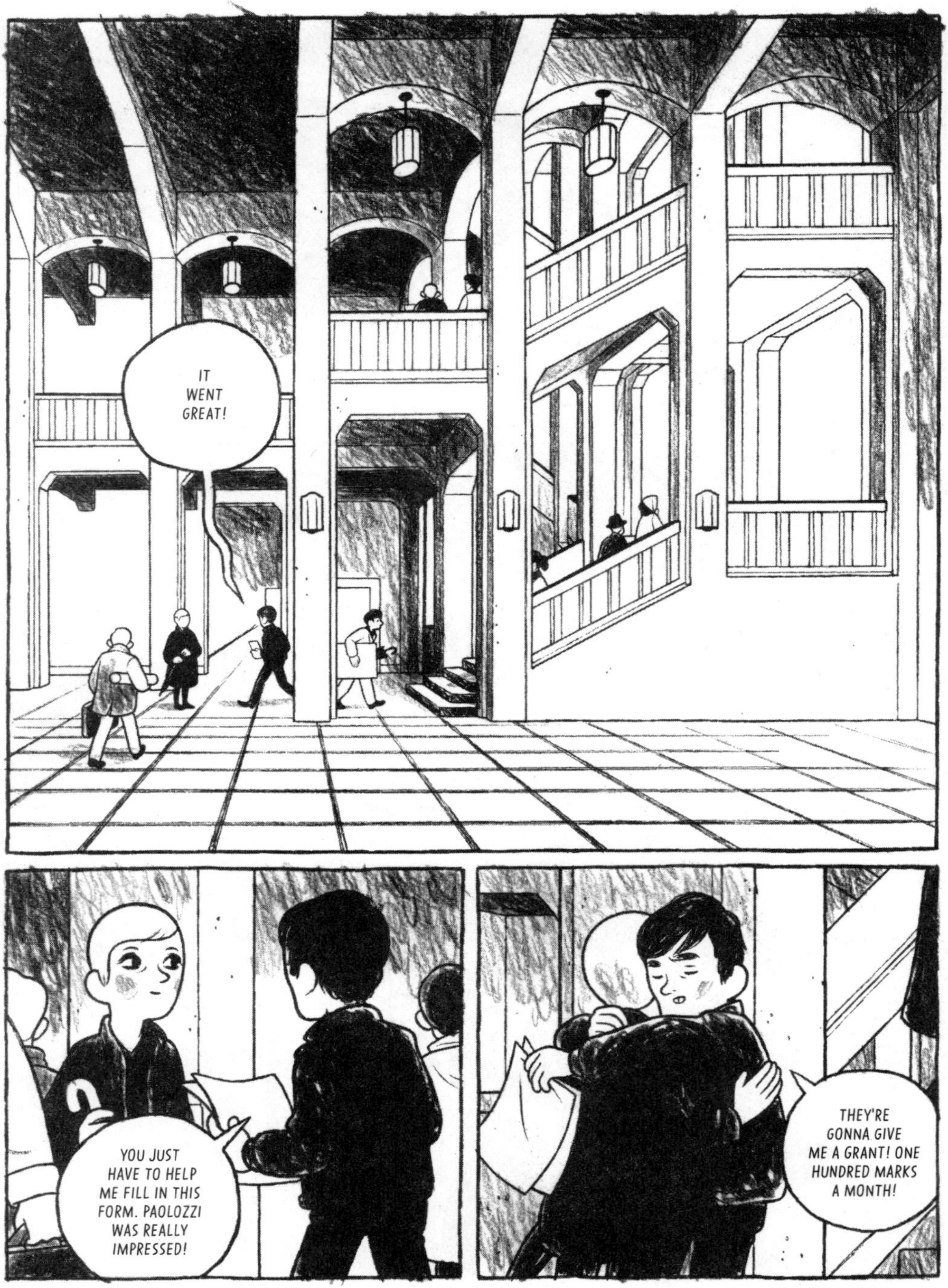
IT WENT GREAT!
YOU JUST HAVE TO HELP ME FILL IN THIS FORM. PAOLOZZI WAS REALLY IMPRESSED!
THEY'RE GONNA GIVE ME A GRANT! ONE HUNDRED MARKS A MONTH!

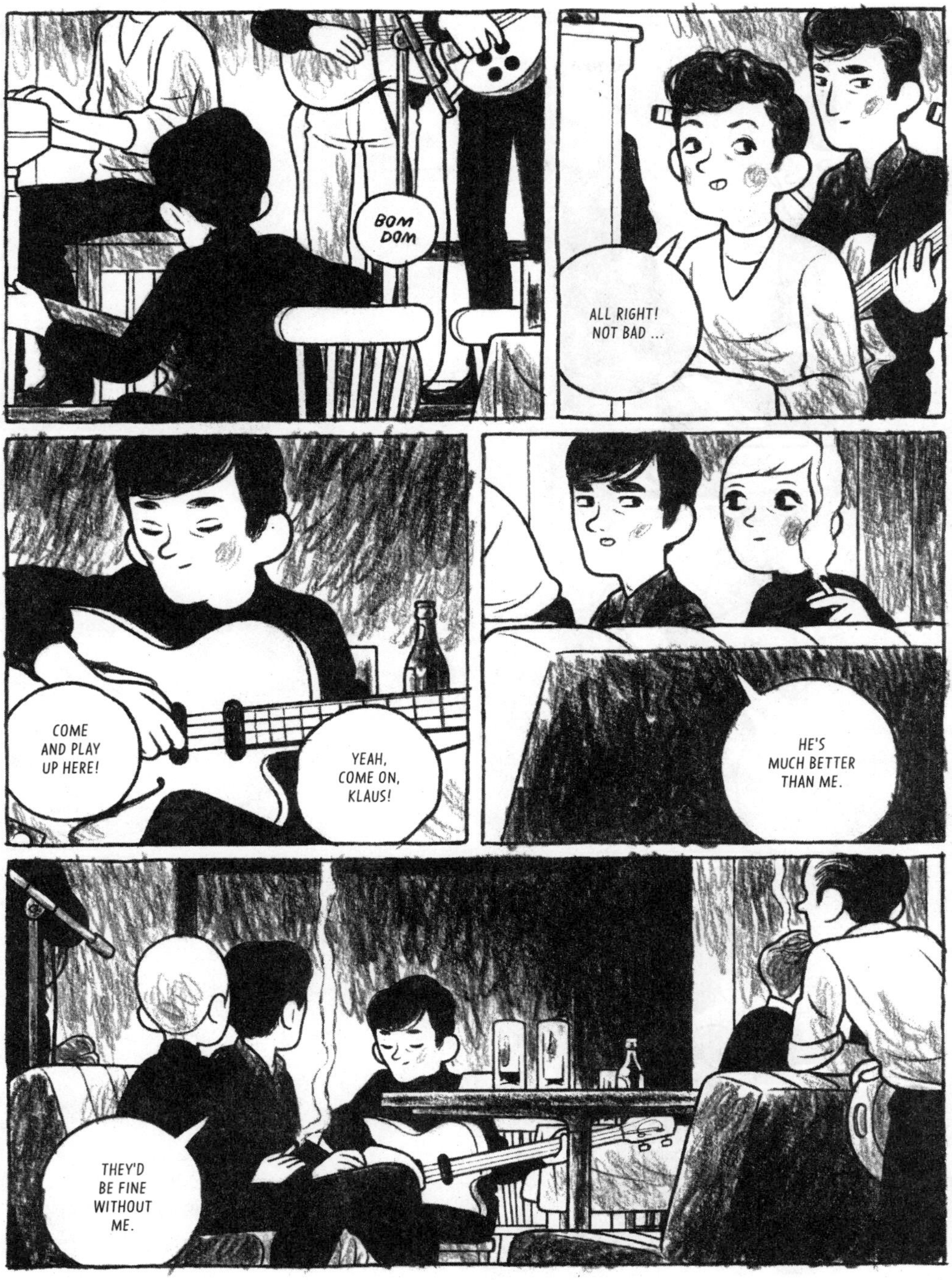
BOM
BOM
ALL RIGHT! NOT BAD ...
COME AND PLAY UP HERE!
YEAH, COME ON, KLAUS!
HE'S MUCH BETTER THAN ME.
THEY'D BE FINE WITHOUT ME.

141

A GASTRITIS PROBLEM LIKE THIS CAN BE DEALT WITH.

HE SHOULD TAKE THE TABLETS IN THE MORNING. AND HE SHOULD EAT FOOD THAT'S GENTLE ON THE STOMACH ... AND REST AFTER EATING.

IF YOU CONTINUE TO HAVE PROBLEMS ...

WE'LL HAVE TO CONSIDER REMOVING THE APPENDIX.

OTHERWISE, I DON'T SEE ANY REASON TO WORRY.

OH YES, AND DON'T FORGET TO PICK UP THE ADDRESS OF THE MASSAGE PRACTICE ON YOUR WAY OUT.

A COUPLE OF SESSIONS AND THE STRESS AND HEADACHES SHOULD DISAPPEAR.

HE SAID IT'S NOTHING TO WORRY ABOUT?

143

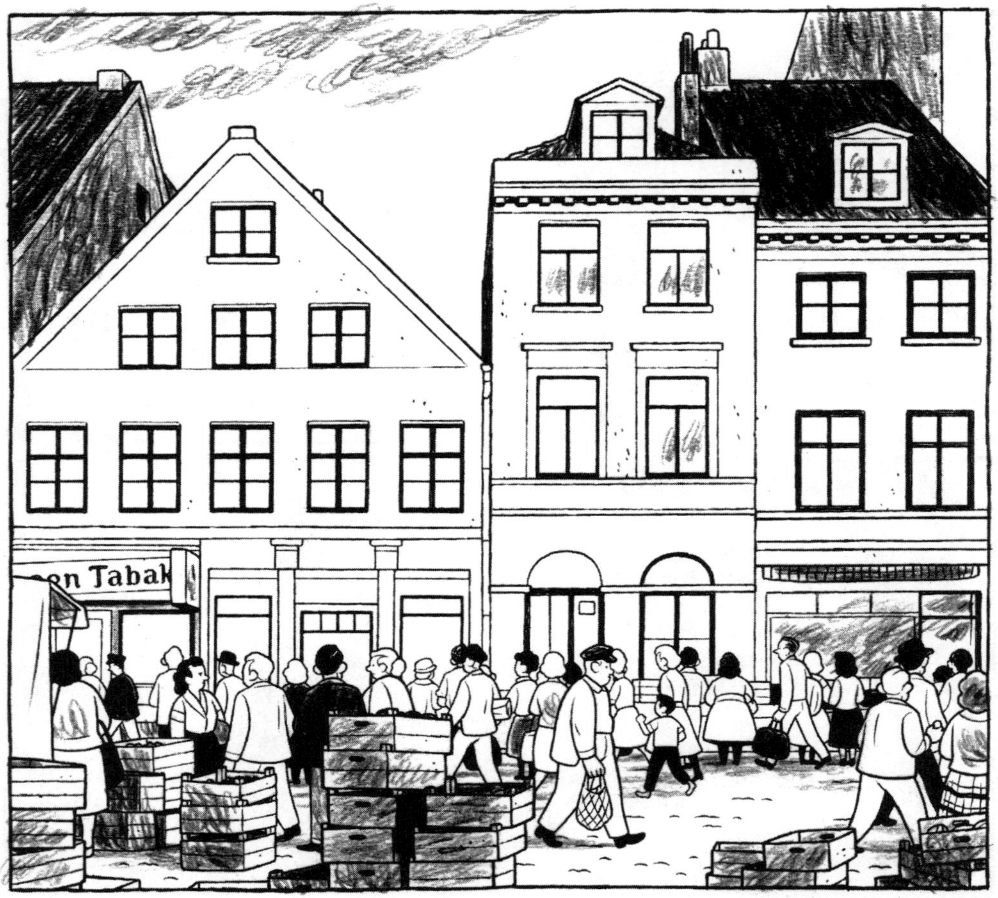
...on Tabak

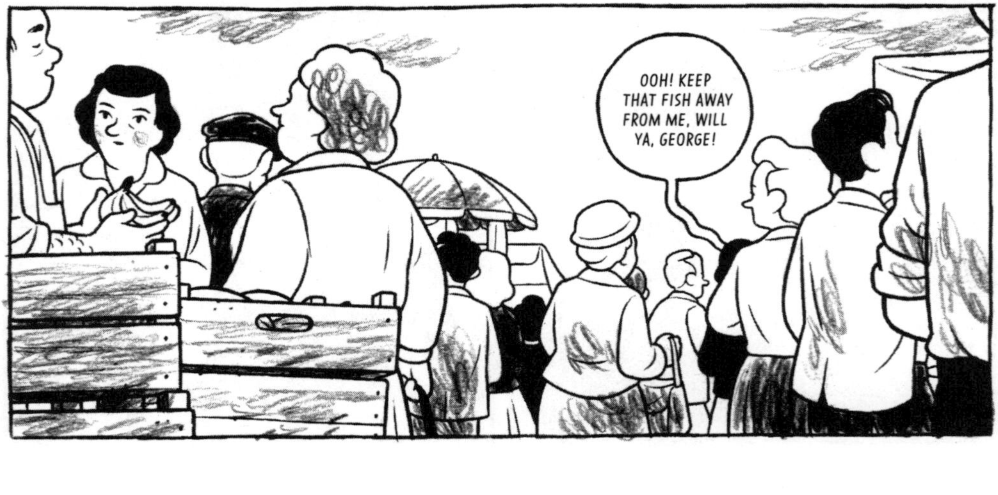
OOH! KEEP THAT FISH AWAY FROM ME, WILL YA, GEORGE!

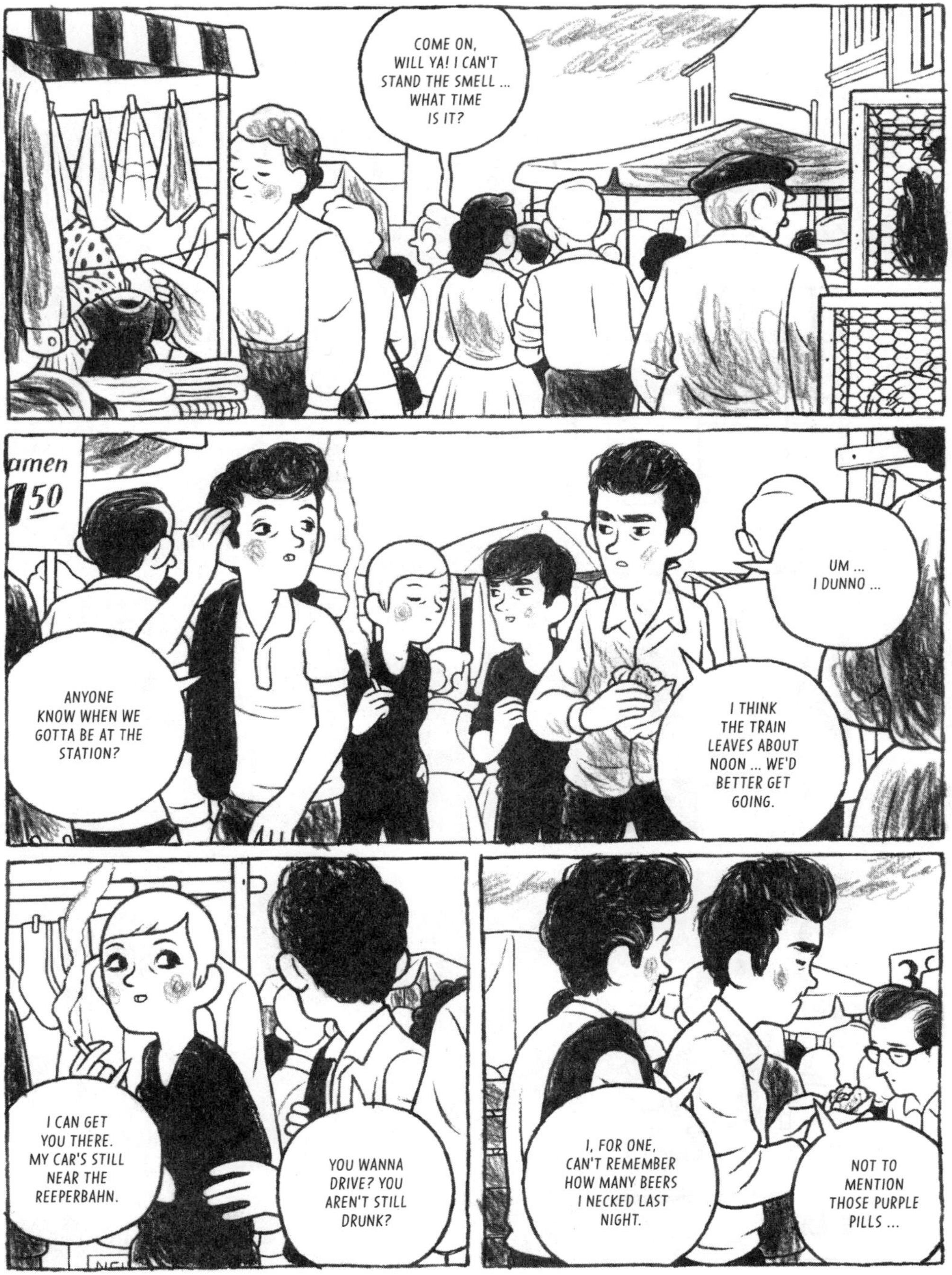
COME ON, WILL YA! I CAN'T STAND THE SMELL ... WHAT TIME IS IT?
amen
1.50
UM ... I DUNNO ...
ANYONE KNOW WHEN WE GOTTA BE AT THE STATION?
I THINK THE TRAIN LEAVES ABOUT NOON ... WE'D BETTER GET GOING.
I CAN GET YOU THERE. MY CAR'S STILL NEAR THE REEPERBAHN.
YOU WANNA DRIVE? YOU AREN'T STILL DRUNK?
I, FOR ONE, CAN'T REMEMBER HOW MANY BEERS I NECKED LAST NIGHT.
NOT TO MENTION THOSE PURPLE PILLS ...

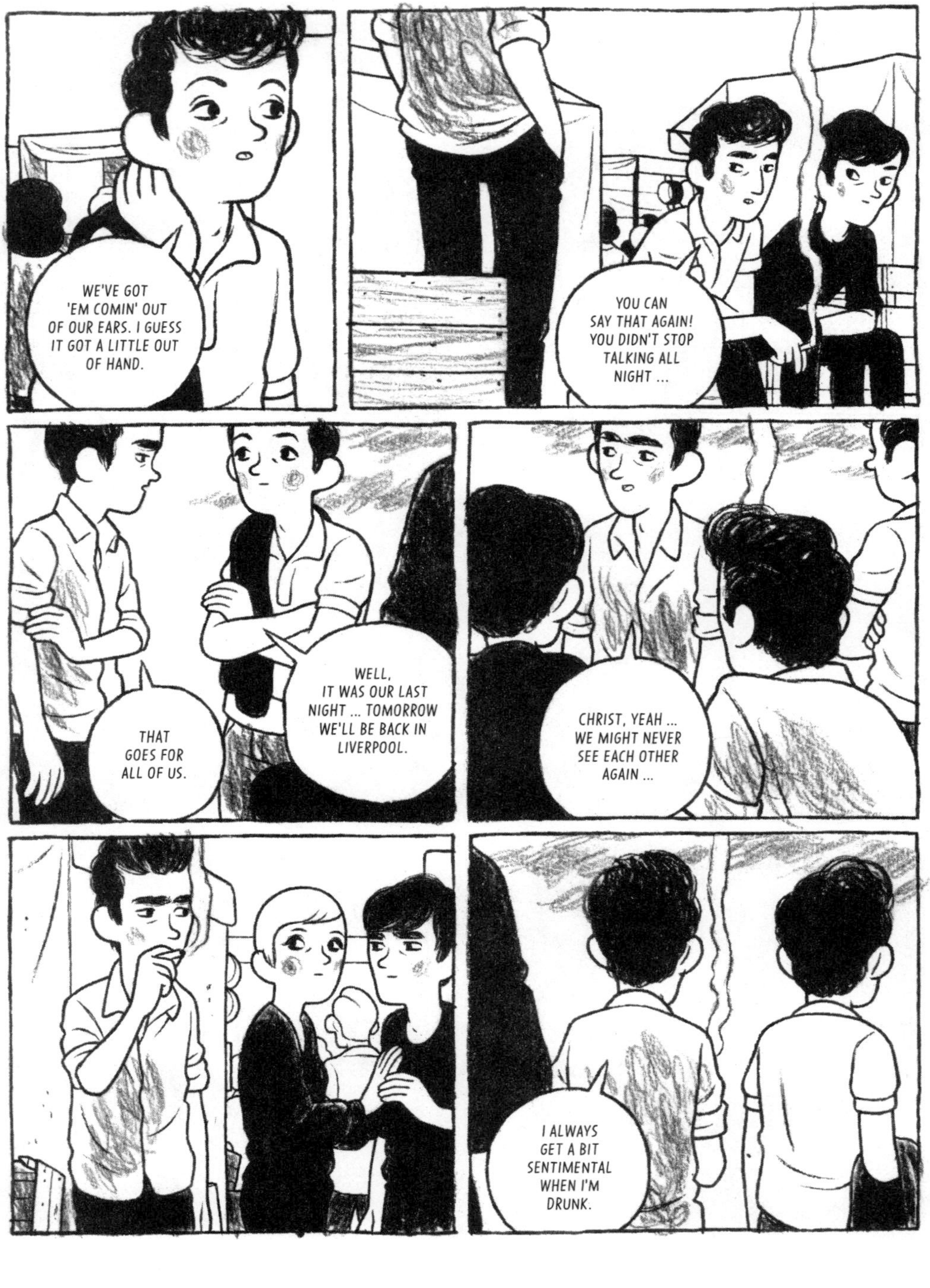
WE'VE GOT 'EM COMIN' OUT OF OUR EARS. I GUESS IT GOT A LITTLE OUT OF HAND.
YOU CAN SAY THAT AGAIN! YOU DIDN'T STOP TALKING ALL NIGHT ...
THAT GOES FOR ALL OF US.
WELL, IT WAS OUR LAST NIGHT ... TOMORROW WE'LL BE BACK IN LIVERPOOL.
CHRIST, YEAH ... WE MIGHT NEVER SEE EACH OTHER AGAIN ...
I ALWAYS GET A BIT SENTIMENTAL WHEN I'M DRUNK.

149

»Stay like that ...«
———
October 1961

153

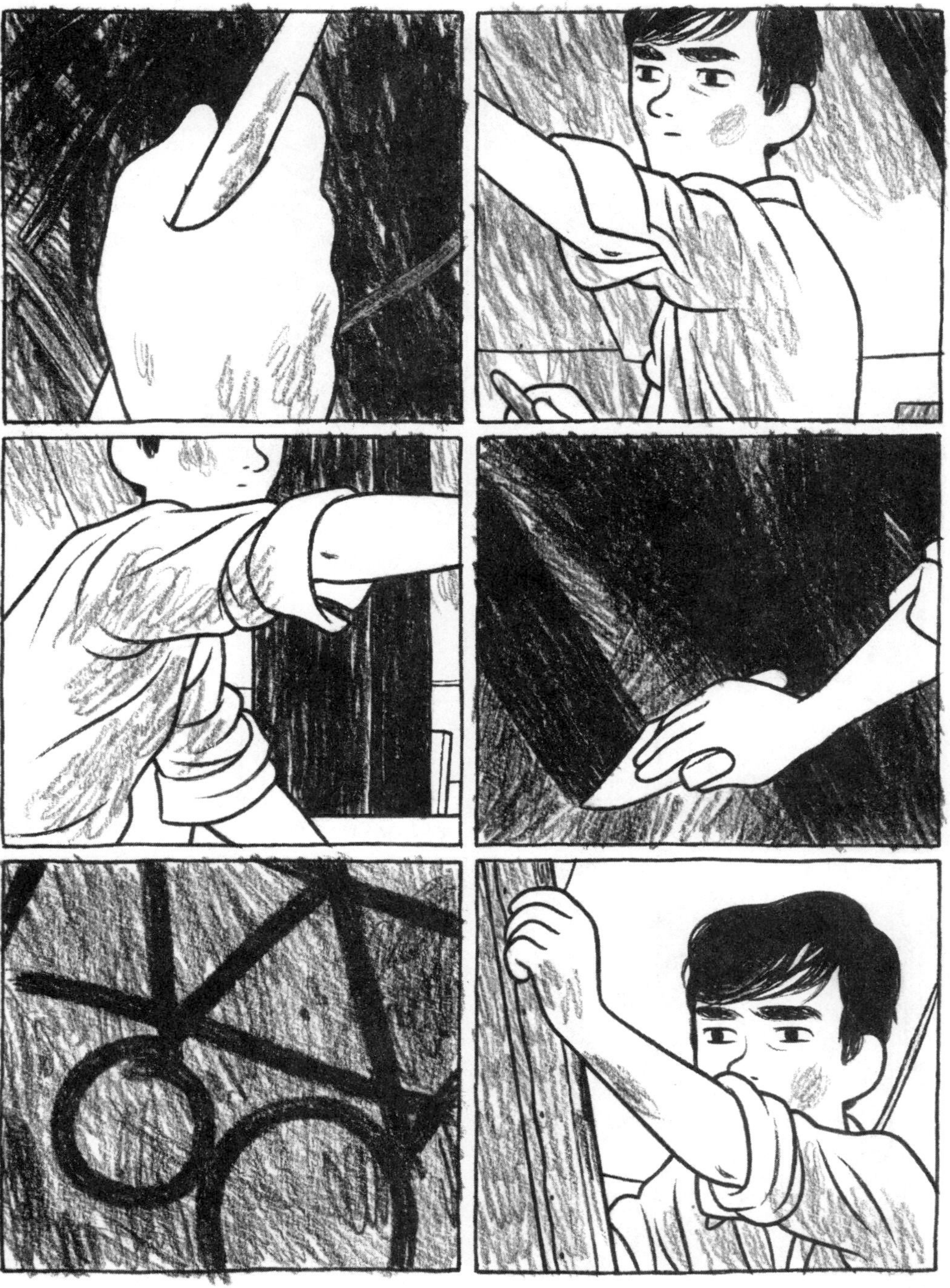

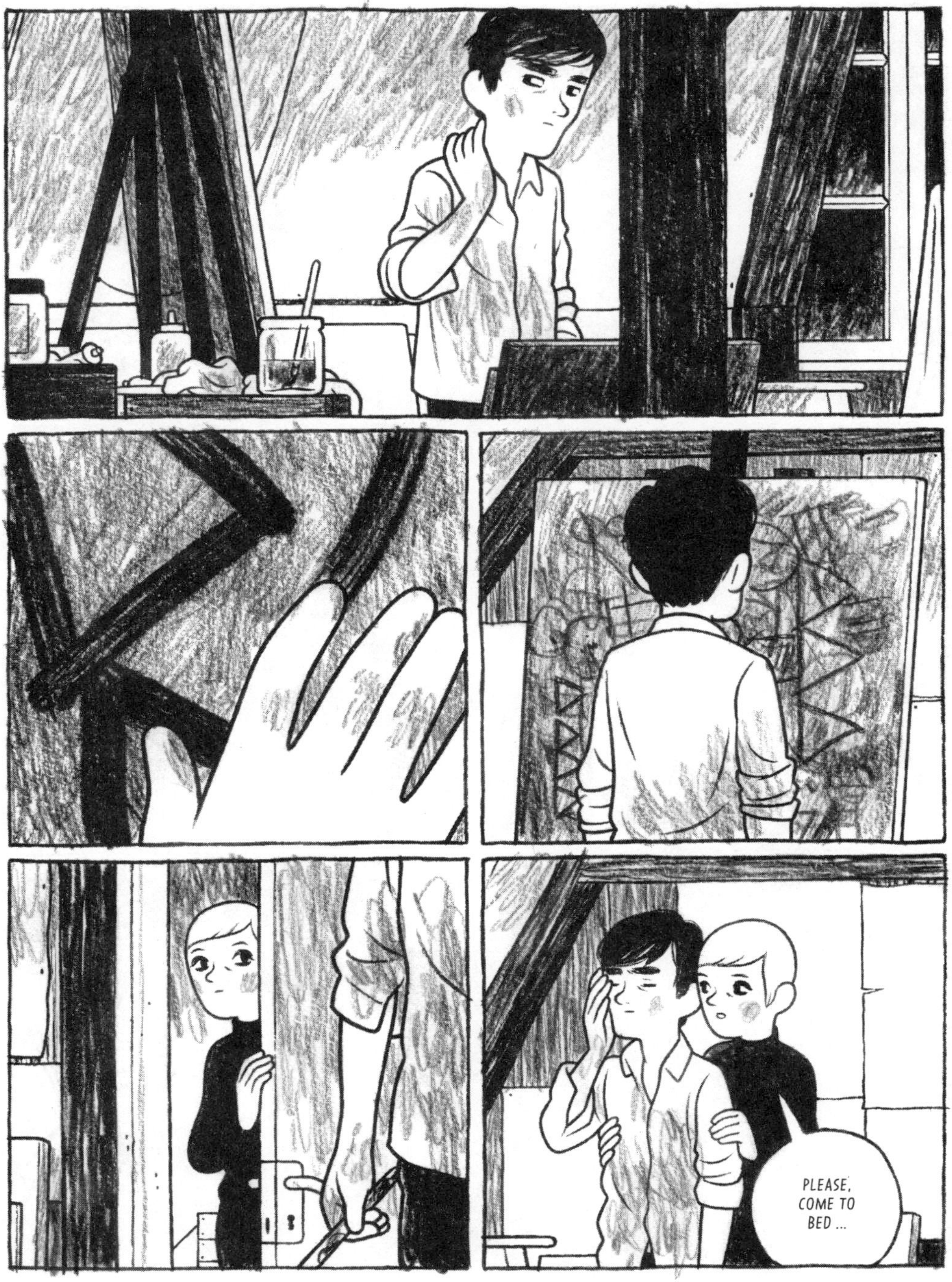
PLEASE, COME TO BED ...

162

164

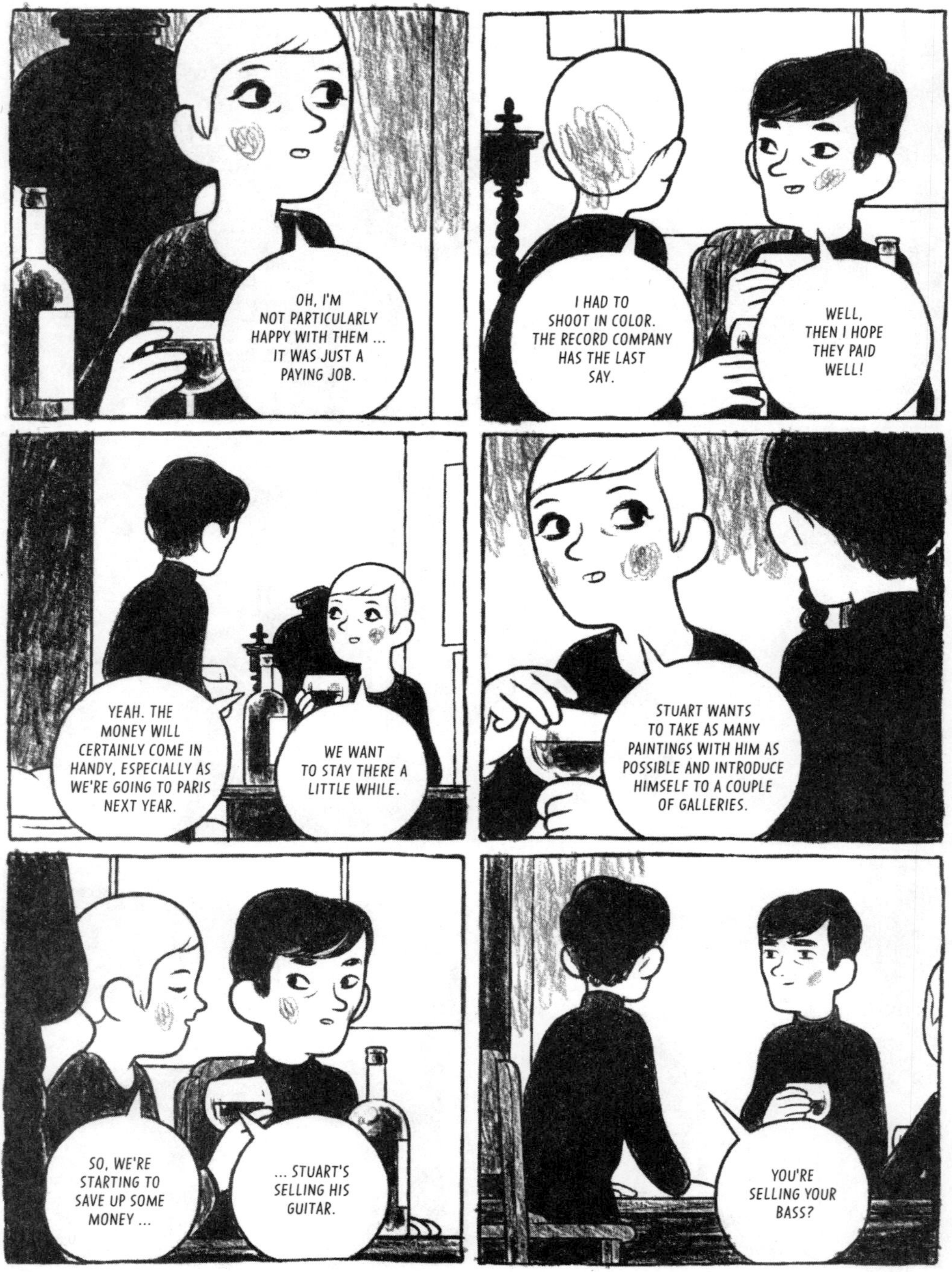
OH, I'M NOT PARTICULARLY HAPPY WITH THEM ... IT WAS JUST A PAYING JOB.
I HAD TO SHOOT IN COLOR. THE RECORD COMPANY HAS THE LAST SAY.
WELL, THEN I HOPE THEY PAID WELL!
YEAH. THE MONEY WILL CERTAINLY COME IN HANDY, ESPECIALLY AS WE'RE GOING TO PARIS NEXT YEAR.
WE WANT TO STAY THERE A LITTLE WHILE.
STUART WANTS TO TAKE AS MANY PAINTINGS WITH HIM AS POSSIBLE AND INTRODUCE HIMSELF TO A COUPLE OF GALLERIES.
SO, WE'RE STARTING TO SAVE UP SOME MONEY ...
... STUART'S SELLING HIS GUITAR.
YOU'RE SELLING YOUR BASS?

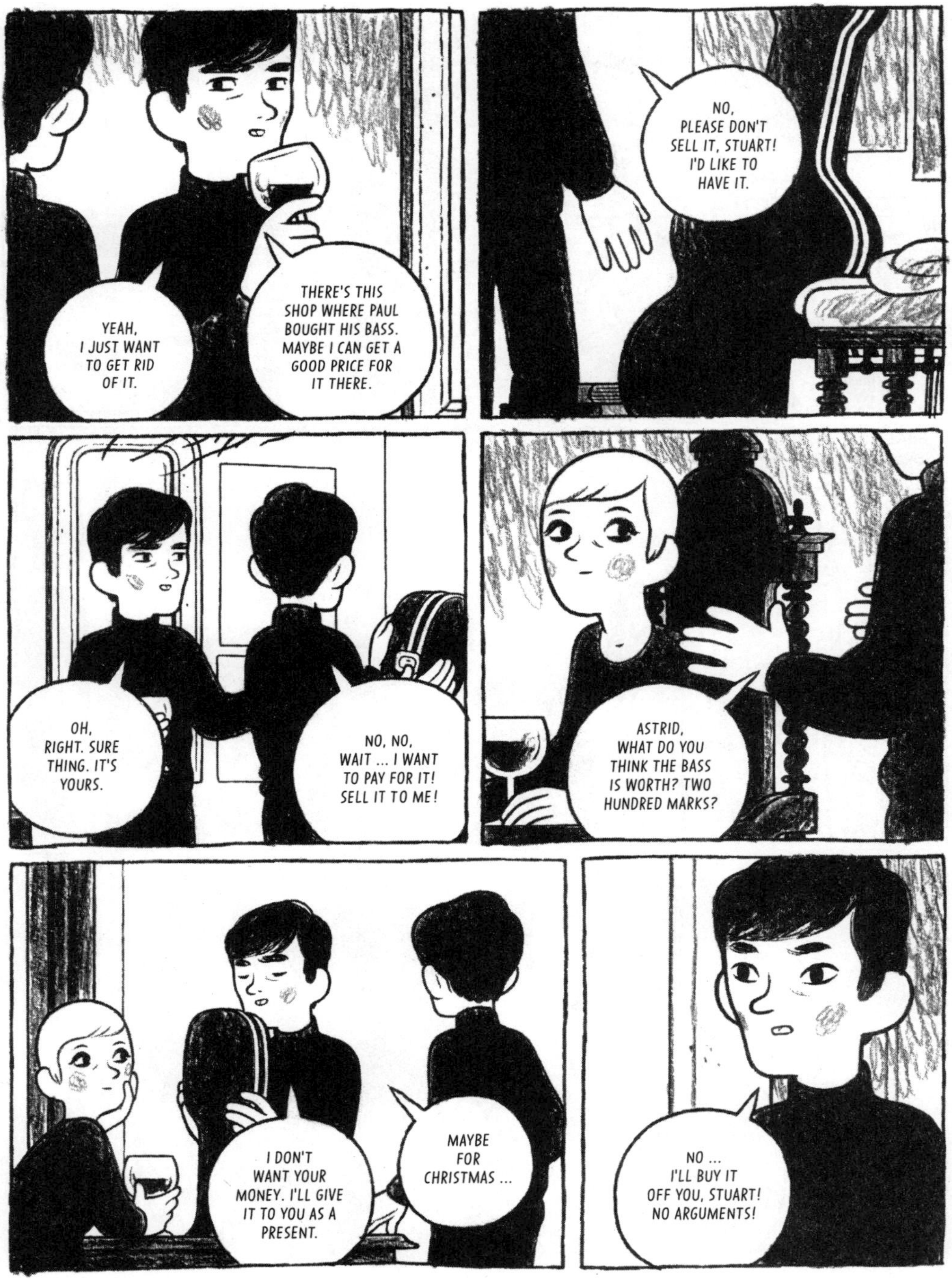

YEAH, I JUST WANT TO GET RID OF IT.
THERE'S THIS SHOP WHERE PAUL BOUGHT HIS BASS. MAYBE I CAN GET A GOOD PRICE FOR IT THERE.
NO, PLEASE DON'T SELL IT, STUART! I'D LIKE TO HAVE IT.
OH, RIGHT. SURE THING. IT'S YOURS.
NO, NO, WAIT ... I WANT TO PAY FOR IT! SELL IT TO ME!
ASTRID, WHAT DO YOU THINK THE BASS IS WORTH? TWO HUNDRED MARKS?
I DON'T WANT YOUR MONEY. I'LL GIVE IT TO YOU AS A PRESENT.
MAYBE FOR CHRISTMAS ...
NO ... I'LL BUY IT OFF YOU, STUART! NO ARGUMENTS!

168

169

»Maybe it's too dark«

February 1962

ASTRID! YOU LOOK GORGEOUS. MY GOODNESS!

OH! THANK YOU!

HAVE YOU SEEN KLAUS AROUND?

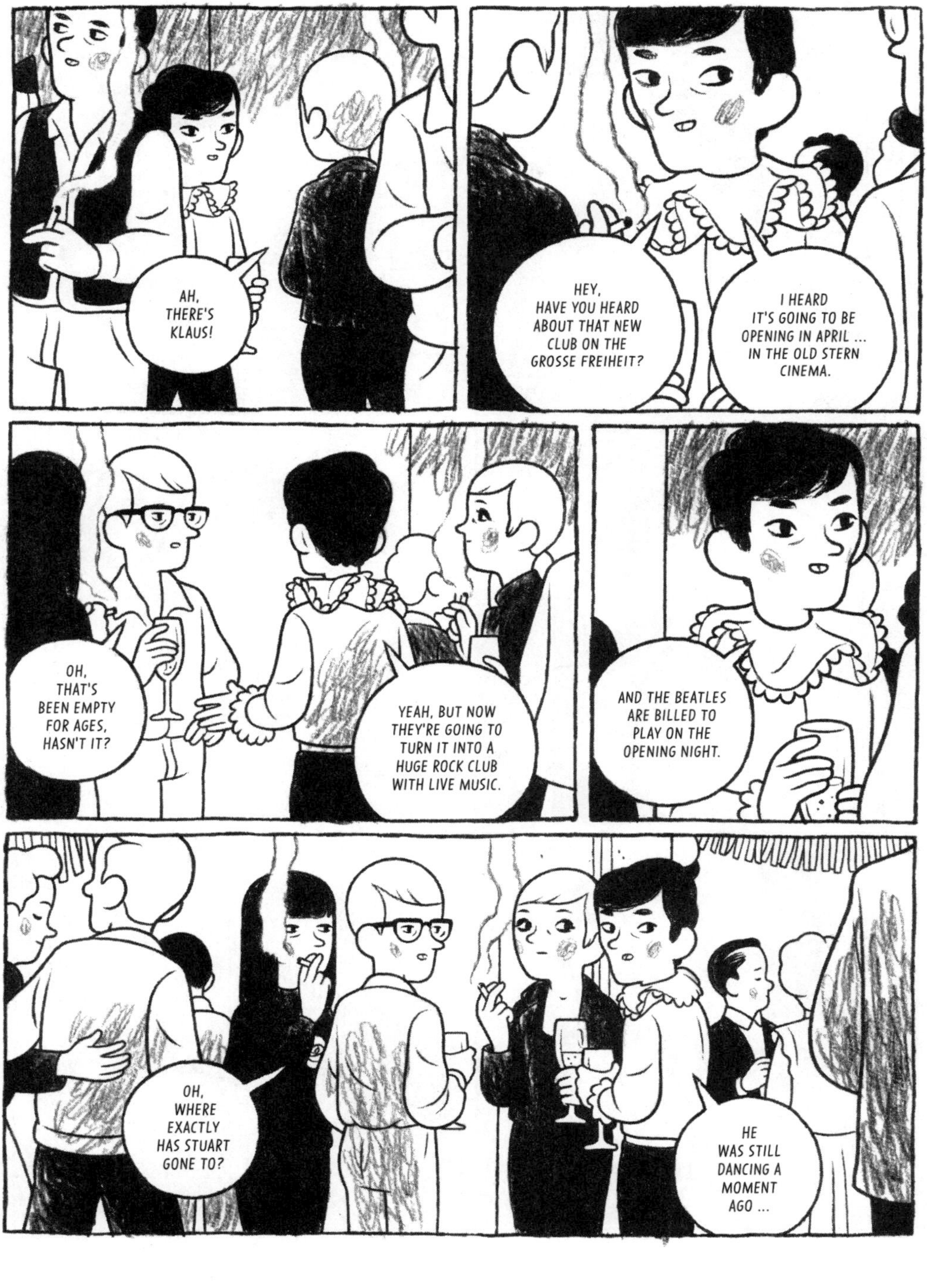
AH, THERE'S KLAUS!
HEY, HAVE YOU HEARD ABOUT THAT NEW CLUB ON THE GROSSE FREIHEIT?
I HEARD IT'S GOING TO BE OPENING IN APRIL ... IN THE OLD STERN CINEMA.
OH, THAT'S BEEN EMPTY FOR AGES, HASN'T IT?
YEAH, BUT NOW THEY'RE GOING TO TURN IT INTO A HUGE ROCK CLUB WITH LIVE MUSIC.
AND THE BEATLES ARE BILLED TO PLAY ON THE OPENING NIGHT.
OH, WHERE EXACTLY HAS STUART GONE TO?
HE WAS STILL DANCING A MOMENT AGO ...

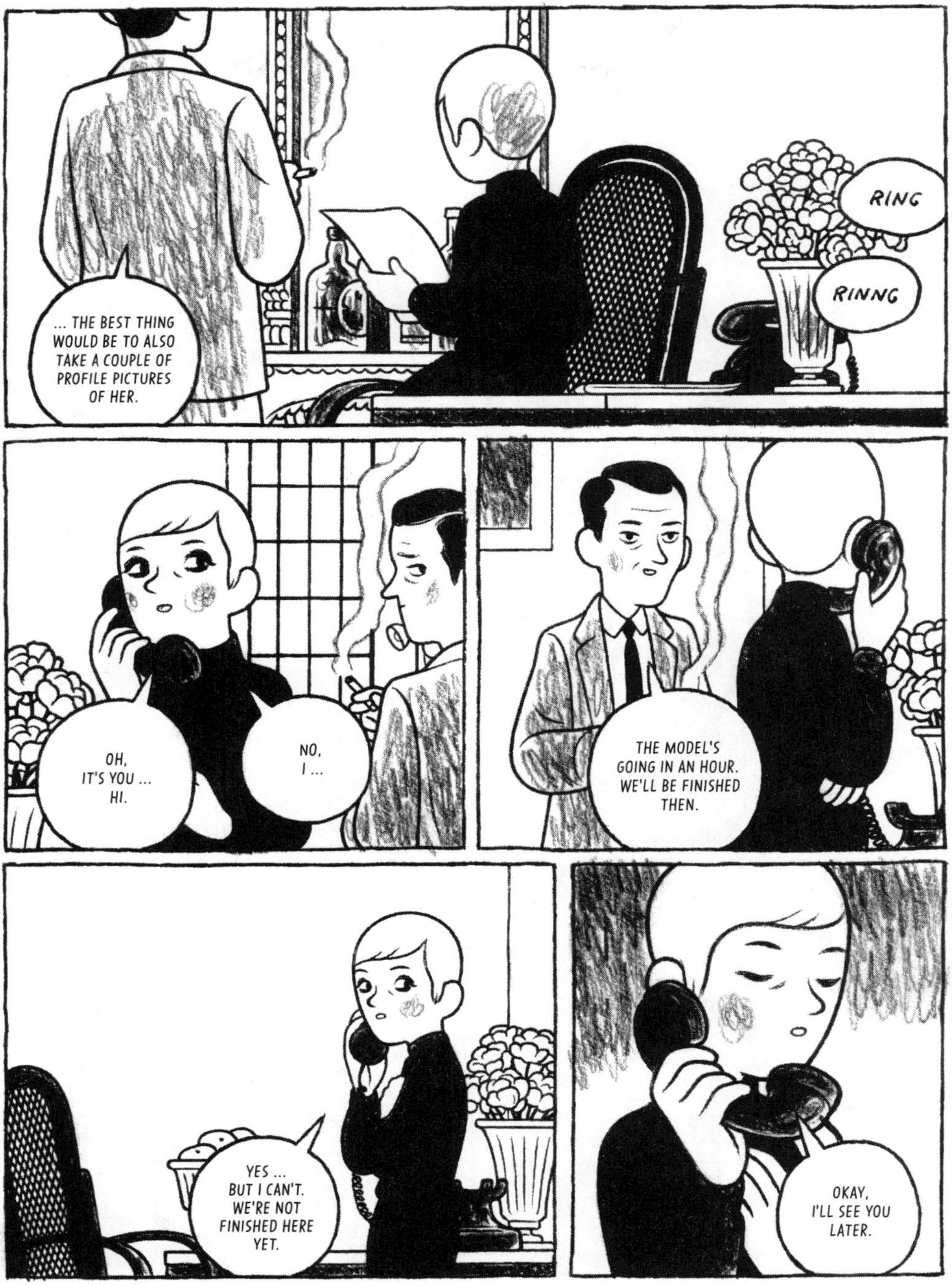
RING
RINNG
... THE BEST THING WOULD BE TO ALSO TAKE A COUPLE OF PROFILE PICTURES OF HER.
OH, IT'S YOU ... HI.
NO, I ...
THE MODEL'S GOING IN AN HOUR. WE'LL BE FINISHED THEN.
YES ... BUT I CAN'T. WE'RE NOT FINISHED HERE YET.
OKAY, I'LL SEE YOU LATER.

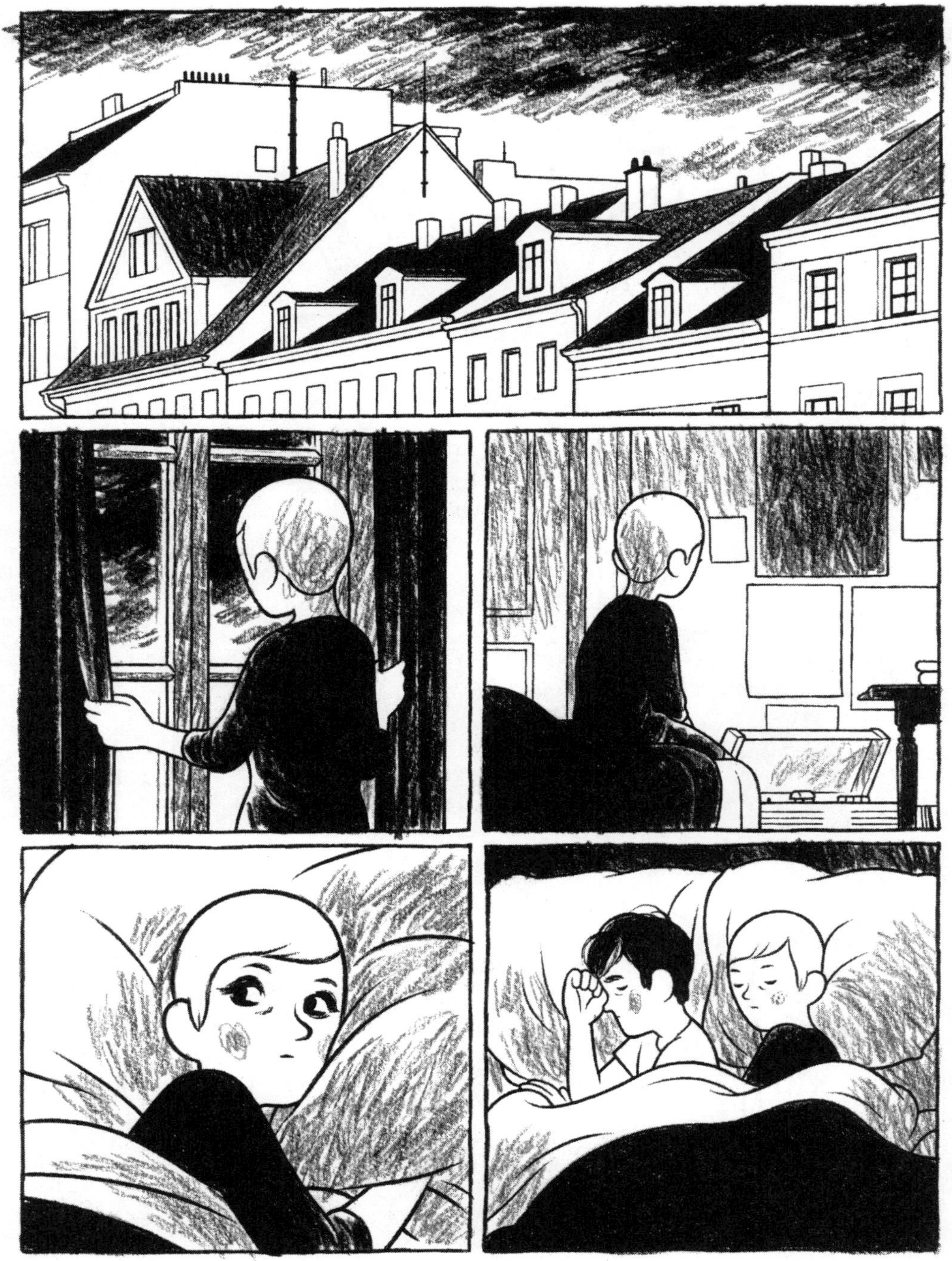

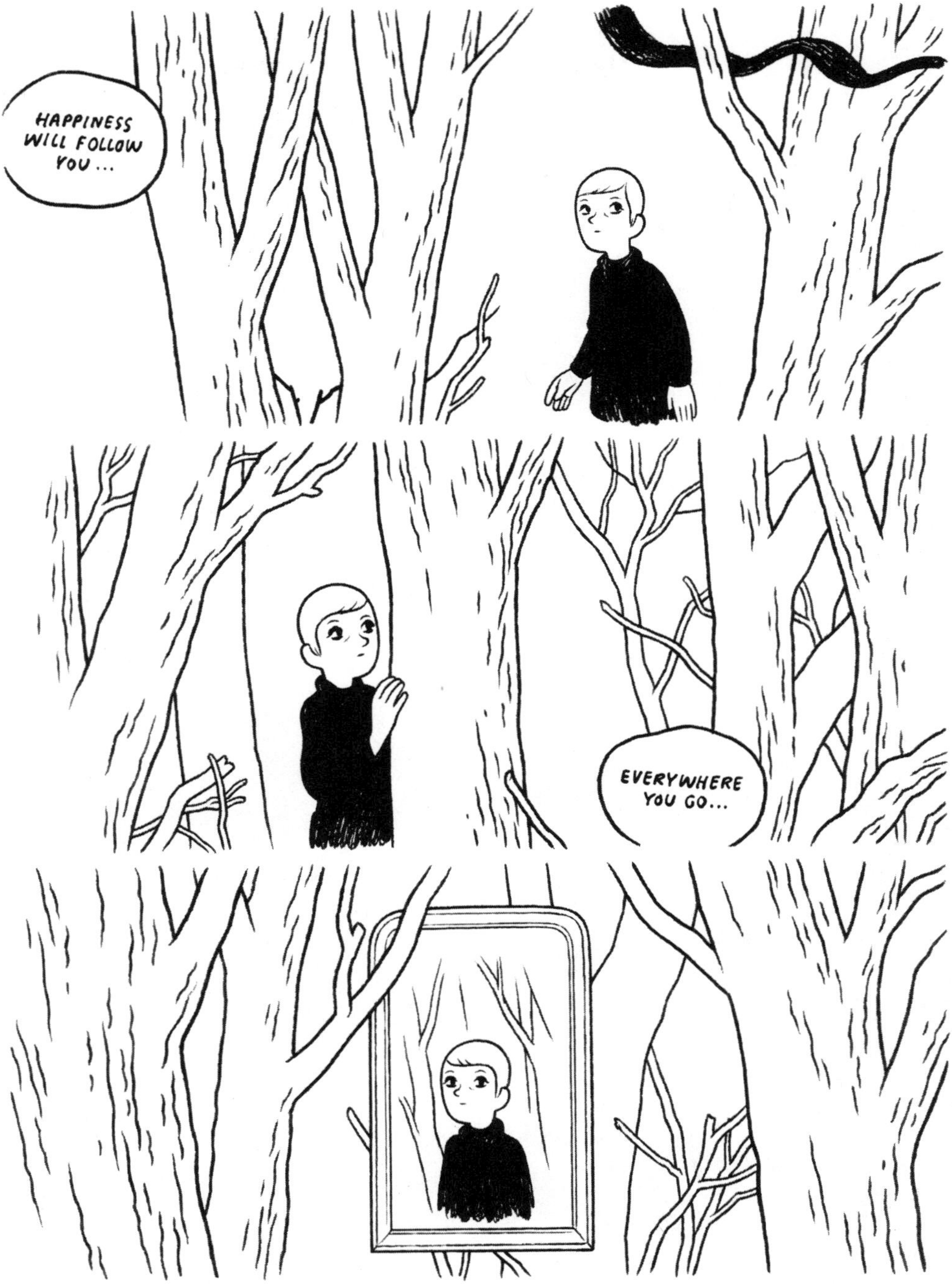
HAPPINESS WILL FOLLOW YOU...
EVERYWHERE YOU GO...

»What's wrong with you?«

April 1962

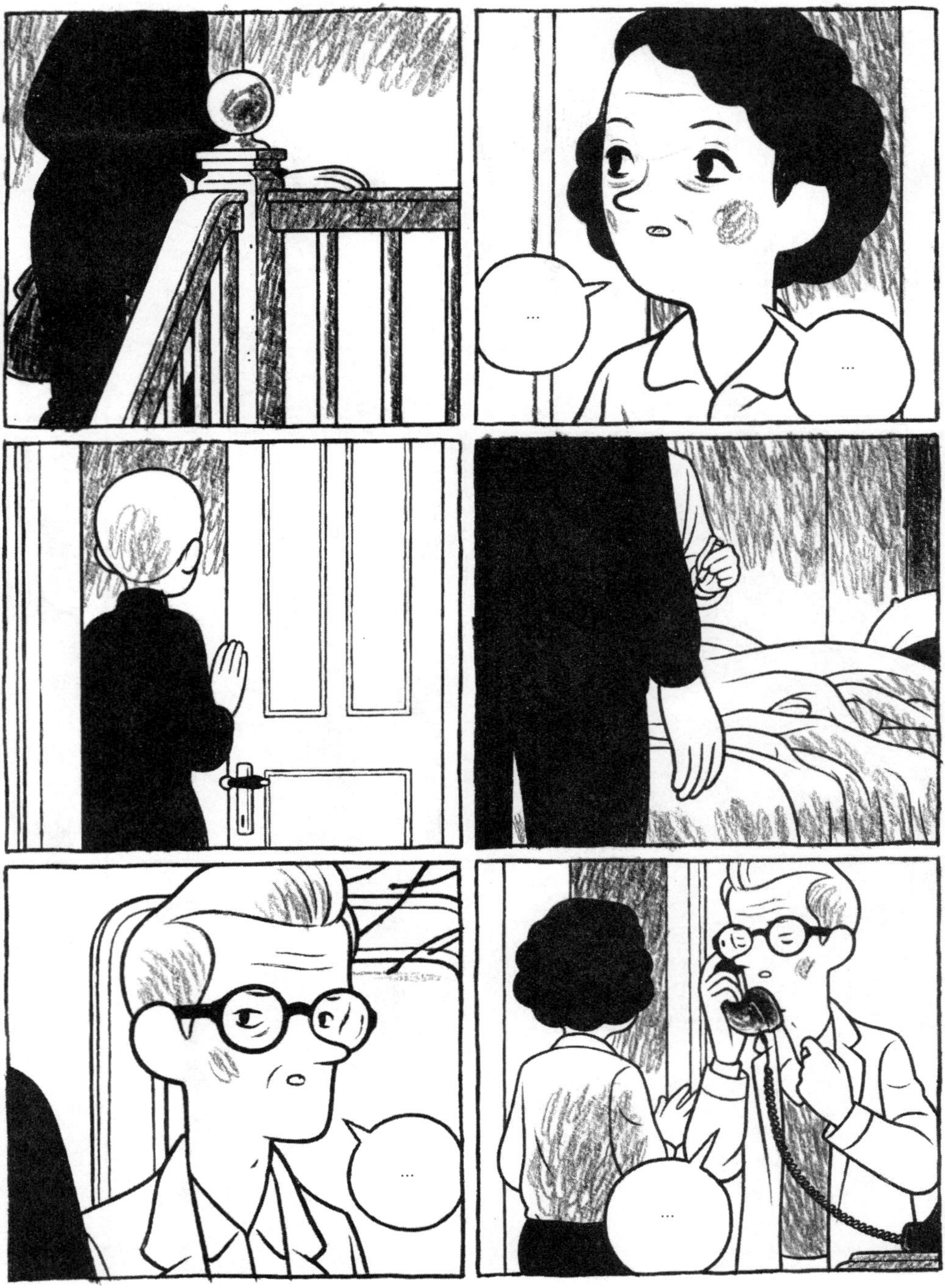
…
…
…
…

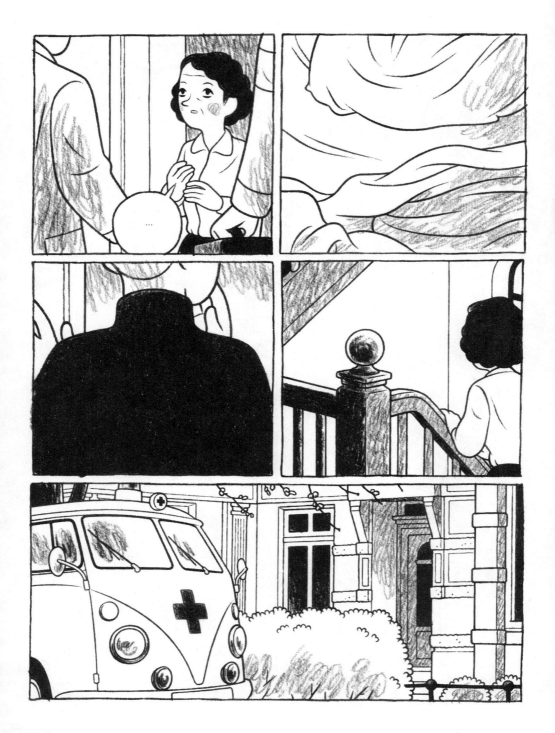

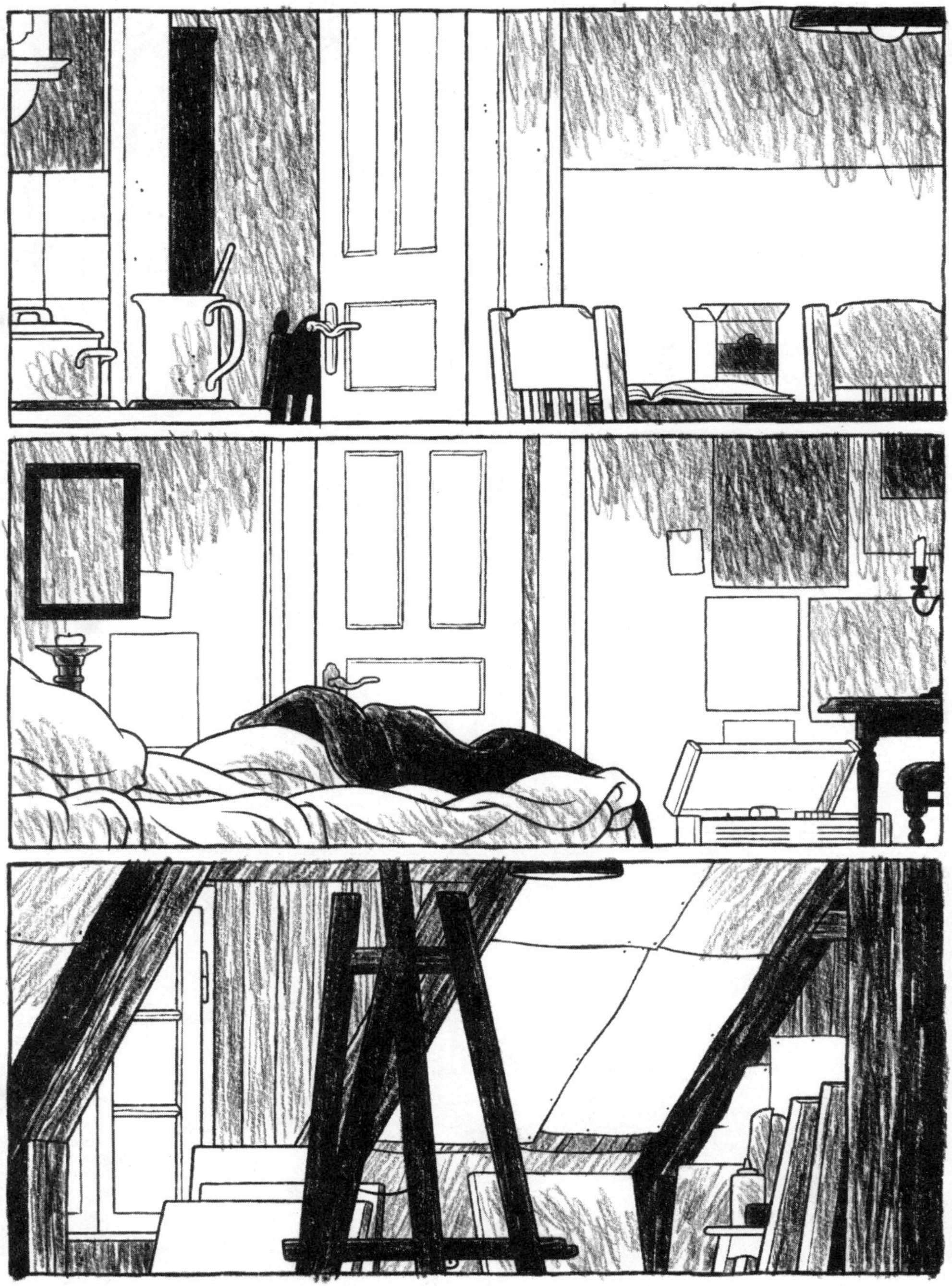

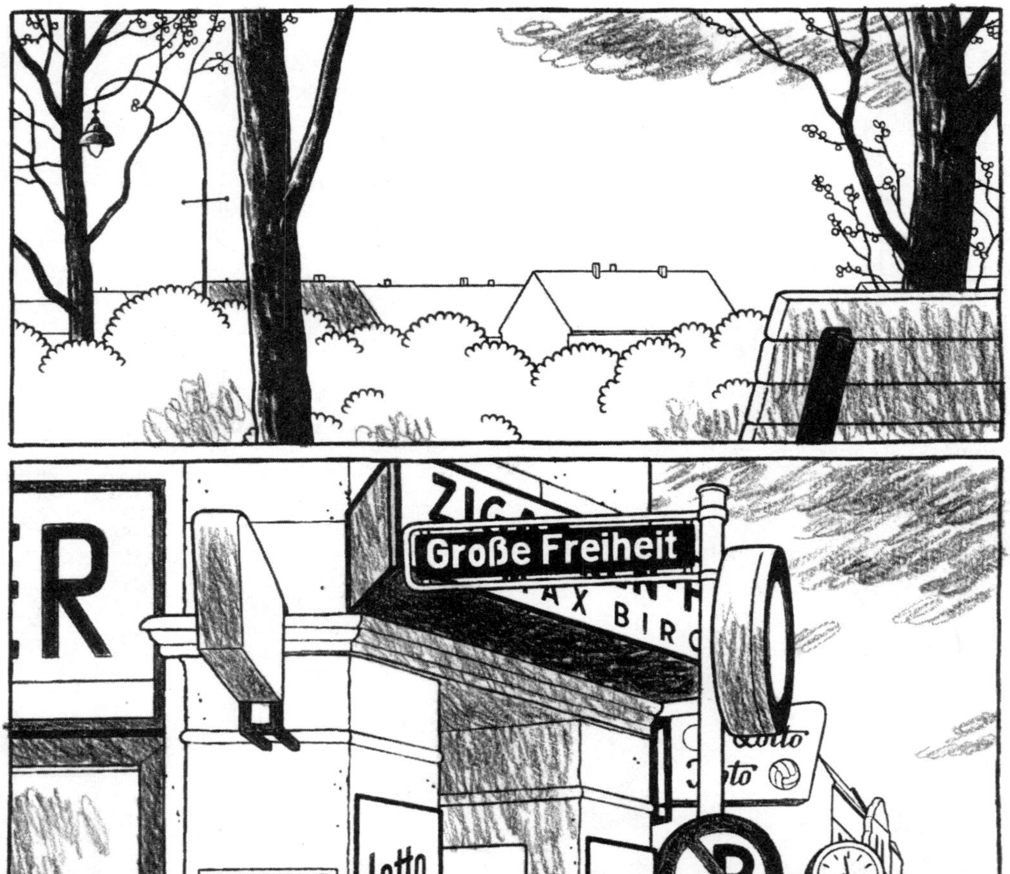
ER
Große Freiheit
lotto
Star-Club
Rock n' Twist-Parade 1962
Monica
Erotic

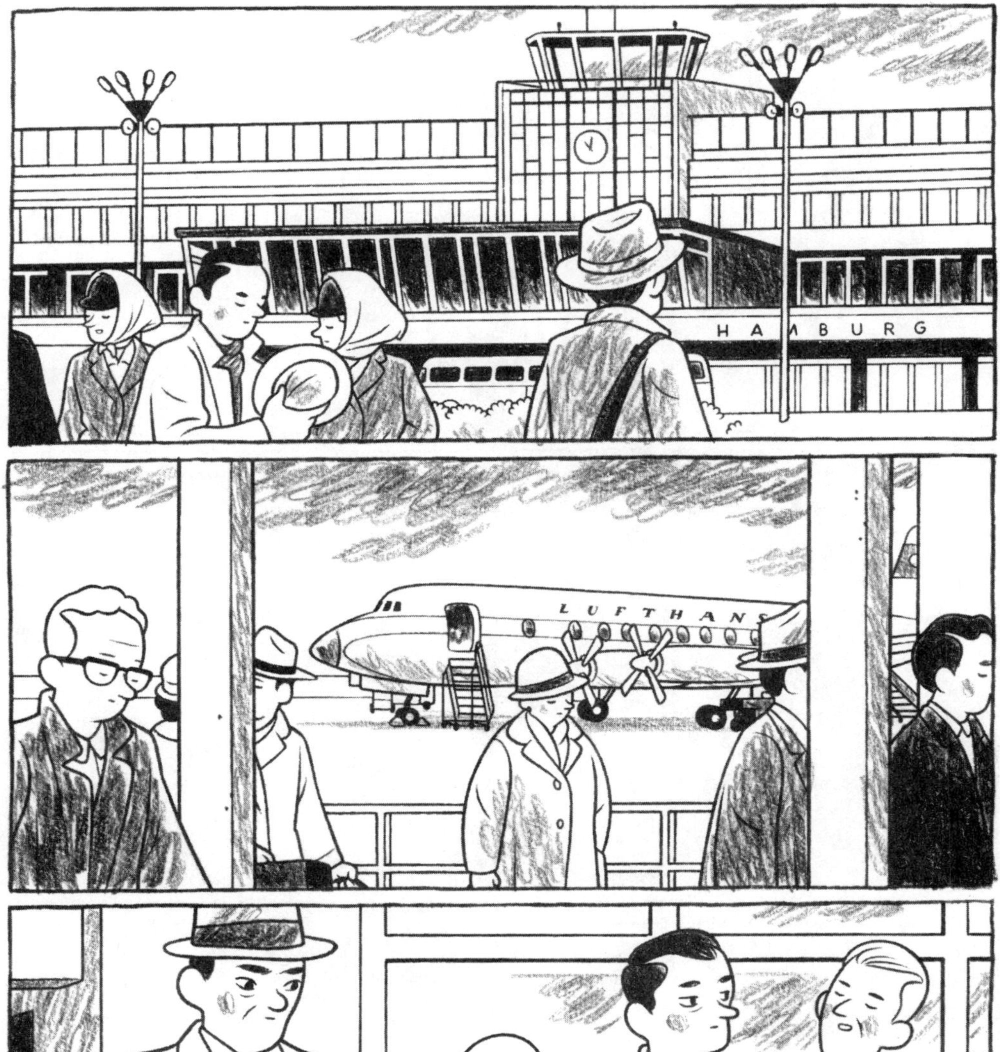
HAMBURG
LUFTHANS

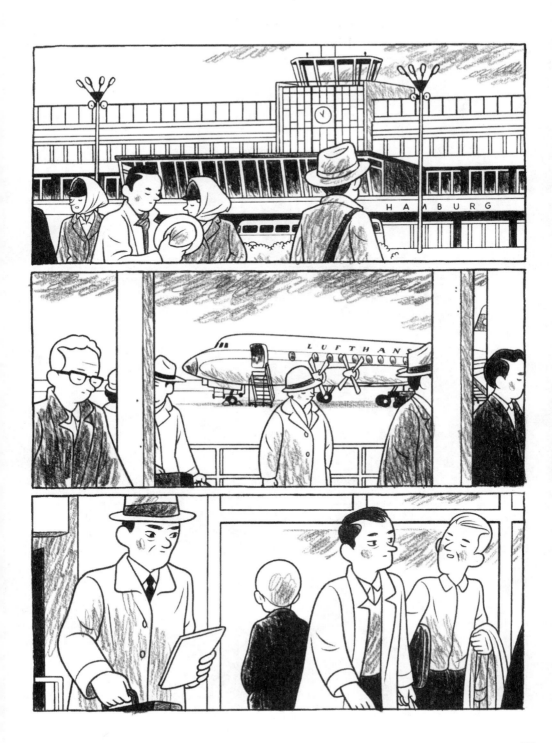